PLANT CLOSINGS AND LABOR RIGHTS

COMMISSION FOR LABOR COOPERATION

NORTH AMERICAN AGREEMENT ON LABOR COOPERATION (NAALC)

PLANT CLOSINGS AND LABOR RIGHTS

A REPORT TO THE COUNCIL OF MINISTERS
BY THE
SECRETARIAT OF THE COMMISSION FOR LABOR COOPERATION
ON

THE EFFECTS OF SUDDEN PLANT CLOSINGS ON
FREEDOM OF ASSOCIATION AND THE RIGHT TO
ORGANIZE IN CANADA, MEXICO, AND
THE UNITED STATES

COMMISSION FOR LABOR COOPERATION
NORTH AMERICAN AGREEMENT ON LABOR COOPERATION (NAALC)

Co-published by Bernan Press and the Commission for Labor Cooperation

Secretariat of the Commission for Labor Cooperation
One Dallas Centre
350 North St. Paul Street
Suite 2424
Dallas, TX 75201-4240 USA

www.naalc.org
214.754.1100
fax 214.754.1199

Distributed by
Bernan Associates
4611-F Assembly Drive
Lanham, MD 20706-4391 USA

www.bernan.com
800.274.4447
fax 800.865.3450

ISBN (English):   0-89059-077-X
ISBN (French):   0-89059-078-8
ISBN (Spanish):   0-89059-079-6

COMMISSION FOR LABOR COOPERATION
COMISIÓN PARA LA COOPERACIÓN LABORAL
COMMISSION DE COOPÉRATION DANS LE DOMAINE DU TRAVAIL
SECRETARIAT   SECRETARIADO   SECRÉTARIAT

Office of the Executive Director   Oficina del Director Ejecutivo   Bureau du Directeur éxécutif

June 9, 1997

Council of Ministers of the Commission for Labor Cooperation

Hon. Javier Bonilla, Secretary of Labor and Social Welfare, Mexico
Hon. Alfonso Gagliano, Minister of Labour, Canada
Hon. Alexis Herman, Secretary of Labor, United States of America

Dear Ministers:

I am pleased to submit for publication the first "special study" prepared by the
Secretariat in response to a request from the Council of Ministers under the provisions of
the North American Agreement on Labor Cooperation, entitled, **Plant Closings and Labor
Rights.** This study was requested in February 1996 as part of an agreement following
Ministerial Consultations initiated by the Government of Mexico.

I would like to express my thanks for the cooperation of your departments of labor, your
senior representatives, the National Administrative Offices, and the various labor
tribunals and administrative agencies throughout North America who assisted in the
preparation of this study.

It is my hope that this study will educate and inform the public on an important area of
labor law and so fulfill your objectives in calling for it to be prepared.

Sincerely,

John S. McKennirey

The principal authors of this report are

John McKennirey
Lance Compa
Leoncio Lara
Eric Griego

Additional assistance was provided by the staff of the Secretariat.

Interns: Laurie Lamb, Carlos Mallen, Katherine McLellan, and
Alvaro Rodriguez de la Vega

ACKNOWLEDGMENTS

The Secretariat acknowledges the assistance of the following agencies:

United States: National Labor Relations Board, Office of the General Counsel; NLRB Statistical Service branch; regional directors and regional office staff of NLRB Region 16 (Fort Worth, Texas) and Region 30 (Milwaukee, Wisconsin); Bureau of Labor Statistics.

Canada: The federal and provincial labor boards and the labor commissioner offices of the Canada Labour Relations Board and the provincial jurisdictions; Statistics Canada.

Mexico: The Federal Conciliation and Arbitration Board of Mexico; the Local Conciliation and Arbitration Board of Chihuahua; the Local Conciliation and Arbitration Board of Nuevo León; the General Coordination of Labor Statistics; the Mexican Institute of Social Security.

The National Administrative Offices of the three NAALC parties.

Research assistance was provided by

United States
—Prof. James J. Brudney, *Ohio State University College of Law*
   Research Assistants: Arlus Stephens and David Winston

—Prof. David Weinstein, *Temple University School of Law (Emeritus)*
   Research Assistant: Jeffrey Wolken

—Attorney Jeffrey Bryant, *San Antonio, Texas*

—Attorneys Arthur Heitzer and Susan Gramling, *Milwaukee, Wisconsin*

—Dr. Kate L. Bronfenbrenner, *Cornell University*
   Research Assistants: Chad Apoliski, Cara Beardi, Beth Berry, Katie Briggs, Jason Coulter, Becky DiMarinis, Nicole Lindstrom, Megan O'Brien, and Clay Samford

Canada

—Prof. Brian Etherington, *University of Windsor*

—John C. Murray, *Genest Murray DesBrisay Lamek*

—Jeffrey Sack, Q.C., *Sack Goldblatt Mitchell*
  Research Associate: Andrea Bowker, *Sack Goldblatt Mitchell*

Mexico

—Dr. Juan Jose Ríos Estavillo, *National Autonomous University of Mexico*

—Dr. Mario Humberto Gamboa,
  Former President of the Local Conciliation and Arbitration Board of the State of Nuevo Leon

—Lic. Humberto Flores Salas,
  Former President of the Local Conciliation and Arbitration Board of the State of Chihuahua

—Dr. Néstor de Buen Lozano and Lic. Carlos de Buen Unna, *Bufete de Buen, Ciudad de México*

—Lic. Arturo Alcalde Justiniani, *Ciudad de México*

CONTENTS

List of Tables

EXECUTIVE SUMMARY

This report by the Secretariat of the Commission for Labor Cooperation responds to a request from the Council of Ministers for a study of the effects of plant closings on the principle of freedom of association and the right to organize in the three countries that negotiated the North American Agreement on Labor Cooperation (NAALC).

In February 1996, the Council of Ministers called for this report following ministerial consultations initiated by Mexico on a plant closing that occurred in the United States during a union organizing campaign. This is the first special report by the Secretariat under Article 14 of the NAALC, which provides for special reports on "any matter as the Council may request."

Under terms of reference for this report adopted by the Council, the Secretariat was asked to look at the implications of plant closings as related to (1) the right to organize, (2) how workplace closings are addressed in the legal systems and how laws related to closings are enforced, (3) the experience of labor tribunals and courts with this issue, (4) implications for labor market adjustment, and (5) other issues for future consideration. The Secretariat was instructed to complete its report in 6 months.

INTRODUCTION: BACKGROUND AND TERMS OF REFERENCE

The introduction to the report provides general information on the background and terms of reference. Mexico requested ministerial consultations after a report issued by its National Administrative Office (NAO) expressed concern about the effectiveness of U.S. law in dealing with a plant closing related to union organizing. The Mexican NAO report followed a submission by the Mexican telephone workers union on the 1994 closing of *La Conexion Familiar*, a California-based division of the Sprint Corporation, 1 week before a union representation election was to be held.[1]

---

[1]   This report does not revisit the specific case that gave rise to the consultation, which is under consideration by domestic labor law authorities of the United States. In August 1995, an Administrative Law Judge (ALJ) found that the employer committed numerous unfair labor practices, including threats of plant closing. However, the ALJ ruled that the plant closing itself was motivated by economic considerations, not by anti-union animus.

In December 1996, the National Labor Relations Board (NLRB) overruled the ALJ decision, finding that the closing was unlawful discrimination for anti-union reasons. The NLRB upheld the ALJ decision with respect to other unfair labor practices. The Board ordered Sprint to rehire affected workers into positions at other company facilities. The Board's decision has been appealed to a federal appeals court. See LCF, Inc., d/b/a La Conexion Familiar and Sprint Corporation, 322 NLRB 137 (1996).

1

NOTES ON METHODOLOGY

The notes on methodology describe the research plan for the report. The terms of reference called for a study of the effects on freedom of association and the right to organize. In an effort to develop a new factual basis to improve understanding of these issues, a research plan was developed to be as empirical as possible within the given time frame. The research plan was formulated in consultation with the labor departments of the three NAALC countries and was adapted to differences in the legal systems and the union organizing systems of the three countries. The plan also took into account differences in the availability of resources and research infrastructure needed to complete the study in the specified 6-month time frame. The research plan called for legal research into the different labor law systems, commentary and analysis by knowledgeable labor specialists, examination of the actions of labor boards and courts, review of literature, and a special survey of union representatives in the United States.

PART ONE: LEGAL FRAMEWORKS

Part One of the report describes the relevant legal framework for resolving plant closing cases in the three NAALC countries. In the United States and Canada, plant closings or threats of closing motivated by anti-union sentiment are defined as unfair labor practices. As such, they are prohibited under law and are subject to remedial action when an employer is found to have committed an unfair labor practice. The Mexican labor law system does not use the unfair labor practice concept. Instead, Mexican labor law specifies the permissible reasons for closing a plant.

In all three NAALC countries, an employer may not close a plant or threaten to close a plant in reprisal for union activity, but may close a plant for valid economic considerations. In the United States, the law allows an employer to express "any views, argument, or opinion" about plant closings or other possible consequences of unionization, as long as such expression contains no "threat of reprisal or force or promise of benefit." However, an employer may close a plant, even for anti-union reasons, when the plant closing is at the same time a cessation of the entire business. U.S. labor law is enforced throughout the United States by the National Labor Relations Board (NLRB or Board).

Determining liability in an unfair labor practice (ULP) case is a multi-layered procedure under U.S. labor law. After a ULP charge is filed in a regional office of the NLRB, the regional director decides whether or not the charge has merit. If so, the regional director issues a complaint. A hearing on evidence is held before an Administrative Law Judge (ALJ) of the NLRB. The ALJ decision may then be appealed to the NLRB in Washington, D.C., for a review of the record and an affirmation or reversal, in whole or in part, of the ALJ determinations. The NLRB's decision may then be appealed to a federal court of appeals, and that court's decision can be appealed to the U.S. Supreme Court.

In Canada, statutes generally permit employers to express views on unionization as long as the employer does not use "coercion, intimidation, threats, promises, or undue influence" (an example drawn from the Ontario statute—other provinces have similar rules). Canadian labor boards and courts generally prohibit an employer from acting, even in part, on the basis of anti-union motives, regardless of the existence of a valid business justification for the employer's actions.

Canadian labor law is mainly within provincial jurisdiction and is enforced by the provincial governments. Provincial jurisdiction covers approximately 90 percent of the national workforce. Federal authorities enforce the law with respect to the other 10 percent of the workforce that come under federal jurisdiction.

Unfair labor practice cases in Canada are processed in more of a single-layered procedure. The relevant labor board or, in Quebec, the labor commissioner receives complaints, conducts investigations, holds hearings, and issues decisions in a single overall proceeding. Their decisions are generally not susceptible to appeal to the courts except on constitutional or jurisdictional grounds.

In general, U.S. law permits wider latitude for employers to close a plant or to make statements about plant closings in connection with a unionization drive by workers. Where both an anti-union motivation and an economic motivation exist, U.S. law looks for the predominant motive. Under Canadian law, any degree of anti-union motivation is generally sufficient to find an unfair labor practice.

Mexico does not use the unfair labor practice system, and anti-union motivation does not arise explicitly as an issue for administrative or judicial determination. However, a plant closing can be found to be unlawful in Mexico by labor authorities if the closing is not undertaken for specified, legally valid reasons as defined in the Federal Labor Law (FLL). Provisions for "collective conflict of an economic nature" in Mexico's FLL create a detailed procedural mechanism for determining whether a plant closing conforms to the legal requirements.

A plant closing threat is not unlawful in Mexico because the labor law addresses acts, not statements. Therefore, there are no administrative or judicial cases under Mexican labor law alleging anti-union threats of plant closing that can be included for study in this report. Such cases do arise in the United States and Canada. In both countries, the labor authorities determine liability on a case-by-case basis after analyzing alleged plant closing threats in the overall context of employer conduct. Thus, the same employer statement alleged as an unlawful threat may be found to be lawful in one case and unlawful in another, depending on the overall context.

PART TWO: UNION ORGANIZING SYSTEMS

Part Two discusses the typical process of organizing a union in each country. In the United States, workers may petition the NLRB to conduct a representation election if at least 30 percent of the employees request it. Unions normally wait until a majority of the employees have joined the union before petitioning for an election.

NLRB representation elections are normally held within 30–60 days after the filing of a petition for the election. Of all elections, 20 percent are held more than 60 days after the filing of a petition. The period between filing a petition and holding an election is often marked by vigorous pro- and anti-union campaigning in the workplace by employees and by management. Such campaigns appear to be the typical settings that give rise to plant closings or threats of plant closing in response to union organizing efforts.

The NLRB may certify a union as the collective bargaining representative where an employer's unlawful conduct has destroyed the union's majority support and made a fair election impossible. If a union is certified, the employer must bargain in good faith with the union.

In Canada, the federal jurisdiction and a majority of provinces provide for union certification on the basis of authorization cards signed by a majority of workers and without the need to hold an election. This is known as the "card-check" method of union certification. When an election is held, it is usually within 5 days of the union's application for certification. Both the card-check system and the rapid election procedure minimize the extent of sustained, aggressive campaigning in the workplace, although campaigning does take place.

Labor authorities may certify the union without an election when the employer's unlawful conduct destroys the conditions for free choice by employees. The employer must bargain in good faith with a certified union. Some provinces set forth conditions in which failure to achieve a first collective bargaining agreement in a newly certified bargaining unit can lead to binding arbitration for a first agreement.

In Mexico, any group of 20 or more workers may form a union without an election taking place. They need not be a majority of the workforce. There is not normally a campaign for or against union organization in the workplace. With some regional and sectoral exceptions, unions are generally accepted as a normal feature of Mexico's labor relations system.

After duly registering with the authorities, the union may demand that the employer sign a contract submitted by the union. If the employer signs, that union is considered to hold "title" to the collective bargaining agreement. If the employer refuses to sign, the union may strike to obtain a contract. The employer may then demand a strike vote to determine if a majority of workers support the strike. If not, the strike must end and workers must return to work. The union continues to exist, but without title to a collective agreement. If a majority of workers supports the strike, the employer must cease operations, and the relevant Conciliation and Arbitration Board (CAB) of the federal or state jurisdiction generally mediates a settlement leading to *titularidad* (the holding of title to the collective agreement) for the registered union.

If another registered union claims support from workers already represented by a union that holds title to the collective agreement, the labor authorities conduct an election to determine which union enjoys majority support. Thus, union representation elections in Mexico are held only when two unions compete for bargaining rights in an already organized workplace.

PART THREE: REVIEW OF ADMINISTRATIVE AND JUDICIAL DATA

Part Three reviews official records of labor tribunals in plant closing cases, yielding an appreciation of the frequency of cases in each country and how the labor law system deals with them. For the United States, additional survey research was undertaken.[2]

United States

U.S. labor law authorities actively prosecute unfair labor practice cases involving plant closings and threats of plant closing. They demonstrate a high level of success in litigation before the NLRB and the courts. However, despite this effective enforcement, the incidence of anti-union plant closings and threats of plant closing continues with some frequency. There appears to be significant variation in the types of statements employers are permitted to make about plant closings in connection with a union organizing effort.

The Secretariat examined all 89 federal appeals court decisions in cases involving plant closings and threats of plant closing published between 1986 and 1993. Of the cases, 70 arose in the context of a new union organizing campaign. Closings or partial closings prompted 32 cases, and 57 cases involved threats of closing. Courts of appeals upheld NLRB determinations that employers unlawfully closed or threatened to close plants in 84 of the 89 cases.

---

[2] Experts in Canada and Mexico advised the Secretariat that a comparable survey could not be carried out in the 6-month time frame allotted for the study. Such a survey was not possible within the time both for technical reasons (immediate availability of databases, model questionnaires, mail-and-response systems, trained staff for telephone follow-up and for coding/tabulating/ entering data, etc.) and because of differences in legal systems. (In Mexico, and in many Canadian provinces, there is not an election and related campaign to achieve union representation, making a comparable survey on campaign conduct not feasible.)

The Secretariat studied 319 decisions of the NLRB between 1990 and 1995 involving plant closings and threats of closing. Of the total, 109 cases involved closings or partial closings, and 210 involved threats of closing. New union organizing campaigns in non-union workplaces were involved in 275 of these cases, while 44 involved existing unions. The NLRB found a violation by the employer in 283 of the 319 cases.

The Secretariat also looked at case files in two regional offices of the NLRB to determine the volume and disposition of cases that do not reach the level of a published determination by an adjudicator. Findings suggest that for every case that reaches a published decision, 10 cases are initiated at the regional office level. More than half of these are withdrawn or dismissed.

In more than 40 percent of cases where the regional office found merit in the charge, the NLRB General Counsel took the case to trial before an ALJ. This is 10 times the rate of enforcement in other cases of meritorious unfair labor practice charges against employers. These findings indicate that the NLRB takes plant closing cases very seriously and actively pursues them to a litigated conclusion. The General Counsel prevails in nearly 90 percent of such cases.

In the United States, resources were readily available to conduct survey research for information that could not be gleaned from administrative and judicial records. Union representatives surveyed reported what they believed to be plant closing threats occurring in half of the sampled union organizing campaigns during the 3-year period studied, with a higher incidence in industries more susceptible to closing such as manufacturing, trucking, and warehousing. Perceived plant closing threats were the largest single factor identified by respondents who decided to withdraw an election petition they had earlier filed, thus discontinuing the organizing campaign. When unions proceeded to an election, the overall union win rate where plant closing threats were reported to have occurred was 33 percent, compared with 47 percent in elections where no threats were reported to have taken place.

Canada

Canadian federal and provincial labor laws on union organizing have generally established rapid procedures for union certification, either by card check or by an election within 5 days. This minimizes the "campaign" aspects of union organizing where plant closings or threats of closing tend to arise.

Most Canadian jurisdictions hear and decide unfair labor practice cases in a single-stage proceeding before the relevant labor board or commissioner. Those decisions normally are not appealable to the civil courts. This single-stage approach makes for relatively prompt final determinations. Canadian law appears to be quite strict in limiting statements about plant closings made by employers during a union organizing effort. In general, enforcement appears to have a significant effect on anti-union plant closings and threats of closing in Canada.

The Secretariat examined 36 cases involving issues of anti-union closings and threats from 1986 to 1995. These were apparently all the cases on this subject decided by Canada's labor boards, labor commissioners, and civil courts combined during this 10-year period.

British Columbia and Ontario were the sites of 25 of the Canadian cases. In contrast to the U.S. experience, where most cases involved threats of plant closing, the majority of Canadian cases involved plant closings rather than threats. Among the Canadian cases, 21 involved new union organizing or first-contract bargaining, and 15 involved incumbent unions. Employers were found liable for unlawful conduct in 23 of the 36 cases.

Mexico

In Mexico, the labor law system and the union organizing system are fundamentally different from the systems of the United States and Canada in the treatment of plant closings and threats of closing. There are not union organizing "campaigns" in Mexico where employers might seek to deter unionization by closing or threatening to close the plant. The certification process of union formation that occurs in the United States and Canada through an election or other determination of majority status does not exist in Mexico. Threats of plant closing that are not followed by an actual closing are not unlawful. Thus, there is no opportunity for "threat" cases to emerge in Mexican administrative and judicial data as they do in the United States and Canada. Moreover, once a union is formed, the law makes it difficult to carry out a threat to close without the union's consent. The employer must turn to the relevant CAB to obtain approval for closing in a proceeding where the union can challenge the closing.

Mexican workers may normally form a union without elections, except where unions compete for representation rights in an already organized workplace. With exceptions in some *maquiladora* regions, most medium and large employers in the formal sector of the economy accept unions as an inevitable part of the industrial relations landscape in Mexico. Controversies sometimes arise in connection with disputes over *titularidad* between two unions or leadership disputes within a union, but they generally do not give rise to legal cases or decisions where plant closings or threats of closing are at issue.

The Federal Labor Law creates a complex procedure called "collective conflict of an economic nature" where employers must secure the permission of a federal or state labor board before closing a plant. A closing is justifiable only for a specific cause defined in the law, and unions have the opportunity to appear before the board to contest the closing on the grounds that it does not meet one of the statutory causes for closing. The procedure involves extensive hearings and testimony by financial experts and other expert witnesses.

Secretariat researchers confirmed that this procedure is almost never used. In the Federal CAB and two state CABs visited by Secretariat researchers who examined thousands of case files, only five cases in 5 years involved the "collective conflict" plant closing procedure, which is contemplated in the law as the mechanism for undertaking a plant closing. In contrast, more than 1,000 cases followed an alternative "voluntary termination" procedure under other provisions of the FLL.

The most common alternative procedure in plant closings takes place under a provision for voluntary termination of the employment relationship through a "mutual consent" clause of the law. Workers and unions appear to prefer this more rapid, flexible procedure, which results in a faster provision of severance pay to affected workers in place of a long, complex, and costly procedure that delays receipt of severance pay. It must be noted that statutorily required severance pay in Mexico, which can equal 3 months' pay plus 12–20 days' pay for each year of service, is significantly greater than customary or contractual severance pay in the United States or Canada.

PART FOUR: ECONOMIC AND SOCIAL CONTEXT

Part Four presents relevant contextual information on plant closings and worker displacement in labor markets in the three countries, and describes labor adjustment and social security systems to address such dislocations. This section discusses the constant "churning" in the labor markets of the three countries, reflected in frequent plant closings and high numbers of affected workers in all three countries.

The U.S. Worker Adjustment and Retraining Notification (WARN) Act requires advance notice of plant closings in large workplaces. Canadian federal and provincial statutes also provide for advance notice of closings. Many statutes in Canada compel the creation of joint committees through which employers are to cooperate with employee representatives to search for alternative solutions to mass termination or to minimize the impact of termination on employees. Mexican law contains a procedure requiring permission from the appropriate CAB before a plant can be closed, although an alternative procedure for "mutual consent" usually replaces it.

PART FIVE: SUMMARY AND ISSUES FOR FUTURE CONSIDERATION

Part Five summarizes the report and offers, pursuant to the terms of reference, "important issues for future consideration regarding this matter." Issues for future consideration include possible improvements to the quality and accessibility of administrative data, particularly from dispersed regional, state, and local labor law authorities, which would help to advance prospects for comparative international studies. Possibilities for further research are also indicated.

Also to be considered are links to labor relations initiatives in each country and in international organizations such as the Organization for Economic Cooperation and Development (OECD) and the International Labor Organization (ILO). These models are variously known as "codes of conduct," "model business principles," "principles of ethics in labor relations," and "guidelines for multi-national corporations."

BACKGROUND AND TERMS OF REFERENCE

THE COMMISSION FOR LABOR COOPERATION AND THE NAALC

The Commission for Labor Cooperation is a new international organization created by Canada, Mexico, and the United States under the North American Agreement on Labor Cooperation (NAALC). Along with an agreement on environmental cooperation, the NAALC is one of two supplementary or "side" agreements to the North American Free Trade Agreement (NAFTA). The NAFTA and the two side agreements came into force on January 1, 1994.

The NAALC sets forth *Objectives* that include promoting 11 basic labor principles promoting international cooperation, improving working conditions and living standards, and ensuring the effective enforcement of labor laws. Following these objectives, the NAALC countries agree to a set of six *Obligations* that relate specifically to the effective enforcement of labor law.

The NAALC's 11 *Labor Principles* define the scope of the agreement. Covering nearly all aspects of labor rights and labor standards, the principles are ones that the countries are committed to promote but those principles do not establish common laws or standards. However, the countries agree to open themselves up to reviews and consultations among themselves on all labor matters within the scope of the Agreement.

The NAALC is the first international labor agreement linked to a trade treaty. It creates an international discipline on the enforcement of domestic labor law, a major innovation in international labor affairs. In addition to review and consultation, the countries' obligations on effective labor law enforcement are subject to an *Evaluation* by an independent committee of experts and, in certain circumstances, to *Dispute Resolution* by an independent arbitral panel.

The Agreement also establishes an organizational structure. It involves a Commission for Labor Cooperation headed by a Council of Ministers responsible for labor in each nation, and an international Secretariat, located in Dallas, to support the Council. Each government has also established a National Administrative Office (NAO) within each department or ministry of labor to receive communications from the public in that country, provide information, and generally facilitate participation under the Agreement.

ROLE OF THE SECRETARIAT

As the permanent staff organization of the Commission, the Secretariat has two main responsibilities. First, it assists the Ministerial Council in carrying out any of the Council's functions under the agreement, such as supporting an independent Evaluation Committee of Experts or Arbitral Panel, which the Council may establish. Second, the Secretariat prepares both periodic reports and special studies. Periodic reports cover four broad areas: (1) labor law and administrative procedures, (2) the implementation and enforcement of labor law, (3) labor market conditions, and (4) human resource development issues. Special studies can be called for at any time on any matter that the Council considers necessary. This report on the effects of plant closings on workers' right to organize is the first such special study carried out under the NAALC.

MINISTERIAL CONSULTATIONS

Under Article 22 of the NAALC any country can formally request consultations at the level of the Council of Ministers to consider any matter within the scope of the Agreement. Ministerial Consultations may address issues pertaining to the enforcement of labor laws, but are not restricted to such issues. Ministerial Consultations are a flexible mechanism by which the countries can engage one another formally, in a cooperative manner, at the highest political level (involving the Secretary or Minister of Labor) on issues of importance relevant to their Agreement.

For most matters arising under the NAALC, Ministerial Consultations are a necessary step before proceeding to independent evaluation and dispute resolution mechanisms. However, matters regarding the enforcement of labor laws related to the first three labor principles (freedom of association and protection of the right to organize, the right to bargain collectively, and the right to strike) can be the subject of only Ministerial Consultations. Such matters cannot be taken further in the evaluation and dispute resolution procedures of the NAALC. As a result, the conduct of Ministerial Consultations is very important for these matters.

To date there have been two Ministerial Consultations completed under the NAALC, one at the request of the United States and the other at the request of Mexico. This study is an outcome of the second consultation. Both consultations have raised issues related to the enforcement of labor law regarding freedom of association and the right to organize a union. Both have originated as public communications that were submitted to and reviewed initially by the respective NAOs of the United States and Mexico. In both cases, the Ministers have concluded their consultations with announcements of follow-up programs involving conferences, workshops, studies, and other measures. In the consultation giving rise to this report, the results included a forum open to the public conducted by officials of the governments.

CURRENT MINISTERIAL CONSULTATION AND SECRETARIAT SPECIAL STUDY

Under Article 14 of the NAALC, the Secretariat is authorized to undertake special studies as directed by the Council. This report was directed by the Council as part of its action plan following the Ministerial Consultation initiated by Mexico after review by the Mexican NAO of Submission No. 9501/NAOMEX. The Mexican NAO review was released May 31, 1995. The Ministers announced the results of their consultation on February 13, 1996 (see Appendix A). They called for a trinational study by the Secretariat on "the effects of the sudden closing of a plant on the principle of freedom of association and right of workers to organize in the three countries" to be completed within 6 months.

Submission No. 9501/NAOMEX was filed by the *Sindicato de Telefonistas de la República Mexicana* (STRM) on February 9, 1995. The submission addressed the closing by Sprint Corporation of its *La Conexion Familiar* (LCF) facility in San Francisco on July 14, 1994. Sprint closed the LCF operation shortly before workers there were to vote in an NLRB-supervised election for union representation by the Communication Workers of America (CWA). The election had been scheduled for July 22, 1994.

The LCF closing affected 235 workers engaged in "telemarketing" long-distance telephone service to the Spanish-speaking population in the area. The union and employees filed a charge with the NLRB alleging that the closing of the workplace was the culmination of a series of illegal practices by the employer during the organizing campaign and was itself motivated by anti-union animus. The employer argued that the closing was motivated by the fact that the business was losing money and its place in the market.

The regional office of the NLRB, acting as an arm of the General Counsel of the NLRB (which operates independently from the Board itself), issued a complaint in the case after determining that there was enough evidence to take the case to trial before an Administrative Law Judge (ALJ), part of another independent branch in the NLRB structure. In August 1995, the ALJ ruled that the employer committed over 50 unfair labor practices prior to the closing, including threats of plant closing, but that the closing itself was economically motivated. The union and the General Counsel appealed the ALJ decision to the Board.

In December 1996, the NLRB issued a determination on the appeal of the ALJ decision. The Board overruled the ALJ on the plant closing issue, finding that the closing was motivated by unlawful anti-union considerations. The NLRB upheld the ALJ findings on other unfair labor practices committed by the employer. The Board ordered the employer to offer affected workers reinstatement at other operations of the employer and to pay back wages lost because of the unlawful closing.[3]

---

[3] See note 1.

In addition to calling on the Secretariat to undertake this study, the Ministers announced that a public forum on the events surrounding this Ministerial Consultation would be held in San Francisco. The forum took place on February 27, 1996. A transcript of the forum is included at the end of this report.

The NAALC does not provide the basis for any rehearing at an international level of the merits of any particular case that has been treated by domestic authorities. This report does not re-examine the originating case, but is devoted to a general examination of practices in all three countries over a period of years on general or systemic issues posed by that specific case, especially as they relate to the administration of labor law.

Terms of Reference

The Council adopted the following terms of reference for the Secretariat's study:

Effects of Sudden Plant Closings on Principle of Freedom of Association

The Secretariat is instructed by the Council of the Commission for Labor Cooperation to conduct a study on the effects of the sudden closing of a plant on the principle of freedom of association and the right of workers to organize in the three countries: Canada, the United States, and Mexico.

Terms of Reference

1. *What are the primary implications of sudden plant closings for the right to organize a union, and the ability of workers and unions to adjust?*

2. *How are the principle of freedom of association (including the right to union organization) and the question of workplace closings addressed in the legal system in each country, and how are those laws enforced?*

3. *What has been the experience in the labor tribunals and the courts with this issue in each country? In particular, how has the question of "intent" been addressed?*

4. *How is this issue currently being affected by labor market developments in North America and what are the implications for labor market adjustment?*

5. *What are important issues for future consideration regarding this matter?*

Conduct of the Study

1. *The study is to be completed 180 days from February 13, 1996, which is the date it was formally authorized by the Council.*

2. *The study is to be undertaken and authored by the Secretariat itself, allowing for the use of experts on contract on a limited basis only to provide necessary background information.*

3. *The study is to be based on existing publicly available information. The Secretariat may take into consideration any relevant information, including any written contributions provided voluntarily by the public. The Secretariat may seek relevant information from appropriate government, business, labor, and academic sources.*

4. *The Secretariat shall make periodic reports on the progress of the study to the Council.*

NOTES ON METHODOLOGY

The Secretariat study focuses mainly on the effectiveness of the law, and of administrative and judicial enforcement, as they have dealt with plant closings and threats of plant closing to prevent union organization in a previously unorganized workplace. The study also looks at the period following formation of a new union and, where an existing union is already present at the workplace, at closings or threats where the potential objective is to eliminate the union.

For the study to have comparative value, a mix of methods suited to each country's labor system was required. Labor rights in relation to plant closings and threats of plant closing have varying and complex dimensions in the three NAALC countries. Plant closings themselves take various forms.[4] The first obvious difference is one between total closings and partial closings of a plant or workplace. There is a further difference, under U.S. and Quebec labor law, between a total plant closing that is also a total closing of the entire business and a total plant closing that affects only part of a business—closing one plant of a multi-plant enterprise, for example.[5]

Partial plant closings themselves can take several forms: closing a department, closing a shift, closing a product line or service function, relocating work, subcontracting work, converting employees to independent contractors, and so on. Cases before labor authorities reveal that any of these measures can be employed to deter union organization by workers. Of equal importance, employers can affect workers' choice of union representation by making statements about plant closing, which may or may not amount to unlawful threats under U.S. and Canadian labor law. Such statements themselves can take different forms and arise in different contexts.

In all three NAALC countries the challenge for labor law enforcement is to determine the *motivation* for an employer's decision to close a plant, and to decide whether it is motivated by legitimate business considerations or by anti-union bias. In the United States and Canada, issues of anti-union motivation can be litigated, while in Mexico

---

[4] Note that the term "plant closing" is used generically in this report. It includes any workplace shutdown, not just a closing of a "plant" in the usual sense of a manufacturing plant. The Secretariat uses the term "plant closing" to conform to the terms of the ministerial agreement. The "plant" in the case that prompted the Ministerial Consultation was a telemarketing facility, not a "plant" in the more common, industrial sense of the word.

[5] See text accompanying notes 15 and 29.

the only issue is the legitimacy of the claimed business consideration for an actual closing. Evidence about other motivations is not relevant in Mexican labor law.

In legal proceedings on this issue, labor tribunals must take into account complex issues involving the burden of proof, the use of expert witnesses, the financial documents, and the other means of proving financial difficulty or economic necessity for a plant closing. In the United States and Canada, there is the added complexity of evidence about other motives that may demonstrate unlawful anti-union discrimination. In all three countries, experts in labor law and union organizing matters contributed to the research effort.

All outside researchers' reports and supporting documentation are on file and available upon request for a fee from the Secretariat.

UNITED STATES

U.S. research first examined all decisions by U.S. federal appeals courts in the period 1986–1993 in which the courts upheld, modified, or reversed the findings and orders of the NLRB in cases involving plant closings or threats of closing. This information was drawn from a pre-existing database and methodology for typifying court decisions in unfair labor practice cases.[6]

The U.S. research also covered administrative data in plant closing cases, reviewing all NLRB decisions in cases involving plant closings and threats of plant closing from 1990–1995. The cases were found through an electronic search of all NLRB decisions using appropriate key words.[7] Researchers also reviewed case files in two regional offices of the NLRB to sample how cases that do not reach the level of a published Board decision are handled by the regional offices. This review required a

---

[6]   Federal appeals court research was performed by Professor James J. Brudney of the Ohio State University College of Law using a database he had earlier created of 1,224 cases decided between October 1986 and November 1993. While the time frame does not precisely match that of the NLRB decisions, the immediate availability of the database and methodology made it possible to include this information in the Secretariat's study within the allotted time for this report.

At the Secretariat's request, Professor Brudney's research deals with cases involving unfair labor practices under Sections 8(a)(1) [coercion] and 8(a)(3) [discrimination], not under Section 8(a)(5) [refusal to bargain]. Thus, for example, it does not treat a case like the recent decision of a U.S. appeals court reversing a Board order that a Canadian-owned company reopen a plant it had closed during negotiations with the union. See *Stroehmann Bakeries, Inc. [Division of George Weston Ltd.] v. NLRB*, CA 2, Nos. 95–4159(L), 95–4207(XAP), September 9, 1996.

[7]   NLRB case research was performed by Professor David Weinstein of the Temple University School of Law.

physical examination of thousands of case files in two regional offices recommended by the NLRB General Counsel's office as generally reflective of national data.

The sample research in NLRB regional offices indicated that for every case involving a plant closing or a threat of plant closing that reaches the level of a published NLRB decision, 10 other cases are initiated in Board regional offices and disposed of through withdrawal, dismissal, or settlement, or by an administrative judge's decision.

Survey research was undertaken to obtain information that cannot be gleaned from records of unfair labor practice charges filed with the NLRB. Unions that had recently attempted organizing campaigns were surveyed for data on the factors, including perceived plant closings and threats of plant closing, that influenced their decisions to withdraw election petitions or to proceed to elections, as well as factors affecting the results of elections and first-contract negotiations.[8]

The Secretariat also sent letters to four major U.S. employer associations describing the study, attaching the ministerial agreement, provisions of the NAALC on Secretariat studies, and the terms of reference, and inviting any views and information relevant to the project.[9]

CANADA

In Canada, researchers reviewed unfair labor practice cases involving plant closings and threats of plant closing before the administrative labor boards and commissioners of the 10 provinces and the federal government. Court decisions dealing with these issues were also examined, although the court decisions are few since labor board decisions are normally not accepted for appeal by the courts.[10]

---

[8] The survey research was designed and directed by Dr. Kate L. Bronfenbrenner, Director of Labor Education Research at the New York State School of Industrial and Labor Relations at Cornell University. The Cornell group used an existing database of information on union petitions, withdrawals, elections, and first contracts drawn from records of the NLRB. Survey questionnaires were mailed to a random sample of 1,000 U.S. union representatives who had filed petitions with the NLRB to hold a representation election in workplaces with bargaining units of more than 50 workers. Responses and follow-up phone calls from researchers obtained information about the incidence and effects of plant closings and threats of plant closing in union organizing campaigns, certification elections, and first-contract bargaining in the United States.

[9] The four associations were the U.S. Council for International Business, the Business Roundtable, the National Association of Manufacturers, and the U.S. Chamber of Commerce.

[10] Research on Canadian administrative and judicial data was performed by Professor Brian Etherington of the Faculty of Law, University of Windsor, and editor of the *Canadian Labour and Employment Law Journal*, with John C. Murray, chairman and partner, Genest Murray DesBrisay Lamek, and Jeffrey Sack, Q.C., Sack Goldblatt Mitchell, co-editors of the *Journal*.

An electronic search using appropriate key words, with follow-up review of texts, exposed the entire field of plant closing and threat cases in all Canadian jurisdictions since 1986. Each case could be examined in detail for its key characteristics, with extensive comparative information on a provincial basis. Important cases that arose in earlier years were also examined, especially for their importance as legal precedent.

MEXICO

Mexican labor law requires employers to exhaust a complex legal proceeding before a state or federal Conciliation and Arbitration Board (CAB) to justify a plant closing and ensure that the reason for closing is among those permitted in the Federal Labor Law. The proceeding is called a "collective conflict of economic nature" in which the employer, the union (if there is one), and workers must appear. If a union were to resist a plant closing, the challenge would be raised in this proceeding.

No published records of the results of such proceedings are generally available in libraries or electronically. Case files and decisions are housed in the offices of the CABs. Secretariat researchers visited the offices of the federal CAB and two state CABs and examined thousands of case files in "collective conflict" cases brought before the CABs of selected jurisdictions.[11] The collective conflict proceedings covered several other common types of labor grievances, which meant that extracting those on plant closings was a daunting task.

The review of CAB records revealed that the collective conflict mechanism described above is rarely invoked in plant closing cases. This led researchers to examine records of another means of resolving plant closing disputes: a "voluntary termination" clause of the law in which the critical issue is the provision of severance pay to workers as quickly as possible and under the most favorable terms.

For Part Four of this report on the labor market context, the Secretariat relied on reports from the three governments' labor departments and statistical agencies, as well as a review of reports on plant closing issues produced by non-governmental groups. The Secretariat also used information from its own *North American Labor Markets: A Comparative Profile,* prepared for publication in May 1997.

---

[11] Empirical research in Mexico was performed by Dr. Juan Jose Rios Estavillo of the Institute of Juridical Research at the National Autonomous University of Mexico; Lic. Humberto Flores Salas, former president of the Central CAB of the state of Chihuahua; and Dr. Mario Humberto Gamboa, former president of the Central CAB of the state of Nuevo Leon. Legal analysis and advice were provided by expert labor attorneys Nestor de Buen Lozano, Carlos de Buen Unna, and Arturo Alcalde Justiniani.

Systematic Differences Among Mexico, Canada, and the United States

Mexico does not normally have union organizing "campaigns" in which employers might seek to deter unionization in an unorganized workplace by closing or threatening to close the plant. In Canada there are several days, and in the United States several weeks, leading up to a union representation election. In a majority of Canadian provinces, however, no election is necessary. Workers obtain union certification by signing authorization cards.

This campaign period—prolonged in the United States and short in Canada—is the setting for most threats or decisions to close a plant to block unionization. In Mexico, the process of union formation through an election or other determination of majority status does not exist. Thus, Mexican administrative data offer little opportunity for examining plant closings or threats of plant closing as U.S. or Canadian case law does. This limited the applicability of the method of examining published labor board and court decisions in plant closing cases with respect to anti-union motivation, although important new data were obtained on how plant closing cases are resolved within the legal system.

While actual plant closings are unlawful in the Mexican system if they do not conform to specified legal requirements, threats to close a plant if workers form a union are not unlawful under Mexican law. Mexico does not employ an unfair labor practice concept, such as that used in Canada and the United States, which defines such threats as illegal. The protection against threats in the U.S. and Canadian systems is directly linked to the union election campaign process, which is not contemplated in Mexican labor law.

Mexican labor law targets employer *actions*, not employer statements. The relevant issue under Mexican law is whether the employer met one of the specified, permissible reasons for closing a plant. Since it is not unlawful, the phenomenon of the anti-union threat to close a plant, as it occurs in the United States or Canada, cannot be discerned in Mexican labor law records.

Systematic Differences Among Mexico, Canada, and the United States (continued)

Some academic researchers have discussed a phenomenon of localized business cultures where there exists a widespread sentiment among workers that their employer would close a plant rather than accept a union. Some of these accounts point to *maquiladora* areas that are along the U.S.-Mexico border and that are said to be anti-union, while other areas are seen to have developed a culture of company unionism.[12] Similar academic and journalistic accounts discuss an anti-union culture in areas of the southern United States, and in "Silicon Valley" and other high-technology manufacturing centers.[13] But examining a culture of anti-unionism in which workers have internalized a fear of plant closing would have to be undertaken in another study that would range far beyond the terms of reference of this report. Thus, no anecdotal accounts of anti-union behavior could be confirmed and incorporated into this study on the same basis as administrative and judicial records, or as a methodologically sound social science survey.

---

[12] See, for example, Guillermo Marrero, "Labor Issues for Maquiladoras," 4 *Latin America Law and Business Report* (May 31, 1996), citing "an anti-union attitude held by many *maquiladora* operators in most locations; the perception by some *maquiladora* workers and managers that trade unions will have little to offer them; and the inability or unwillingness of unions to zealously represent workers against foreign manufacturers." See also Alfredo Hualde, "Industrial Relations in the Maquiladora Industry: Management's Search for Participation and Quality," in Maria Cook and Harry Katz, eds., *Regional Integration and Industrial Relations in North America* (1994); Jorge Carillo and Alfredo Hualde, "Maquiladoras: La restructuración industrial y el impacto sindical," in Bensusán and León, eds., *Negociación y conflicto laboral en México* (1990); María Eugenia De la O. and Cirila Quintero, "Sindicalismo y contratación colectiva en las maquiladoras fronterizas," *Frontera Norte* 8 (July–December 1992); Monica Claire Gambrill, "Sindicalismo en las maquiladoras de Tijuana: regresión en las prestaciones sociales," in Jorge Carrillo, ed., *Reestructuración industrial: Maquiladoras en la frontera MéxicoEstados Unidos* (1986); Edward J. Williams, "Attitudes and Strategies Inhibiting the Unionization of the Maquiladora Industry: Government, Industry, Unions and Workers," VI *Journal of Borderlands Studies* 51 (1991); Susan Tiano, *Patriarchy on the Line: Labor, Gender, and Ideology in the Mexican Maquila Industry* (1994); Kathryn Kopinak, *Desert Capitalism: Maquiladoras in North America's Western Industrial Corridor* (1996).

[13] See, for example, AnnaLee Saxenian, *Regional Advantage: Culture and Competition in Silicon Valley and Route 128* (1994), noting that "No high technology firm has been organized by a labor union in Silicon Valley during the past 20 years, and there have been fewer than a dozen serious attempts," at 55; Kathy Sawyer, "Unions Striking Out in High-Tech Firms," the *Washington Post*, March 18, 1984, at C1.

PART ONE

LEGAL FRAMEWORKS[14]

United States

The U.S. legal framework regarding the effects of plant closings on freedom of association and the right of workers to organize encompasses two central issues in labor law jurisprudence: (1) motivation for closing a plant, and (2) the difference between a lawful expression of any views, argument, or opinion, and an unlawful threat of reprisal.

The key issue in a plant closing, except where an employer goes completely out of business (see 1 below), is whether the closing is motivated by anti-union considerations, often called "anti-union animus" in legal proceedings, or by unbiased economic considerations. An anti-union plant closing is unlawful and may be remedied by an order to reopen the facility and rehire the workers. An economic closing is lawful, although there may be related legal obligations such as advance notice requirements, accrued benefits, health insurance continuation, or contractually required severance pay.

In threat cases in which an employer makes statements about the possibility of the plant closing if workers unionize, the issue is whether such statements amount to a threat of reprisal against workers' organizing efforts, or are simply an expression of views, argument, or opinion that do not contain a threat of reprisal. A threat of reprisal is an unfair labor practice, whereas expressions of any views, argument, or opinion are allowed under the law.

Decisions of the National Labor Relations Board (NLRB or the Board) and federal courts have established the following basic principles in cases involving plant closings or threats of plant closing in connection with workers' organizing efforts:

1. An employer may not close a plant to avoid dealing with a union, to retaliate against workers for forming a union, or to discourage union organizing at another facility of the employer. Such an unfair labor practice may be remedied by an order to reopen the plant and rehire the employees. However, an employer may lawfully decide

---

[14] The legal frameworks presented here cover general private sector labor law. Each country has special constitutional or statutory regimes for public sector employment in federal, state or provincial, and subordinate jurisdictions. The countries also have special legislation for certain private sector industries or occupations. These specialized legal systems are not treated here.

to go completely out of business and cease operating altogether, even for an anti-union motivation.[15]

2. An employer may close a plant for legitimate economic considerations if the closing is not motivated by anti-union considerations.

3. An employer may not threaten to close a plant in reprisal for union activity.

4. An employer may express any views, argument, or opinion about plant closings or other possible consequences of unionization, as long as such expression contains no threat of reprisal or force, or promise of benefit.

The cases that arise in U.S. labor law posing issues of plant closings or threats of plant closing in connection with the workers' right to organize are among the most difficult and complex in labor jurisprudence. There is no "rule" for such cases, because proving motivation (anti-union versus economic), or proving whether certain statements amount to an unlawful threat or a lawful expression of views, argument, or opinion, is always a matter of interpretation of the evidence.

Each case depends on a unique set of facts and circumstances that are brought out in a trial before an Administrative Law Judge (ALJ) of the NLRB. The judge's decision may then be appealed to the NLRB in Washington, D.C., and the Board's decision may be appealed to 1 of 12 federal circuit courts of appeals, whose own decisions may be appealed to the U.S. Supreme Court.

Elements of the U.S. Legal Framework

Common Law Rights of Ownership

As a general principle, the common law places no restrictions on an owner's power to dispose of means of production through sale, lease, transfer, relocation, shutdown, or other form of alienability because of such a transaction's effects on workers. Until passage of the National Labor Relations Act of 1935 (NLRA or "Wagner Act," after the name of its author in the U.S. Senate) and its upholding by the U.S. Supreme Court in 1937, U.S. employers enjoyed unfettered power to close a plant in response to unionization drives by their employees, or to threaten plant closings if their employees chose union representation.

Notwithstanding this, much of U.S. heavy industry was unionized in the 1930s and 1940s through mass organizing drives and "sit down" strikes. An actual closing was not so easy at large-scale industrial plants representing huge investments, which

---

[15] See *Textile Workers Union v. Darlington Mfg. Co.*, 380 U.S. 263 (1965).

characterized the period of the early 20th century. Many of these plants in the steel, auto, electrical, rubber, aircraft, and other mass production industries were relatively new, vertically integrated, and highly productive, so employers could not easily "walk away" from them, or credibly threaten to close them, if workers unionized.[16]

The NLRA

The NLRA changed the law regarding plant closings and threats of plant closing related to workers' organizing efforts. The Wagner Act affirmed workers' freedom of association, defined certain anti-union conduct as an "unfair labor practice," and prohibited such conduct.

Section 7 of the NLRA extended to most private sector employees "the right to self-organization, to form, join, or assist labor organizations, to bargain collectively through representatives of their own choosing, and to engage in other concerted activities for the purpose of collective bargaining or other mutual aid or protection."

The Wagner Act also created a means to protect these rights by defining unfair labor practices in Sections 8(a)(1) and 8(a)(3) of the NLRA. An unfair labor practice violates the law and is subject to the remedies provided by the Act.

An anti-union plant closing, or a threat to close a plant in reprisal for workers' organizing activity, violates Section 8(a)(1) of the NLRA, which makes it an unfair labor practice to "interfere with, restrain, or coerce employees in the exercise of the rights guaranteed in Section 7." The Act empowers the NLRB to issue "cease-and-desist" orders and other remedial steps to prevent 8(a)(1) violations.

Closing a plant in retaliation for union activity also violates Section 8(a)(3) of the Act, which defines the unfair labor practice of "discrimination in regard to hire or tenure of employment to encourage or discourage membership in any labor organization."

The Act provides for reinstatement and back pay (or other "make-whole" remedies) for workers who are discharged or otherwise discriminated against for such activity. For workers affected by a plant closing, the remedy may include an order to reopen the plant and re-employ the workers. The Act also empowers the Labor Board to set aside an election and order a new election if plant closing threats destroyed "laboratory conditions" for employee free choice of representation, whether or not an unfair labor practice charge is filed.

---

[16] Recall that in the case that gave rise to submission no. 9501 OAN/Mex and the Ministerial Consultations that prompted this report, the workplace was a telemarketing facility consisting essentially of offices, cubicles, and telephone lines and phones. The work was shifted to another U.S. city after the closing of the facility. For another example of capital mobility in the new global economy, see Mike Mills, "With Click of a Mouse, White-Collar Jobs Go Overseas," the *Washington Post*, September 17, 1996, at A1.

The Employer Free Speech Clause of the Taft-Hartley Act

While the Wagner Act of 1935 has been described as "Labor's Magna Carta," the 1947 Labor Management Relations Act (LMRA or "Taft-Hartley Act," after its legislative sponsors) reflected management interests. Opposed by U.S. unions as an anti-labor law while supported by management as a restoration of balance in the law, the LMRA added a new clause, Section 8(c), known as the "employer free speech" provision. It states that

> The expressing of any views, argument, or opinion, or the dissemi-
> nation thereof, whether in written, printed, graphic or visual form,
> shall not constitute or be evidence of an unfair labor practice under
> any of the provisions of this Act, if such expression contains no threat
> of reprisal or force or promise of benefit.

Section 8(c) codified a trend in court rulings that established the employer's right to communicate its views on unionization to employees. In the decades since then, the NLRB and the courts have introduced complicated and often shifting rules about how strongly, directly, or aggressively employers may speak out against unionization, including through such devices as "captive audience meetings" where workers are required to hear management speeches against union organization. Under these rules, employers are allowed to discuss with employees the possible consequences of union-ization, including plant closings, as long as the employer's statements do not contain a "threat of reprisal or force or promise of benefit."

Critics have long argued that management's ability to discuss plant closings, how-ever apparently neutral the discussion may be, inherently amounts to a threat of re-prisal given the employer's acknowledged power to close a facility. Defenders of 8(c) argue that management cannot be denied its free speech rights to convey its opposi-tion to unionization and to objectively discuss issues, including plant closings, as long as the discussion does not amount to a threat. Since this is a matter of interpretation of management statements, the NLRB and the courts closely scrutinize such statements in the overall context of company actions in an organizing campaign. The result is that the Board or the courts might find the same words permissible in one case and an unlawful threat in another case. Each case rises and falls on its own unique facts and circumstances as to whether employer statements stop short of a threat, or cross the line and become a threat.

Significantly, the Taft-Hartley Act did not diminish Section 7 rights or change the Wagner Act's definitions of unfair labor practices by employers. Sections 8(a)(1) and

(3) of the Act remained intact. The statute preserved the unlawfulness of threats to close a plant to discourage union activity, and of the actual closing of a plant in reprisal for union activity.

Plant Closings: The Wright Line Test

In plant closing cases, the issue of motivation is paramount. Did the employer close for legitimate economic reasons or for unlawful anti-union reasons? This issue is even more difficult in "mixed motive" cases where both considerations are present.

The NLRB and the courts apply the same test to plant closing cases that they apply to unfair labor practice cases involving the alleged discriminatory discharge of an individual employee for attempting to form a union. The employer usually responds that the employee was terminated for legitimate reasons such as absenteeism, misconduct, poor performance, and so on. Such cases can be either a "pretext" case, alleging that the employer's excuse is completely false and fabricated, or a "mixed motive" case, where there is some evidence of employee wrongdoing as well as evidence of anti-union motivation of the employer.

The test for such cases was elaborated in the NLRB's *Wright Line* decision.[17] Under this ruling, the NLRB General Counsel first has the burden of proving that the employee's union activity was a motivating factor in the employer's action. If the General Counsel establishes a case of apparent anti-union motivation, the burden of proof shifts to the employer to demonstrate that the discharge was for legitimate, job-related causes. If the employer fails to prove any legitimate cause, it is a pretext case, and the employee is reinstated regardless of the degree of unlawful anti-union motivation. If the employer succeeds in proving some level of legitimate, business-related motivation, it is a mixed motive case. The employer must prove that the employee would have been terminated even in the absence of an anti-union motivation.

Plant closing cases usually pose the issue even more starkly. An employer can nearly always present some legitimate business reason for closing a plant, which is a much weightier action than discharging an individual employee. Thus, these cases usually present the mixed motive posture. The General Counsel first has the burden of showing that anti-union motivation is an element in the decision to close. Evidence could include such matters as the timing of the closing in relation to the union organizing effort, or statements by managers and supervisors suggesting that the closing is related to the unionization. The burden then shifts to the employer to show that the decision to close would have been made anyway, and to provide evidence of business, accounting, marketing, or other economic considerations motivating the decision.

---

[17] Wright Line, A Div. of Wright Line, Inc., 251 N.L.R.B. 1083(1980), *enf'd*, 662 F.2d 899 (1st Cir. 1981), *cert. denied*, 455 U.S. 989 (1982).

Threats of Plant Closing: The Gissel Balancing Test

In the landmark *Gissel* case,[18] the U.S. Supreme Court established the standards for balancing an employer's right to express any views, argument, or opinion on plant closings with the employees' right to organize. The court stated that balancing those rights "must take into account the economic dependence of the employees on their employers" and the "necessary tendency" of employees to perceive implied threats in statements "that might be more readily dismissed by a more disinterested ear."

An employer may make a prediction as to the precise effect he believes unionization will have, but such a prediction must be carefully phrased on the basis of objective fact involving demonstrably probable consequences beyond his control. If there is any implication that the employer may take action for reasons unrelated to economic necessity, the statement is an unlawful threat.

Remedies

The NLRB normally views an order to reopen the plant and rehire the workers as the proper remedy for an anti-union plant closing, unless the employer can demonstrate that reopening would endanger its continued viability. In this case, remedies are usually limited to back pay. The Board may order the employer to offer employment to affected workers at other facilities of the employer and to pay workers the costs of moving to a new location. It should be recalled, however, that such remedies apply only when the employer relocates work or maintains operations elsewhere. Under the *Darlington* doctrine, there is no remedy when an employer goes entirely out of business for antiunion motivations.

NLRB decisions are routinely appealed to the federal courts. While generally the courts maintain a doctrine of "deference" to the Board's specialized expertise in labor relations matters, federal courts may reverse or modify Board decisions. In plant closing cases, some federal courts make the test one of "undue burden" on the employer rather than the viability of the enterprise. Under this standard, NLRB orders to reopen a plant are sometimes overturned by the federal court reviewing the Board's decision.

The remedy for plant closing threats is different from the remedy for a closing. The normal remedy for plant closing threats is a "cease-and-desist" order. The NLRB orders the employer (1) to cease and desist from threatening to close the plant, and

---

[18] *NLRB v. Gissel Packing Co.*, 395 U.S. 575 (1969).

(2) to repudiate the earlier threats by posting a notice at the workplace promising not to repeat the threat. In some cases the Board orders the employer to repudiate the threat in the same manner that the threat was made—in a letter to employees' homes, for example, or in a meeting with employees.

Critics argue that the mere posting of a notice or other promise not to repeat the threat is an empty remedy. They maintain that the effect of the threat remains, despite the employer's new statements to the contrary as ordered by the NLRB, because of the employer's inherent power to carry out the threat. This argument is not accepted in U.S. labor law jurisprudence. However, U.S. law does provide that in extraordinary cases where plant closing threats are part of a pattern of massive unfair labor practices that would destroy a union's majority support and make a fair election impossible, the NLRB is empowered to issue an order to the employer to recognize and bargain with the union, either without an election or even if the union lost the election. This is also based on the *Gissel* ruling of the U.S. Supreme Court.

Plant Closings and Threats at an Already Unionized Plant

The discussion up to now has focused on the effects of plant closings or threats of plant closing on workers attempting to form a new union. Another line of labor jurisprudence involves cases affecting workers who have already formed a union and established a bargaining relationship with the employer through one or more collective bargaining agreements.[19]

The same basic issues of anti-union motivation versus economic justification, and prediction versus threat of reprisal, arise in cases where already unionized plants are closed or where threats of plant closing are made in the course of collective bargaining. Normally in such cases, however, closings or threats are seen as reflecting an employer's desire to achieve cost reductions. A viable unfair labor practice case exists only if the employer demonstrates, by some action susceptible to proof, an anti-union motivation or a desire to discourage union organizing at other facilities.

Employers normally have available managers, planners, consultants, and accountants who can provide documentary evidence of the claimed business justification. Workers and unions can only claim to "know" that the closing or the threat is motivated by anti-unionism, while having great difficulty proving it.

---

[19] Because of the limits of this study and its focus on the effects of plant closings on workers' right to organize, as distinct from the right to collective bargaining, the issue of the employer's duty to bargain with the union over a *decision* to close the plant (as opposed to the *effects* of the decision to close), and the distinction between mandatory and permissive subjects of bargaining (a distinction that does not exist in Canadian or Mexican labor law), are not discussed here. See *First National Maintenance Corp. v. NLRB*, 452 U.S. 666 (1981).

This poses the central, unresolved problem of plant closings and their effects on workers' right to organize under U.S. labor law: how can the right be sufficiently protected when the law subordinates it to a plausible economic motive for closing? Since union organization and collective bargaining are normally seen by managers as imposing additional costs, there is almost always in management's view an element of

Unfair Labor Practice Proceedings Under U.S. Law

1. Investigation of the Charge

Acting under the authority of the General Counsel, the NLRB Regional Director first conducts an investigation of the unfair labor practice charge. The investigation includes taking sworn statements. It also allows opportunity for union or employer counsel to submit position papers and to argue on behalf of their client for the issuance of a complaint or dismissal of the charge.

2. Complaint or Dismissal

The Regional Director issues a complaint upon a finding that the charge is "meritorious"—that is, if the findings of a preliminary investigation support the facts alleged in the charge, and the facts alleged, if true, would constitute an unfair labor practice. If not, the charge is dismissed. No appeal is allowed to the NLRB or to the courts of a decision by the General Counsel to dismiss an unfair labor practice charge.

3. ALJ Hearing

If the parties do not settle a complaint, the case goes forward to a trial of the facts before an ALJ. The ALJ hears the examination and cross-examination of witnesses and rules on the admissibility of evidence and testimony. The General Counsel (that is, an NLRB staff attorney representing the General Counsel) prosecutes a case before the ALJ, with assistance of counsel for the charging party. The ALJs evaluate witnesses' credibility, examine documents and other exhibits for their probative weight, and make findings of fact and findings of law. They issue a written decision in the case determining whether the charged party has committed an unfair labor practice, and explaining the reasons for such a determination. (See Table 1 for statistics on NLRB unfair labor practice proceedings through these stages, 1990–1995).

4. Appeal to the NLRB

ALJ decisions may be appealed to the NLRB for a review of the record in the case, which includes the transcript of the trial before the ALJ and all documentary evidence. The Board can affirm or reverse, in whole or in part, the ALJ decision. In complex or novel cases, the NLRB might hear oral arguments by parties to the case. The Board issues a written decision in the case either adopting the ALJ decision without further comment, or offering its own reasoning for deciding how to treat the case. In contrast to Canadian and Mexican law, U.S. NLRB decisions are not self-enforcing. A party may refuse to abide by the Board's ruling, forcing the NLRB to initiate new legal proceedings to have its order enforced by the courts.

5. Appeal to the Federal Courts

The NLRB's decision may then be appealed to a federal court of appeals in 1 of 12 judicial circuits, divided geographically among several states. The courts of appeals maintain a general policy of deference to the administrative expertise of the NLRB, but at the same time the courts will consider the substance of a case and may overrule the Board on the merits. Some circuit courts are more deferential to the NLRB. Others are more forceful in reviewing the substance of Board decisions and overturning them when the court disagrees.

Decisions by the federal circuit courts of appeals may be appealed to the U.S. Supreme Court. Only a small percentage of cases are accepted for review by the Supreme Court. As a result, despite the general rule of uniform federal law governing labor relations in the United States, conflicting doctrines on certain aspects of the law may prevail in different judicial circuits.

economic rationality or business justification in avoiding or eliminating a union.[20] This rationale applies equally to a closing where a new union organizing campaign is under way, where a union has won bargaining rights and is seeking a first contract, or to the closing of an already unionized plant.

Table 1

U.S. NLRB Handling of Unfair Labor Practice Charges Against Employers, 1990–1995[a]

FY	Charges Filed Under §8(a)	Charges Withdrawn	Dismissed	Complaints Issued	Informal/ Formal Settlement	Hearing Held	Post-Hearing Settlement
1990	24,075 (26,265)	7,294 (28%)	7,251 (28%)	3,182 (12%)	7,891 (30%)	523 (2%)	124 (.5%)
1991	23,005 (25,661)	7,433 (29%)	6,470 (25%)	3,225 (13%)	7,881 (31%)	559 (2%)	93 (.4%)
1992	23,119 (25,652)	7,541 (29%)	6,778 (26%)	3,013 (12%)	7,689 (30%)	536 (2%)	95 (.4%)
1993	24,500 (26,270)	7,467 (28%)	6,887 (26%)	3,069 (12%)	8,354 (32%)	362 (1.4%)	131 (.5%)
1994	26,058 (26,592)	7,705 (29%)	6,877 (26%)	3,162 (12%)	8,304 (31%)	422 (1.6%)	122 (.5%)
1995	26,244 (27,123)	8,175 (30%)	6,213 (23%)	3,271 (12%)	8,870 (33%)	465 (1.7%)	129 (.5%)
Average	24,500 (26,262)	7,603 (29%)	6,746 (26%)	3,154 (12%)	8,165 (31%)	478 (1.8%)	116 (.4%)

[a] Numbers in parentheses under Charges Filed are the number of dispositions of unfair labor practice charges against employers during the year. The percentages supplied here in parentheses refer to these dispositions. The number of dispositions is higher than the number of charges filed in a given year because some are dispositions of charges filed in *prior* years. This trend reflects the progress of the NLRB in taking care of the backlog of cases from earlier years.

---

[20] See, for example, Roger W. Schmenner, *Making Business Location Decisions* (1982), a study that equated "favorable labor climate" with non-union status, and concluded that "[a] new workforce that is nearly impossible to organize is perhaps the most prized side benefit of a new plant site, and it is the controlling consideration for many companies." (at 37, 156–157); Thomas A. Kochan et al., *The Transformation of American Industrial Relations* (1986), discussing union avoidance as a factor in U.S. corporate investment and plant closing decisions (at 66–76).

Canada

Plant closings and threats of plant closing in the context of Canadian labor organizing give rise to unfair labor practice complaints.[21] A complaint normally alleges that an employer has interfered in the formation or selection of a trade union or the representation of employees by a union, or that the employer has disciplined or discriminated against employees for exercising their rights to organize or bargain collectively under the legislation, or both.[22]

As in U.S. labor law, some Canadian statutes contain an employer "free speech clause." The Ontario Act states that "nothing in this section shall be deemed to deprive an employer of the employer's freedom to express views so long as the employer does not use coercion, intimidation, threats, promises, or undue influence." Whether statements about plant closing are coercive or not depends on the overall context of employer conduct, but Canadian jurisdictions generally limit the scope of what employers may lawfully say in light of potential coercion inherent in the employer's position of authority over employees.[23]

---

[21] Note that in U.S. terminology, affected workers or unions file a "charge." In Canada, this initial filing is called a "complaint." In the United States, a "complaint" is issued by the Regional Director acting as an arm of the General Counsel upon finding merit to the charge. The finding of merit is preliminary; it is not a determination of guilt.

[22] See for example, Ontario *Labour Relations Act, 1995*, S.O. 1995, c.1. (hereinafter "*OLRA*"), s. 70: "No employer or employers' organization and no persons acting on behalf of an employer or an employers' organization shall participate in or interfere with the formation, selection or administration of a trade union or the representation of employees by a trade union or contribute financial or other support to a trade union"; and *OLRA*, s. 72: "No employer, employers' organization or person acting on behalf of an employer or employers' organization (a) shall refuse to employ or continue to employ a person, or discriminate against a person in regard to employment or any term or condition of employment because the person was or is a member of a trade union or was or is exercising any other rights under this Act; (b) shall impose any condition in a contract of employment or propose the imposition of any condition in a contract of employment that seeks to restrain an employee or a person seeking employment from becoming a member of a trade union or exercising any rights under this Act; or (c) shall seek by threat of dismissal, or by any other kind of threat, or by the imposition of a pecuniary or other penalty, or by any means to compel an employee to become or refrain from becoming or continue to be or to cease to be a member or officer or representative of a trade union or cease to exercise any other rights under this Act."

[23] See, for example, the *American Airlines* and *Wal-Mart* cases described in Part Three. The statements "I hope you will think very seriously before taking any action that will make your job a union job" and "It would be inappropriate for your company to comment on what it will or will not do if the store is unionized" were found to be unlawful closing threats in the context in which they were delivered.

Closings or threats of closing may result in complaints that an employer has breached its duty to bargain in good faith with the union, or has engaged in an unlawful lock-out. In Newfoundland and Saskatchewan, a union may bring a complaint that an employer has closed, relocated, or threatened to close a plant or business during a labor-management dispute, conduct which is expressly prohibited by statute.[24]

Several principles are applied consistently and uniformly across jurisdictional lines. In unfair labor practice cases, the presence of anti-union animus is the prime determinant. Canadian tribunals and courts generally prohibit an employer from acting even in part on the basis of anti-union motives, regardless of the existence of a valid business justification for its actions. The predominant motive approach was specifically rejected by the Ontario Labour Relations Board (OLRB) in its oft-cited decision in *Westinghouse.*[25] There, the OLRB held that, despite the existence of several valid business reasons for moving operations, the employer acted in part based on anti-union motives and thus committed an unfair labor practice.

In plant closing cases, evidence of economic considerations and business justifications are critical in applying the mixed motive test. A majority of Canadian jurisdictions place the burden of proof on employers to show that the closing was not motivated by anti-union animus.[26] In practice, the presence or absence of anti-union motive will often have to be determined without direct evidence and will depend upon inferences drawn from the timing of decisions and other contextual factors.

The most difficult unfair labor practice cases tend to arise when employers claim they are acting solely on the grounds of economic considerations, part of which are the economic costs of collective bargaining. The employers' argument is twofold: (1) they are not attempting to forestall the exercise of union rights; rather they are reacting to the economic consequences of collective bargaining; and (2) labor legislation must not prevent them from responding to the marketplace. Unions maintain, conversely, that statutory rights to bargain will be meaningless if, on the basis of increased costs, employers can simply move elsewhere when a union is certified.

---

[24]   See Newfoundland *Labour Relations Act*, R.S.N. 1990, c. L-1 (hereinafter "*Nfld. LRA*"), s. 26; and Saskatchewan *Trade Union Act*, R.S.S. 1978, c. T-17 (hereinafter "STUA"), s. 11(1)(I).

[25]   *UEW, Local 504 v. Westinghouse Canada Inc.* (1980), 80 C.L.L.C. 16,053 (O.L.R.B.); upheld on judicial review *Westinghouse Canada Inc. v. UEW, Local 504* (1980), 80 C.L.L.C. 14,062 (Ont. Div.Ct.).

[26]   See British Columbia, s.8(6); Manitoba, s.7; Ontario, s.89(5); Quebec, s.17; Prince Edward Island, s.11(5); Canada, s.98(4).

Canadian labor law contains the same tension noted previously, in connection with U.S. law, of protecting workers' right to organize in a context in which economic motivations justify plant closings. For example, the OLRB distinguished the *Westinghouse* case, where the employer explicitly made non-union operation as the goal to be achieved, from another case where "there was no evidence that the fact that the employees ... were represented by a trade union played any part in the employer's decision ... a decision to save money and thereby increase profits is not equivalent to anti-union animus simply because the money saved would otherwise have been paid as wages to employees in the bargaining unit."[27]

A later Ontario board decision involving the same employer cautioned that its earlier decision did *not* stand for the proposition that "so long as an employer can point to cost savings in justifying the business decision he has made, it cannot be found he has breached the Act."[28] Instead, labor boards have attempted to resolve these difficult cases through the use of the mixed motive approach, the drawing of inferences and presumptions, and the use of a flexible approach to remedies in cases where there is evidence of legitimate business justifications. Cases tend to be decided against an employer when it has taken precipitous action in the context of an organizing drive, failed to resort to collective bargaining to resolve economic difficulties with employees, or reacted to the process of collective bargaining as opposed to its actual economic impact.

In general, Canadian labor boards make no distinction between full and partial closures in finding that an unfair labor practice has been committed. Except in Quebec, and then in just one reported case, Canadian adjudicators have generally rejected the view that an employer has a fundamental right to completely close down operations, even if motivated by anti-union animus.[29] An unfair labor practice may also be found when an employer, during negotiations for a new collective agreement, fails to disclose an impending decision, or the high probability of a decision, to close, relocate, or contract out operations even for purely economic motives.[30]

---

[27] See *Kennedy Lodge Nursing Home* (1980), 81 C.L.L.C. para. 16,078 (O.L.R.B.), at 473. Analyzing this passage, one commentator argued that "this simply collapses the distinction between discriminatory (anti-union) and economic motives, at least in a good number of cases. The rational employer, intent on avoiding the collective bargaining process is protected through this test." See Brian Langille, "Equal Partnership in Canadian Labour Law" (1983), 21 *Osgood Hall Law Journal* 496.

[28] See *Kennedy Lodge Inc.* (1984), O.L.R.B. Rep.931.

[29] In *City Buick Pontiac (Montreal) Inc.* (1981), 81 C.L.L.C. 14,108, the Quebec Labour Court held that as long as the closure was permanent and complete the employer could go out of business with impunity, despite the presence of anti-union motive.

[30] See *Int'l Woodworkers of America, Local 2–69 v. Consolidated Bathurst Packaging Ltd.*, (1983), 83 C.L.L.C. 16,066 (O.L.R.B.); upheld on application for judicial review on another point; *Consolidated Bathurst Packaging Ltd. v. Int'l Woodworkers of America, Local 2–69* (1990), 68 D.L.R. (4th) 524 (S.C.C.).

Labor boards are generally given fairly broad remedial powers, not only to make cease-and-desist orders but also to require one of the parties to rectify violations. Statutes often contain explicit powers to order reinstatement or award damages. However, no Canadian labor board has actually ordered an employer to resume operations at a closed facility. Many have expressed concern about the practicality of such an order, although at the same time several decisions have suggested that they have the jurisdiction to order reopening.

However, labor boards have ordered an entire bargaining unit to be reinstated where employers unlawfully contracted out the work of that unit. In another case, where a legitimate closing was moved up by 8 months as a result of anti-union animus, the board ordered the employer to either maintain operations for 8 months and reinstate the employees, or pay employees their wages and benefits as if they were employed throughout that period.[31]

Generally, labor boards have sought to formulate alternatives such as providing affected employees with transfer rights at other locations or compensating employees and unions as fully as possible in the circumstances.[32] While courts do not usually disturb labor board rulings, the Supreme Court of Canada has made it clear that labor boards' innovative remedies must be reasonably related to an employer's breach of the statute and must meet constitutional criteria. For example, it overturned a CLRB order that an employer pay its savings from closing a unionized facility into a trust fund to promote the objectives of the statute on the grounds that such an order is not within a labor board's jurisdiction. The Court also suggested that the federal board's

---

[31] See *Insurance Courier Services and UFCW, Loc. 175* (1993), 18 Can. L.R.B.R. (2d) 286 (Can); *Westfair Foods and RWDSU, Local 454*, (1993) S.L.R.B.D. No. 2.

[32] In *Humpty Dumpty Foods Ltd.* (1978), 78 C.L.L.C. 16,136 (O.L.R.B.), a case involving the transfer of operations to a location beyond the coverage of the collective agreement, the board ordered the employer either to reopen operations at its original location, or to agree to extend the scope of the recognition clause in the collective agreement to cover its new locations. Subsequently, in *Westinghouse, supra* note 3, the employer relocated its operations to avoid a collective agreement, at the same time creating considerable employment. Because of the intermingling of old and new employees, the board refused to extend the collective agreement to cover the new locations. Instead, existing employees were given the right to claim job openings in other divisions of the old location or at the new locations (without loss of benefits and full relocation expenses) and, the employer was ordered to compensate the union for organizing expenses at the new locations and to provide the union with information relevant to organizing employees.

practice of requiring an employer to sign and send to its employees a board-dictated pledge of future compliance may violate the employer's freedom of expression under the Canadian Charter of Rights and Freedoms.[33]

Unfair Labor Practice Proceedings Under Canadian Law

As a result of the structure of Canadian federalism, Canada has 11 labor relations regimes: one federal and 1 in each of the 10 provinces. The Canada Labour Code, administered by the Canada Labour Relations Board (CLRB) and the Federal Mediation and Conciliation Service, governs labor relations in the federal jurisdiction, which covers approximately 10 percent of the nation's workforce. The acts and authorities for the provinces are

Alberta Labour Relations Code / Alberta Labour Relations Board
British Columbia Labour Relations Code / British Columbia Labour Relations Board
Manitoba Labour Relations Act / Manitoba Labour Board
New Brunswick Industrial Relations Act / New Brunswick Labour and Employment Board
Newfoundland Labour Relations Act / Newfoundland Labour Relations Board
Nova Scotia Trade Union Act / Nova Scotia Labour Relations Board
Ontario Labour Relations Act, 1995 / Ontario Labour Relations Board
Prince Edward Island Labour Act / Prince Edward Island Labour Relations Board
Saskatchewan Trade Union Act / Saskatchewan Labour Relations Board
Quebec Labour Code / Office of the General Commissioner of Labour (Labour Ministry)

Unfair labor practice law enforcement is complaint driven. Details of procedures differ from province to province, but most jurisdictions empower their labor boards (or commissioners in Quebec) to investigate a complaint, receive evidence and hear arguments of the parties, and issue a decision. Note that there is no equivalent in Canada to the independent General Counsel of the NLRB, who decides (through the Regional Director) if a charge has merit, then issues a complaint and takes over the prosecution of the case on behalf of the charging party. In Canada the complaining worker or union, and the complained-against employer, represent themselves through counsel before the board or commissioner.

---

[33] *National Bank of Canada v. Retail Clerk's Int'l Union* (1984), 9 D.L.R. (4th) 10 (S.C.C.). There, the employer closed one of its bank branches and transferred work to a non-union branch following certification of a union. The Supreme Court of Canada upheld the remedy of automatic certification at the new branch and other aspects of the Board's remedial order. With respect to the trust fund and the written pledge, one justice called these "clearly punitive in nature ... the Canada Labour Relations Board has no power to impose punitive measures. This type of penalty is totalitarian...."

Provincial Example: Ontario

The Ontario Labour Relations Board (OLRB) is an independent enforcement agency composed of a chairperson, an alternate chairperson, 27 vice chairs, and 34 board members—17 each of employer and employee representatives. Many of the vice chairs and board members serve part-time, maintaining separate employment.

The OLRB employs 20 labor relations officers as its full-time staff. The Board normally operates in three-member *ad hoc* panels to hear cases based on investigations carried out by the staff. The chair appoints one representative from each of the employer and employee members of the OLRB, as well as a vice chair to preside over the panel.

Upon receiving a complaint, the OLRB will normally appoint a permanent staff officer to investigate it and report to the Board. In practice, officers are trained to encourage the parties to settle the matter without need for further legal proceedings. Of unfair labor practice complaints in Ontario, 80 percent are resolved without a hearing, compared with 98 percent for the U.S. NLRB.

Although a greater percentage of Canadian cases go forward to a hearing, they are handled in a streamlined fashion. Instead of having multiple stages of investigation, hearings, and appeals, the case is handled in a single proceeding. The OLRB hears the case and issues a final decision. Unfair labor practice procedures before the OLRB are usually concluded relatively rapidly.[34]

Although the OLRB can reconsider its own decisions, its rulings are final and binding, and are immediately enforceable by the civil courts, backed by contempt-of-court power. There is no right of appeal, but there is a limited right to judicial review in the Ontario Court (General Division) on grounds of natural justice, jurisdictional error, and constitutional matters. Courts have exercised caution in reviewing decisions of the OLRB on the grounds that the Board is a specialized tribunal charged with balancing competing interests. For example, in 1994–1995, the Ontario Court dealt with just five applications for judicial review among hundreds of OLRB decisions. All five appeals were dismissed.

Ontario Board Statistics

During fiscal year 1993–1994, the OLRB received 4,525 cases and carried over 894 from the previous year for a total caseload of 5,419. Compare this figure to 711 cases received by the federal CLRB for an indication of the relative importance of

---

[34] See Peter G. Bruce, "State Structures and Processing of Unfair Labor Practice Cases in the United States and Canada," in Jane Jenson and Rianne Mahon, eds., *The Challenge of Restructuring: North American Labor Movements Respond* (1993), at 180.

provincial jurisdiction in labor matters. The OLRB processed 1,297 unfair labor practice cases alleging contravention of the Act. Of those, 856 were disposed of, proceedings were adjourned indefinitely in 160 cases, and 281 unfair labor practice cases were pending at the end of the fiscal year.

From the date of initial filing, 80 percent of all dispositions were accomplished in 3 months or less. A median of 26 days was taken to proceed from filing to disposition for the 3,287 cases completed in the year. Certification applications were processed in a median of 24 days, while unfair labor practice cases took 33 days. In all categories of cases, the processing time was shorter than the year before.

The experience of the CLRB contrasts sharply with the OLRB case-handling experience. The average time taken to process a CLRB case without a hearing in 1994–1995 was 168 days, or 5-1/2 months. The average for a CLRB unfair labor practice case with a hearing was 447 days, with averages of about 4 months to prepare a report, 3 months waiting for a scheduled hearing, and 6 months to write the decision.[35]

The Quebec Commissioners and the Labour Court

While the Quebec statute is like other Canadian laws in its definition and prohibition of unfair labor practices, labor law enforcement is structured differently in Quebec. Quebec does not have a separate board empowered to adjudicate cases and issue remedies largely free of judicial review. Quebec's enforcement is carried out by a specialized branch of the Ministry of Labour: the Office of the General Commissioner of Labour. The commissioners' decisions are subject to review by the Labour Court, part of the judicial branch.

The General Commissioner of Labour

An individual Labour Commissioner investigates an unfair labor practice charge after a complaint is filed. The Commissioner receives evidence and makes determinations on lawful or unlawful conduct. The Commissioner is empowered to order an employer to cease and desist from unlawful conduct and to reinstate with full back pay or otherwise make whole an employee who suffered discrimination for union activity.

---

[35] See *Seeking a Balance: Canada Labour Code Part 1 Review*, Ministry of Labour Task Force (1996), at 187. Using this report, the federal government in November 1996 proposed amendments to the Canada Labour Code that would streamline and accelerate unfair labor practice proceedings. A new Canada Industrial Relations Board (CIRB) would replace the CLRB. This new, tripartite Board would be made up of a neutral chair and vice chairs, and equal numbers of members representing labor and management.

The Labour Court

The Court hears appeals from final decisions of a Labour Commissioner, and is empowered to affirm, reverse, or modify the commissioner's decision. The Court's decision is final, and there is no appeal. The Labour Court has original jurisdiction in penal cases involving criminal liability for labor law violations, a powerful but rarely used remedy.

The Labour Court is a judicial entity, not an administrative one. The Court is composed of judges chosen among those of the Quebec Court after consultation with the General Counsel of the Quebec Bar and the Consultative Labour and Employment Council, a labor-management advisory body created by law. Their number is not fixed, but must be "sufficient to rapidly dispose of matters submitted to the Court."

As in all Canadian jurisdictions, decisions of the Labour Commissioners or the Labour Court are self-enforcing upon deposit of the decision in Superior Court, with the same obligatory effect as a decision of the Superior Court itself. The decision may then be carried out as with any decision by a common law court under the Quebec Code of Civil Procedure, enforceable in a contempt of court proceeding upon non-compliance with the order, backed by incarceration and fines.

MEXICO

Mexico's legal framework regarding plant closings and freedom of association is substantially different from that of the United States and Canada.[36] Mexico does not use the unfair labor practice (ULP) concept. Instead, rather than defining prohibited acts, Mexican labor law sets forth affirmative requirements for employment-related decisions.

The Federal Labor Law (FLL) requires companies to secure permission from the relevant Conciliation and Arbitration Board (CAB) before closing a plant. There are over 100 such boards in federal and state jurisdictions for various regions and industrial sectors. Whether in federal or state jurisdiction and regardless of geographic or sectoral reach, all CABs enforce the same provisions of the FLL.

---

[36] The Secretariat's preparation of this section of the report draws on two legal memoranda supplied to the Secretariat for this purpose: "Effects of Sudden Plant Closings on the Principle of Freedom of Association and the Right of Workers to Organize in Mexico," by Nestor de Buen Lozano and Carlos de Buen Unna, and "Trade Union Effects of Plant Closings," by Arturo Alcalde Justiniani.

A temporary plant closing creates a "collective suspension" of the employment relationship under FLL Article 427, and a permanent closing creates a "collective termination" of the employment relationship under Article 433. In short, an employer
must obtain the labor board's approval *before* closing a plant, rather than having a
union file a complaint with the labor board *after* a closing.

In another key difference, the FLL does not consider threats in general or plant
closing threats in particular as unlawful acts. The law only addresses cases where an
employee threatens the employer, which can result in a justified discharge under FLL
Article 47 (II). However, Mexican law does address the effects of a plant closing
threat if the threat is carried out. The issue in such proceedings is whether the employer closed for one of the permissible causes specified in the FLL. The employer
would seek to prove that the closing was motivated by legitimate economic cause specified in the law, through testimony of financial analysts, expert witnesses, examination
of books and records, and so forth. Anti-union motivation is not a permissible cause.
However, the burden always rests with the employer to show legitimate cause. Evidence of anti-union motivation is not relevant in a plant closing case, so threats are not
an issue.

Failing proof of a permissible cause, employees are considered to have been unjus-
tifiably discharged. The employer must then, under the Constitution, reinstate or pay
severance pay to affected workers. In any event, as will be seen, the specified procedure for plant closing is rarely invoked.

Job Stability and Discharge

A key concept in Mexican labor law, without which a plant closing situation cannot
be understood, is that of job stability and discharge. Job stability is understood in
Mexico as a right of the worker to keep his or her job either for a time specified in a
contract or, without such specification, indefinitely. The employer may not discharge a
worker arbitrarily, but must prove a specific cause defined in the law.

This job stability is recognized as a constitutional right in Article 123, Part A,
Paragraph XXII, which states, "The employer who discharges a worker without just
cause, or for having joined an association or a union, or for having participated in a
lawful strike, shall be obligated, at the worker's choice, to fulfill the employment contract or to indemnify the worker with an amount of three months' salary...." Parallel
to the remedy of reinstatement or indemnification, FLL Article 48 gives the unjustly
discharged worker the right to lost salary for the period between the discharge and the
reinstatement or indemnification.

The principle of job security gives rise to two basic protections: first, that the employment contract can only be terminated for cause; second, that additional rights and

benefits accrue with time on the job and increasing seniority. Job security can be absolute, preventing any discharge before a labor tribunal has found cause for discharge and granted a dissolution of the employment relationship or contract. In practice, however, job security is treated as relative, providing security but not necessarily permanence. Section XXII of the Constitution states that "The Law shall determine those cases in which the employer shall be relieved of the obligation to fulfill the employment contract through payment of an *indemnización*...."

Thus, Article 49 of the FLL allows the employer to refuse reinstatement and pay indemnification to discharged workers with less than 1 year of service, or who come into direct contact with the employer, or to confidential, domestic, or casual workers. Article 50 sets forth a formula for indemnification payment, generally 3 months' pay with additional seniority-based payments (usually 12–20 days' pay per year of service) as well as payment of lost salary for the period between the unjust discharge and the payment of the indemnification. Individual discharge cases are heard by the relevant federal or state CABs, where the burden of proof in discharge cases always rests with the employer to show just cause for the discharge.

Workers frequently accept severance pay in liquidation of their claim for reinstatement. According to data from the Office of the Federal Labor Ombudsman (the free legal service for workers claiming unjustified discharge), only 1 worker among 154 who won a claim for unjustified discharge in 1995 opted for reinstatement.[37] In a case study of two state CABs, researchers examined 75 cases of individual claims of unjustified dismissal. None of the workers who prevailed in those cases opted for reinstatement.[38]

Plant Closing Labor Law

The FLL has been fashioned to deal with two types of plant closings: temporary and permanent.

Temporary Plant Closings

Articles 427–432 of the FLL cover temporary plant closings under the title "collective suspension of the employment relationship." In seeking "balance between the factors of production," Article 123 of the Constitution, in its Section XIX, counterpoises the workers' right to strike with the employer's right to cease production "when

---

[37] Information supplied to Secretariat by the *Procuraduría Federal de la Defensa del Trabajo* of the Mexican Department of Labor and Social Welfare.

[38] See Kevin J. Middlebrook and Cirila Quintero Ramirez, "Conflict Resolution in the Mexican Labor Courts: An Examination of Local CABs in Chihuahua and Tamaulipas" (1995), available from the U.S. National Administrative Office.

excess production makes it necessary to suspend operations to maintain prices within limits that meet costs, with prior approval of the CAB." Article 427 of the FLL extends this principle by setting forth extensive procedures for intervention by the CAB, rather than permitting a unilateral decision by the employer on a temporary or permanent closing.

The following are permissible reasons for a temporary plant closing under Article 427:

I. *Force majeure* or an unforeseen circumstance not imputable to the employer, or by his physical or mental incapacity or death, which produces as a necessary, immediate, and direct consequence the suspension of work;

II. Lack of raw materials not imputable to the employer;

III. The excess of production in relation to economic conditions and the circumstance of the market;

IV. The inability to meet the costs of production, of a temporary, clear, and obvious nature;

V. The lack of funds and the impossibility of obtaining them for the normal prosecution of work, if proven by the employer; and

VI. The lack of delivery by the State of payments it had obligated itself to deliver to the enterprise with which it had contracted for goods or services, if such are indispensable.

Under Article 428 of the FLL, a temporary closing of an enterprise or establishment may be total or partial. Under Article 431, if the CAB permits the temporary closing, the union may request every 6 months a reverification of the causes that precipitated the closing. If cause is not found, the Board will order reopening of the workplace within 30 days. Under Article 432, workers have 30 days after the reopening to report back to work, and they must be given their previously held positions.

Permanent Plant Closings

Articles 433–439 of the FLL cover permanent plant closings under the title "collective termination of the employment relationship." Article 434 of Mexico's FLL sets forth specific causes that must be proven, and decided by the CAB, before an employer may permanently close an enterprise or establishment. The permissible reasons for a permanent plant closing are the following:

I. *Force majeure* or an unforeseen circumstance not imputable to the employer, or by his physical or mental incapacity or death, which produces as a necessary, immediate, and direct consequence the suspension of work;

II. The clear and obvious inability to meet the costs of production;

III. The exhaustion of basic material of an extractive industry;

IV. Cases involving employment derived from the exploitation of mines that lack minerals that recover their cost, or in the restoration of abandoned or inoperative mines; and

V. A legally declared personal or corporate bankruptcy, where the creditors have agreed to a permanent plant closing or permanent reduction of work.

In conformity with Mexican law, an enterprise cannot close without following other legal requirements besides the FLL, such as advance notice to the tax authorities. If an employer closes a plant and converts its assets to personal use, the employer will be declared in fraudulent bankruptcy, which carries a 5- to 10-year prison sentence, and will be fined up to 10 percent of the value of the assets. This penal sanction protects the interests of all parties, including workers, tax authorities, social security, creditors, and so on.

In sum, Mexican law protects workers facing a plant closing while recognizing that in certain circumstances closings will be allowed, always with the following two conditions:

1. Workers must receive reasonable severance pay depending on the circumstances and within the parameters of the law (in plant closings, normally 3 months' pay plus 12 days' pay for each year of service), but such severance pay can be higher if so stipulated in the collective bargaining agreement.

2. A plant closing must be approved by a CAB.

Procedures for Temporary and Permanent Plant Closings

The FLL contains different procedures for different types of cases. In temporary plant closing cases, issues of *force majeure* or unforeseen circumstances, and lack of raw materials or payments by the State, are handled through a "special proceeding" before the CAB contained in Articles 892–899 of the FLL. Issues of excess production or failure to meet the costs of production are treated in another procedure for an "economic conflict of a collective nature," which has its own, highly detailed and specific procedural requirements, including reports from expert witnesses on the company's financial status (FLL Articles 900–919).

In permanent closing cases, there are likewise two different proceedings for obtaining the necessary authorization to close a plant, depending on the cause of the closing. For questions of *force majeure* or unforeseen circumstances, such as an earthquake that destroys the workplace, the employer must advise the CAB to invoke a special proceeding under Articles 892–899 of the FLL to approve or disapprove of the closing. When the cause involves failure to meet the cost of production, the employer must initiate a collective conflict of an economic nature before the CAB under Articles 900–919 of the FLL.

Rather than engaging in this complex procedural process, many companies and unions act under Article 53 of the FLL, which permits termination of the employment relationship "by mutual consent of the parties," or under Article 401, which permits termination of a collective contract "by mutual consent." This procedure provides for more rapid, flexible resolution of issues in the plant closing, mainly involving the amount of severance pay and other benefits to affected workers. Under this procedure, which also is overseen by the relevant CAB in a conciliation capacity, the parties reach a voluntary collective agreement on the plant closing.

In addition to this proceeding, at any time workers may exercise their right to strike, which has the effect of halting all proceedings under the collective conflict provisions of the FLL. The matter then shifts to the bargaining table where the parties may reach a settlement, with the intervention of the CAB in a conciliation and mediation role rather than an adjudicatory role. In practice, these alternatives to the "special proceeding" or "economic conflict" procedures are more widely used.

Jurisprudence

Like all systems with origins in Roman and continental European law, Mexican law is a code-based system rather than a common law system. Court decisions are subordinated to the Constitution, laws, and regulations established under the law. Article 17 of the FLL specifies that the Constitution, the FLL and its regulations, international treaties ratified by the Senate, and general principles of law precede jurisprudence, custom, and equity in applying the labor law. In Mexico the legislative authority creates the law. Judges and tribunals resolve only cases that come before them, and their decisions affect only the parties to the cases they decide. They do not establish precedent for other cases with similar facts, unlike in U.S. or Canadian law.

The Mexican Supreme Court has elaborated the following points of jurisprudence regarding plant closings:[39]

1. Definition of Plant Closing

In light of the nature of juridical relations contemplated in labor legislation, it is understood that a plant closing exists when activities for which the service of employees was required has ceased, independently of whether other activities of a different character continue to fulfill the obligations determined by mercantile law.

2. Requirements for Plant Closings

The total closing of an enterprise, which carries with it the termination of contracts of employment, is an economic fact. The FLL does not authorize owners to close an enterprise of their own free will, but considers that the opening of a workplace carries with it the obligation of the owner to remain in business indefinitely, and that the owner may terminate or close it only by fulfilling requirements set forth in the law, and that any failure to fulfill such requirements would make the cessation of operations and the closing of the workplace illegal.

---

[39] See Semanario Judicial de la Federación, época 7A, Tomo XXXIII, p.15, Precedentes: Amparo Directo 6486/68, Unión de Abridores de Ostión, Trabajadores en las Industrias de Empacadores de Pescado, Mariscos y Productos Similares del Golfo de México, 8 de septiembre de 1971, 5 votos. Ponente: María Cristina Salmorán de Tamaño. Cierre Total de Una Empresa, Demanda a la Reanudación de Labores en Caso De;

Semanario Judicial de la Federación, época 6A, Tomo LVIII, p. 9, Precedentes: Amparo Directo 3273/56 Moisés Cosío Gómez, 12 de abril de 1962, 5 votos. Ponente: Agapito Pozo. Contrato Colectivo de Trabajo, Terminación, Causas De;

Semanario Judicial de la Federación, época 5A, Cuarta Sala, Tomo CXIX, p. 2528, Precedentes: Tomo CXIX, p. 2528 Alvarez del Castillo Efrén , 3 de julio de 1953, 4 votos. Contrato de Trabajo, Terminación del Por Cierre Total de la Empresa;

Semanario Judicial de la Federación, Cuarta Sala, época 5A, Tomo CVII, p.1965, Precedentes: Tomo CVII, p. 1965, 14 de marzo de 1951, 5 votos, Tomo CXXV, p.1982, Tomo XCIV, p. 54, Tomo LXXXVIII, p. 2046. Cierre de Empresas, Con Autorización de la Junta. Despido Injustificado;

Semanario Judicial de la Federación, época 5A, Tomo LXXVI, p. 6207, Precedentes: Tomo LXXVI, p. 6207 Ojeda Manuel, 28 de junio de 1943. Cierre de Negociaciones por Incosteabilidad;

Semanario Judicial de la Federación, época 5A, Tomo LX, p. 4276, Precedentes: Tomo LXIX, p. 4267, Muñoz Muñoz, Nieves, 17 de septiembre de 1941; Semanario Judicial de la Federación, época 5A, Tomo LVII, p. 1267.

Semanario Judicial de la Federación, época 5A, Tomo XLVII, p. 1991, Conflictos de Orden Económico.

Semanario Judicial de la Federación, época 5A, Tomo LVII, p.1768, Juntas, Conflictos Económicos Ante Las.

3. Procedure to Follow for Plant Closings

The procedure to follow in the labor field for the temporary or permanent closing of an enterprise is that established in the FLL as an economic conflict to be litigated before the CAB, and which has the nature of public order by which the labor tribunals must issue a justified decision in which both parties, workers and employers, have the opportunity to avail themselves of due process of justice.

4. Termination of Employment Contracts and Plant Closings

The fact that the law allows for such termination of employment contracts for various individual or collective causes does not mean that employers decide the matter on their own, since they cannot halt operations or close a facility, whatever the motivation, except by filing a petition regarding the closing before the CAB, which must then hear the views of the workers so that related dispositions of the FLL are observed.

5. Unjustified Discharges and Plant Closings

The illegal closing of an enterprise undertaken without the intervention of the labor tribunals must be considered as an unjustified discharge because employers are not permitted to simply close without notice on their own volition. Such an action is harmful to workers and undermines the national economy and the general interest of society in preserving sources of employment and increasing the benefits of collective social activity.

The total closing of an enterprise can only take place when there exists a cause that is justified and precisely foreseen in the FLL, and the procedure also preordained in the law for matters of an economic nature is followed (requiring approval by the CAB before closing). When these two requirements have not been complied with, the closing of the enterprise and the separation of the workers amount to unjustified discharge, and the discharged workers are then entitled to their constitutionally guaranteed severance pay under Section XXII of Article 123.

Plant Closing Procedures Under Mexican Law

For temporary closing cases involving *force majeure*, lack of raw materials, and the like, employers must follow "special proceedings" under Articles 892–899 of the FLL. For cases involving failure to meet costs or lack of funds, procedures under Articles 900–919 for a "collective conflict of an economic nature" are used. For permanent closing cases, there are also two procedural routes under the FLL: "special proceedings" for closings caused by unforeseen circumstances, *force majeure*, bankruptcy, or exhaustion of raw materials, and "collective conflict of an economic nature" proceedings for a clear and obvious inability to meet costs.

Special Proceeding (Articles 892–899)

The special proceeding begins with a demand from the employer to the CAB for permission to close the plant, citing the reasons for the closing. The CAB must arrange a hearing with at least 10 days' notice, and within 15 working days, for the employer and the union to appear before it with evidence, witnesses from the workplace, and testimony from expert witnesses. Every attempt is made to fully air the evidence in the hearing so that it is a final rather than a preliminary hearing. Further hearings may be scheduled as needed. After receiving and weighing evidence, the CAB issues an order, or *laudo*, approving or disapproving of the closing.

Collective Conflict of an Economic Nature (Articles 900–919)

Throughout the procedure for a collective conflict of an economic nature, the CAB is obligated to pursue conciliation by agreement of the parties, even as litigation ensues. This procedure is initiated by a written petition from the employer seeking permission to close the plant, with documents demonstrating the economic condition of the company and the necessity of the relief sought. The petition must also contain a list of employees, a statement from an independent expert attesting to the economic situation of the company, and other evidence crediting the claims of the company.

The CAB convenes a hearing for the company and the union within 5 days, and appoints a team of expert witnesses independent of the expert witnesses of the parties. The CAB's expert witnesses undertake the research and studies considered necessary, and may demand of the parties reports and information as needed. The independent experts may also seek information from the public authorities and from independent researchers, union organizations, management associations, and industry groups. They may also visit the workplace and examine books and records, and interview workers and managers. The CAB may undertake its own investigatory action as it deems convenient. At any time this long, complicated process may be immediately halted if the union exercises its right to strike, except in the case of a solidarity strike (Articles 448, 450 fracc. VI, and 902 of the FLL).

The *Amparo* Proceeding as a Guarantee of Due Process in Collective Conflicts

The FLL provides that CAB decisions are final and binding in labor proceedings, including those for special proceedings and collective conflict of an economic nature. Decisions may not be appealed, and the CAB may not revise its own decision. However, either of the parties involved in a case before the CAB has recourse to the *amparo* (shelter) appeal under Article 103 of the Constitution and the federal Law of Amparo.

The right of *amparo* is a cornerstone of civil law in Mexico and in all Latin American countries as a check on administrative authority. Under constitutional and statutory rights of *amparo*, a private party injured by the decision or actions of a CAB may seek review in the civil courts alleging that the CAB has engaged in a violation of fundamental rights or due process of law. An *amparo* appeal must be filed within 15 days of the decision under the Law of Amparo, Article 21. An action for *amparo* can be brought to district court judges, and their decisions may then be appealed to federal circuit courts of appeals and to the Supreme Court. The *amparo* courts may review the decision and the proceedings of an administrative authority, and they are empowered to overturn the CAB where they find a violation of fundamental rights or due process. The findings of the *amparo* court are applicable only to the parties in the case before the court; they do not become precedents for other cases.

In practice, such *amparo* appeals are the most often used recourse in Mexican labor law. The court may issue an injunction in case of irreparable harm or burdensome remedy, or to restore the status quo ante while the case is considered. The *amparo* ruling has the objective of restoring the aggrieved party to the enjoyment of the rights that were violated, and obligates the responsible administrative authority to carry out the ruling, subject to sanctions if it fails to do so.

Collective Termination of the Employment Relationship

In Mexico, it is not lawful for an employer unilaterally to close a plant. The employer must follow the procedures spelled out in the FLL or, alternatively, obtain a collective agreement to terminate the employment relationship. Articles 433–434 of the FLL permit a collective termination of the employment relationship as a consequence of a plant closing by mutual consent of the parties, with payment under Article 436 of severance pay of 3 months' salary plus a seniority-based bonus.

Rather than the complex procedure for collective conflict of an economic nature, using the procedure for collective termination of the employment relationship has emerged as a more frequent practice.[40] The union and the company come before the CAB to declare that they have reached a settlement of their economic conflict between themselves by means of a collective agreement for termination of the collective and individual employment relationships. They present the agreement for CAB approval under Article 901 of the FLL, which empowers the boards to mediate such matters. Article 906 establishes that if the parties reach such an agreement, the collective conflict is considered resolved on that basis, and the agreement ratified by the CAB has the force of a board order or *laudo*.

---

[40]   See Juan B. Climent, *Elementos de Derecho Procesal del Trabajo* (Edit. Esfinge, 1989), at 252.

Whether the parties initiate a collective conflict followed by a voluntary agreement, or come to the CAB directly with a voluntary agreement, they may avoid the long and complicated procedure involving hearings, evidence, three sets of expert witnesses, and the other features of the collective conflict proceeding called for in the FLL. By means of the voluntary agreement for termination of the employment relationship, they find an alternative route that is more rapid, more collaborative, and perhaps, most important, provides higher levels of severance pay for the workers.

The plant closing agreement is treated as a modification of the collective bargaining agreement, which must be approved by the CAB. The accompanying dissolution of the union requires a separate proceeding and declaration by the labor authorities in which no action by the employer in closing the plant can have the effect of harming workers' trade union rights.

The following box compares the legal frameworks for protection of labor rights in the three countries of the NAALC.

Legal Frameworks at a Glance[a]

	Canada	United States	Mexico
Constitutional Foundations	• Constitution is silent on labor rights and standards, except §2 of the Charter of Rights and Freedoms, which guarantees freedom of association and assembly. (Supreme Court ruled Charter protects labor organization and some related activity, but not collective bargaining or the right to strike.)	• Constitution is silent on labor rights and standards. • First Amendment protects freedom of assembly, free speech, and the right to petition the government for redress of grievances; courts have applied this to some labor activity.	• Constitution protects freedom of association, the right to organize, and the right to strike. • Constitution details basic labor standards (i.e., minimum wages, hours of work, seniority, overtime, child labor, leaves, profit sharing, worker housing, etc.).
Labor Law Jurisdiction	• Distinct labor law systems: 1 federal, 10 provincial. • Only 10% of workers are within federal sector. • Administrative labor boards are in federal sector, 9 provinces, and territories; office of commissioner (Labour Ministry) and labor tribunals (judicial branch) in Quebec.	• National system of labor laws: Wagner Act, Taft-Hartley Act, and Landrum-Griffin Act apply throughout the national territory. • Single national administrative labor board (NLRB) is for enforcement; 33 regional offices are throughout the country.	• Federal labor legislation is applied through the national territory; federal labor law is enforced by the federal government for key industries and sectors; states enforce federal law for state-level industries and sectors. • Federal and state tripartite CABs are for enforcement.

[a] "Complete" and "partial" closure here refer to the U.S. *Darlington* doctrine wherein the Supreme Court ruled that a complete closing of an entire business, without continuing in business under any other form or guise, or in any other location, is permissible, but a partial closure of a business for anti-union motives is unlawful, even if the closing is a total closing of a workplace, if the employer remains in business in other locations or reopens operations under another name.

Abbreviation Key:
CA: *collective agreement*
CAB: *Conciliation and Arbitration Board (Mexico)*
FLL: *Federal Labor Law (Mexico)*
NLRB: *National Labor Relations Board (United States)*
ULP: *unfair labor practice*

Legal Frameworks at a Glance (continued)

	Canada	United States	Mexico
Union Registration & Certification	• Majority of jurisdictions certify on basis of signed cards evidencing majority support. • Four provinces require elections in most cases; elections are usually held within days of filing.	• Voluntary recognition may be obtained on basis of cards if employer agrees. • Certification normally requires a majority vote in a secret ballot election; elections are held within several weeks of filing petition. • Pro- and anti-union campaigning occurs between petition and vote.	• Unions may be registered by any group of 20 or more employees. • No election is required for single union formation. • A vote is required when a second union claims majority support for title to collective agreement (CA).
Bargaining Rights	• Exclusive bargaining rights provided to one union per bargaining unit upon certification (i.e., legal recognition of majority desire for representation); normally shown by card check or election; voluntary recognition is also possible.	• Exclusive bargaining rights are provided to one union per bargaining unit upon certification of majority status, normally shown by election; voluntary recognition is also possible.	• Exclusive bargaining rights are given to one union per bargaining unit; bargaining rights are obtained by union upon registration (administrative process).
Protection of Right to Organize	• Key protection is ULP complaint brought by employees or union. • It is prohibited to discharge or discriminate for union activity (see below "anti-union animus").	• Key protection is ULP charge made by employees or union; if charge has merit, NLRB issues complaint. • It is prohibited to discharge or discriminate for union activity (see below "anti-union animus").	• Constitution prohibits discharge for union activities. • Employees discharged within 30 days prior to union formation are still counted as eligible for "20 employees" needed to constitute union.

Legal Frameworks at a Glance (continued)

	Canada	United States	Mexico
Protection for Organizing Activity	• Labor boards balance employees' organizing rights with employers' free speech rights; evidence of "anti-union animus" alone is sufficient to constitute illegal "unfair labor practice," even in presence of other motives.	• NLRB and courts balance employees' right to organize with employers' right of free speech up to limit of "threat of reprisal"; anti-union animus is balanced against other motives to determine predominant motive.	• Anti-union campaigning is exceptional given constitutional right to organize and place of unions in economic/political structure; there is no need for election or other showing of majority status.
Closing Workplace for Anti-Union Purpose	• Illegal; anti-union motivation for closure constitutes unfair labor practice; no distinction is made between complete and partial[a] closures (except in Quebec).	• May be legal or illegal; closure of entire business is not illegal; other closures may be illegal if *predominant motive* is anti-union animus.	• Illegal if unapproved by CAB; all closures require approval by CAB for specified legal cause (*force majeure*, economic failure, bankruptcy, etc.).
Threats of Closure for Anti-Union Purpose	• Threats are illegal; they are unfair labor practice if coercive, intimidating, or undue influence.	• Threats are illegal; unfair labor practice if words contain "threat of reprisal."	• Threat is not defined as illegal unfair labor practice; it does not arise as a legal dispute under labor law.
Penalties & Remedies for Threats of Closure	• Cease-and-desist orders; post notices; certification of union where conditions for objective determination of employee sentiment are destroyed by employer's unlawful conduct.	• Cease-and-desist order; post notices; certification of union where conditions for fair election are destroyed by employer's unlawful conduct.	• Threats as such are not defined as illegal.
Penalties & Remedies for Closure	• Severance pay and transfer rights for workers; extension of contract to new sites; payment of organizing costs to union.	• Order to reopen and rehire workers where feasible; order to bargain over effects of closure; back pay as appropriate.	• Back pay, severance pay for affected workers (rarely arises since unions usually agree on severance terms).

PART TWO

UNION ORGANIZING SYSTEMS

UNITED STATES

In the United States, organizing usually begins when workers concerned about working conditions make contact with a trade union representative. In some cases, union representatives actively seek contact with workers at a particular workplace for strategic purposes, usually when the union already has a collective bargaining relationship with the same employer or one or more other employers in the same industry. However, there is no requirement that a union limit its organizing to a single industry, or that workers seek a union that already represents workers in their company or industry. Many U.S. unions represent groups of workers totally unrelated to their principal industry. For example, the United Steel Workers union represents some nurses' groups, the United Automobile Workers union represents some insurance company clerks, and so on.

The union representative normally arranges a series of meetings with workers in their homes, in a union office, or at restaurants, rented halls, or other meeting places. Workers inform the union representative about conditions in the workplace, and the union representative informs workers about how the union operates. Usually the most interested workers form an "organizing committee" to openly advocate for the union in the workplace.

Organizing in the United States

At some point in the process (it could be at the beginning or later, after the organizing committee has formed), the union representative distributes cards for workers to sign indicating their desire to have the union represent them in collective bargaining. Some unions prefer to have in-plant organizing leaders distribute the cards to co-workers inside the workplace, which is permitted as long as such solicitation takes place in non-work areas on non-work time (typically, in a break or lunch room).

If 30 percent of the workers who are part of the "bargaining unit"[41] sign cards, the union may petition the nearest office of the National Labor Relations Board (NLRB

---

[41] The "bargaining unit" is defined as employees with a sufficient community of interest to bargain collectively for a single agreement. Managers and supervisors are excluded from a bargaining unit, and often workers with apparently divergent interests (professionals and non-professionals, for example) are divided into separate units.

or the Board) to conduct a secret ballot election to determine whether a majority of workers desire representation by the union. Normally, however, union organizers wait until a substantial majority of workers have signed cards (two-thirds is an informal measure often used by experienced organizers). The union then requests recognition from the employer, which is nearly always refused. The union proceeds to petition the NLRB for a representation election.

Slightly fewer than 50 days is the median length of time between the filing of the petition and the holding of the election. Most elections take place in 30–60 days; 20 percent of elections are held more than 60 days after the filing of the petition.[42] The period can be extended when employers challenge the definition of the bargaining unit claimed by the union.

The weeks leading up to the NLRB election are usually marked by vigorous campaigning on all sides. The union organizing campaign often involves wearing buttons and T-shirts, distributing leaflets, holding rallies, and using other tactics. The employer's anti-union campaign usually consists of managers' speeches to assembled employees, letters to workers' homes, and training and instructions to supervisors to convey the employer's opposition to unionization in individual and group discussions with workers. Many employers engage consulting groups or law firms that specialize in directing the "union avoidance" campaign for management.

Typically, some employees within the group being organized are opposed to unionization. They often form a "Vote No" committee and campaign against the union supporters. It is unlawful for the employer to instigate or to assist such a committee. Intensive workplace discussions and arguments are common. After several weeks of such campaigning, the final days before an election usually reach a high level of tension.

NLRB agents conduct a secret ballot vote, usually in the workplace in a time span sufficient to permit all eligible workers to vote during working hours. A voting booth with a curtain to maintain ballot secrecy is normally used. After balloting is completed, the Board agent counts the votes with union and management observers present for the vote count.

Either party may file objections to the election claiming unfair tactics by the other side. If no objections are filed, or if the NLRB disposes of the objections without overturning the election, the election results are certified. If the union has won, the NLRB certifies the union as the exclusive bargaining representative, and the employer is obligated to bargain in good faith with the union.

---

[42] See U.S. Department of Labor and U.S. Department of Commerce, Commission on the Future of Worker-Management Relations, *Fact Finding Report* (May 1994), at 82.

In the 1990–1995 period, unions filed an average of 5,000 petitions for an NLRB election per year. After withdrawals and dismissals, elections took place in 3,200 of those campaigns, and unions won the election in about 1,500 cases (47 percent). (See Table 2 for statistics on union elections conducted by the NLRB, 1990–1995.)

Table 2

U.S. NLRB RC Election Results, 1990–1995[a]

FY	Representation Petitions Filed	Petitions Dismissed or Withdrawn	"RC" Elections	Union Wins ("Success Rate" in Elections)
1990	6,005	2,398	3,607 (60%)	1,773 (49%)
1991	5,162	1,868	3,294 (64%)	1,465 (44%)
1992	4,946	1,852	3,094 (63%)	1,476 48%)
1993	5,084	1,932	3,152 (62%)	1,524 (48%)
1994	4,610	1,428	3,182 69%)	1,481 (47%)
1995	4,571	1,498	3,073 (67%)	1,456 (47%)
Average	5,063	1,829	3,234 (64%)	1,529 (47%)

[a] Most RC (Representation Case) elections are held in connection with new union organizing at an unorganized workplace. These figures do not include decertification or other types of elections.

Bargaining After Certification

The "good faith" requirement is often the subject of new unfair labor practice charges when a union and a company engage in fruitless negotiations. When the employer is found to be bargaining in bad faith, the remedy is an order to return to the bargaining table and bargain in good faith. Nothing in the law compels the employer or the union to agree to any contract clause or to reach an overall agreement. If they bargain to a genuine impasse, the employer may unilaterally implement its last proposal.[43] The union may undertake a strike, or the employer may undertake a lockout, to back up their bargaining position.

---

[43] Whether or not a genuine impasse exists when an employer unilaterally implements its last proposal is often the subject of unfair labor practice charges of failure to bargain in good faith.

CANADA

Union organizing in Canada often begins with unorganized workers contacting a union representative for help forming a union in their workplace. Workers can seek any union to represent them; they are not limited to a union in their company or industry (Canada's largest private sector union, the Canadian Auto Workers, bargains for workers in many industries unrelated to automobiles).

A series of meetings normally takes place in workers' homes or in meeting places. The basic mechanism for union formation is the signing of individual cards authorizing the union as the workers' bargaining agent. In a majority of provinces, signing the card is effectively the vote for union representation. The federal jurisdiction and 6 of the 10 provinces provide for certification of the union as the workers' bargaining agent if the union obtains signed cards from a majority of workers in the bargaining unit (in some provinces, the requirement is 55 or 60 percent to avoid disputes over small numbers of cards). The relevant labor board or labor commissioner in Quebec checks the authenticity of the cards before proceeding to certify the union. This is known as the "card-check" method of union certification.

In those provinces that usually require an election,[44] it is normally held within a few days of the application. In Ontario, for example, which recently switched from the card-check system to a mandatory election system, the election must be held within 5 days of the application. The result of both the card-check system and the rapid-election features of Canadian labor organizing is the relative absence of prolonged, aggressive workplace campaigning for or against union representation.[45]

---

[44] In the United States and Canadian provinces that normally hold representation elections, statutes or judicial doctrines permit the labor authorities to certify a union without an election or in spite of election results when the employer's unfair labor practices make a fair election impossible. In the United States, the union must have attained majority support before its majority was destroyed by employer conduct. In Canada, it is generally not necessary to have obtained a majority.

[45] Many analysts attribute the diverging proportion of union representation in Canada (more than 30 percent) and the United States (less than 15 percent) in part to this key difference in labor law. See Gary N. Chaison and Joseph B. Rose, "Continental Divide: The Direction and Fate of North American Unions," in *Advances in Industrial and Labor Relations*, Sockell, Lewin and Lipsky, eds. (1991); Richard Freeman, "On the Divergence in Unionism among Developed Countries," National Bureau of Economic Research Working Paper no. 2817 (1989); Paul Weiler, "Promises to Keep: Securing Workers' Rights to Self-Organization under the NLRA," 96 *Harvard Law Review* 1769 (1983).

Organizing Results in Canada

A study of certification results in Canada in the 1990–1995 period shows that the two largest provinces, Ontario and Quebec, averaged 953 and 983 applications per year for new union certification received by their board or commissioners. British Columbia averaged 523 applications per year, and 161 per year were received by the federal labor board.

For Ontario and Quebec, applications granted averaged 616 and 712 per year, a 65 and 72 percent success rate, respectively. British Columbia granted 338 certifications per year (65 percent of applications), and the federal board granted 102 per year, a 63 percent success rate. (See Table 3 for statistics on Canadian union certification results, 1990-1995.)

Bargaining After Certification

Canadian labor law establishes the obligation of an employer to bargain in good faith with a certified union. Failure to bargain in good faith is an unfair labor practice. In addition, however, a majority of provinces, and the federal jurisdiction, provide for a special settlement process that may lead to binding arbitration of a first contract when a newly formed union is unable to reach an agreement with the employer.

MEXICO

The union organizing system in Mexico is fundamentally different from the systems of the United States and Canada. In Mexico, unions require a public act of state granting the status needed to legally function. Unions must obtain this official registration with the appropriate government agency. For unions covered by federal jurisdiction, the registry resides in the Department of Labor. In state jurisdiction, registration is obtained from the state CAB. Under the law, the granting of registration is a purely administrative act, as long as the union complies with filing requirements.[46]

Any group of 20 or more workers, even if they are only a minority of the workplace's employees, can form a union by a formal act of registering with the labor authorities. No election is necessary. Normally the union must affiliate with an existing registered

---

[46] An extensive analysis of the union registration system in Mexico is available in a special study by a group of independent experts commissioned by the National Administrative Office of Mexico in connection with ministerial consultations following U.S. NAO Public Communication 94003 (the *Sony* case). See "Estudio del Grupo de Expertos Independientes" in *Consultas Ministeriales: Registro de asociaciones sindicales* (March 1996).

Table 3

Applications for Certification and Certifications Granted in Selected Canadian Jurisdictions, 1989–1995

Canada Labour Relations Board

Certification Applications Received

1989–90	1990–91	1991–92	1992–93	1993–94	1994–95	Avg.
175	175	155	127	173	160	161

Certification Applications Granted

1989–90	1990–91	1991–92	1992–93	1993–94	1994–95	Avg.
89	133	92	81	103	113	102
						(63% success)

Ontario Labour Relations Board

Certification Applications Received

1989–90	1990–91	1991–92	1992–93	1993–94	1994–95	Avg.
910	775	1,092	824	1,166	n/a	953

Certification Applications Granted

1989–90	1990–91	1991–92	1992–93	1993–94	1994–95	Avg.
573	511	660	509	829	n/a	616
						(65% success)

Quebec Office of the General Commissioner of Labour

Certification Applications Received

1989–90	1990–91	1991–92	1992–93	1993–94	1994–95	Avg.
1,267	903	1,320	768	785	854	983

Certification Applications Granted

1989–90	1990–91	1991–92	1991–93	1993–94	1994–95	Avg.
899	640	978	643	556	555	712
						(72% success)

British Columbia Labour Relations Board

Certification Applications Received

1989–90	1990–91	1991–92	1992–93	1993–94	1994–95	Avg.
435	409	347	692	648	607	523

Certification Applications Granted

1989–90	1990–91	1991–92	1992–93	1993–94	1994–95	Avg.
250	244	197	509	437	393	338
						(65% success)

Average "Success Rate" for four jurisdictions combined: 66 percent union within the industrial sector for that employer—food workers with a food workers union, textile workers with a textile workers union, machinists with a machinists union, and so forth.

With registration achieved, a union may then demand a contract from the employer. However, Mexico does not provide for "certification" of a union in the U.S. or Canadian sense, which creates a legal duty of the employer to bargain with the union selected by a majority of workers. Mexico does not require majority status for union registration, and does not use the "duty to bargain" concept. An employer can ignore the union's demand for a contract, which challenges the union to launch a strike. The union must then estimate whether it has the capacity to undertake an effective strike with majority support.

The employer must cease operations when a strike begins. Within 3 days, however, the employer may obtain a vote in which the union must demonstrate majority support for the strike. If the majority is not shown, the strike must end and the workers must return to work or face dismissal. If the union proves its majority, the employer remains closed. The union and the company can continue their test of economic strength until they reach a settlement between them, or seek mediation and arbitration from the CAB. CAB intervention is the normal route.

New union organizing in Mexico (that is, in never-unionized workplaces where workers seek to form a union, register the union, and obtain a contract where none existed before) is relatively low in volume. In private sector industries that are within the federal jurisdiction,[47] which encompasses more than 2.5 million workers, an average of 125 new union registrations were sought from the Department of Labor each year in the 1989–1994 period and an average of 25 registrations granted per year.[48]

In viewing this relatively low volume of new union formation in federal jurisdiction, it should be kept in mind that Mexico has a high density of union organization in the formal, non-agricultural sector. Of manufacturing enterprises in Mexico with more than 100 employees, 85 percent are unionized. More than 50 percent of private sector workers within federal jurisdiction are unionized.[49] (See Table 4 for statistics on union density in private sector industries under federal enforcement jurisdiction in Mexico.)

---

[47] Article 123 of the Constitution grants jurisdiction over FLL enforcement to the states, with the exception of 22 industrial sectors that remain under federal jurisdiction, and enterprises operating in two or more states. The specified private sector industries that remain within federal jurisdiction are contained in Table 4.

[48] *Informes de Labores de la Secretaría del Trabajo y Prevision Social* (STPS), 1989–1994.

[49] Data on federal private sector employment and union membership were obtained by the Secretariat from the General Coordination of Labor Statistic of STPS.

Table 4

Union Density in Mexican Private Sector Industries Under Federal Jurisdiction, 1994

Industrial Branch	Federal Jurisdiction Workers	Unionized Workers in Federal Jurisdiction	Rate of Unionization
Total	**2,557,122**	**1,314,431**	**51.4**
Textiles	97,337	80,536	82.7
Electricity	87,473	77,503	88.6
Cinematography	26,513	18,124	68.4
Rubber	46,232	9,121	19.7
Sugar	184,863	63,631	34.4
Mining	64,427	26,193	40.7
Foundries & Steel Mills	113,614	34,113	30.0
Energy	94,462	81,648	86.4
Cement & Limestone	32,898	11,069	33.6
Automotive	139,772	59,178	42.3
Chemical	123,068	27,339	22.2
Pulp & Paper	47,635	20,066	42.1
Vegetable Oils	16,400	8,529	52.0
Packaged Food Processors	210,316	61,439	29.2
Bottling	152,275	81,197	53.3
Railroad	95,706	36,432	38.1
Lumber	30,765	7,037	22.9
Glass	19,072	12,901	67.6
Tobacco	6,095	3,667	60.2
Banks & Credit Unions	259,164	95,163	36.7
Other Federal Jurisdiction	709,035	499,545	70.5

Source: STPS.

Since most large and medium-sized firms in Mexico's formal sector are already unionized, the potential for new union organizing in the formal sector is greatly reduced. Most workers in established firms are already covered by a union contract. However, they are a minority of the total workforce. In contrast to the United States and Canada, where approximately half the labor force work in enterprises of 500 or more employees, only one-third of the Mexican labor force is employed in enterprises of 50 or more employees. Of all Mexican workers, 60 percent are employed in firms of 15 or fewer employees.[50] Many of these are in the large informal sector. Unions are mostly absent from small firms, small agricultural enterprises, and the informal sector. There are exceptions to this pattern reported in certain *maquiladora* areas where some large firms are not unionized. *Maquiladora* enterprises are normally within state jurisdiction, not federal.

Much of union organizing in Mexico involves one already registered union seeking to supplant another as the collective bargaining representative of the workers. In some instances, workers initiate a change. In others, the challenging union solicits workers' support for a change.[51] In federal private sector jurisdiction, there were an average of 636 such title disputes per year between unions in the 1990–1994 period, compared with the 25 new registrations per year noted above.[52]

When one union claims it has majority support and thus is entitled to take over the collective agreement from an incumbent union, the relevant CAB conducts a vote, called a *recuento*, to determine which union has majority support.[53] The union that gains majority support is awarded title to the collective agreement.

---

[50] See STPS/INEGI, 1995 National Employment Survey.

[51] It should be noted that the same phenomenon, called "raiding," occurs in Canada and the United States as well, although it is relatively rare now (in decades past it was more common as, for example, when the American Federation of Labor [AFL] and the Congress of Industrial Organizations [CIO] were separate, rival federations). The relevant authorities in all three countries conduct votes to determine workers' preference.

[52] *Estadisticas Laborales, Segundo Semestre*, STPS, Subsecretaria "B" at 123.

[53] The voting method is not specified in the statute or by regulations. It may or may not be by secret ballot.

PART THREE

REVIEW OF ADMINISTRATIVE AND JUDICIAL DATA

UNITED STATES

Judicial Findings—Federal Courts of Appeals Case Review

Secretariat researchers examined all 89 U.S. federal appeals court decisions in cases involving plant closings and threats of plant closing published between 1986 and 1993.[54] Among them, 70 cases arose in the context of a new union organizing effort at an unorganized workplace, and 19 cases involved unions with an established bargaining relationship. Significantly, 14 of these 19 cases involved a successor employer or an "alter ego" employer; that is, the same employer claimed to be a successor not bound by a collective bargaining agreement. This suggests that changes in corporate ownership may pose a risk of closing-related, anti-union conduct.

Of the 89 cases, 4 involved a complete plant closing in retaliation for union organizing or union activity. Among the 89 cases, 28 involved some form of partial closing (mass layoffs, subcontracting, shift elimination, failure to rehire union workers after a temporary closing, etc.). Also, 43 cases involved threats to totally close a plant, while 14 involved threats of some other form of systemic (as opposed to individual) job elimination—57 "threat" cases overall.

Appeals Court Findings

The courts of appeals upheld determinations by the National Labor Relations Board (NLRB or the Board) that employers unlawfully closed plants in all four cases of complete closings.[55] In three of those four, the courts upheld a Board order to reopen the facility and rehire the workers.

In the partial closing cases, courts found employers liable for unlawful actions in 26 of the 28 cases. In 22 of those cases, the courts upheld NLRB orders to restore the work and reinstate the affected workers.

---

[54] The period studied covered the last 3 months of 1986 and the first 10 months of 1993. Thus, the time frame for the study is 7 years and 1 month.

[55] In one of the four cases, the court found that the employer closed the facility for a discriminatory, anti-union motive, but found further that the employer would have closed for legitimate business purposes at a later date. The court awarded back pay to affected workers up to the date that the facility would have been closed in the normal course of business, but it ruled that the employer did not have to reopen and rehire the workers.

Employers were found liable for unlawful plant closing threats in 41 of the 43 reported cases, and in 13 of the 14 cases involving partial closing threats.[56]

With regard to plant closing issues, the number of appeals court reversals of NLRB decisions is extraordinarily low. In 32 cases in which the Board found an unlawful closing (full or partial), the courts overruled the Board only three times (9.1 percent). In 57 cases in which the NLRB found an unlawful threat, the decision was reversed only once (1.5 percent). This rate compares to an overall reversal rate of 14.2 percent for all unfair labor practice cases that went to the federal courts in the period studied.[57]

Appeals Court Remedies

The courts nearly always upheld traditional NLRB remedies in unfair labor practice cases: (1) to cease and desist from the unlawful conduct, (2) to post a notice in the workplace promising not to repeat such conduct, and (3) to reinstate and/or to award back pay to affected workers. In one case, the court upheld a Board order for the company president to personally read the notice to assembled workers in the workplace.

Additionally, many of the cases reviewed by the researchers resulted in extraordinary remedies. In more than half the cases, the NLRB had ordered some form of extraordinary relief beyond the normal cease-and-desist order, notice posting, and reinstatement remedies. In one full closing case and 17 of the threat cases that arose in a union organizing campaign before an election could be held, the courts upheld Board orders that the employer must recognize and bargain with the union because the employer's extensive unfair labor practices made a fair election impossible. The courts reversed such orders by the NLRB in four cases.

In 29 cases, the NLRB had issued a bargaining order (these include the 18 cases mentioned above, and 11 cases that resulted in orders to resume bargaining with an existing union). In 12 cases, the Board set aside an election and/or ordered a new

---

[56] Many of the closing cases also involved threats. They were counted as closing cases only. Many of the threat cases involved both types of threats (full or partial closing). All were counted as threats of full closing. Note that in some of these cases the court found in favor of employers on non-plant closing issues, such as individual discharge cases, or remanded the case to the NLRB for further findings or to adjust the remedy.

[57] For purposes of compiling reversal rates, the study here (in contrast to the foregoing) counted cases that involved both closing and threats of closing as separate cases.

election. In seven cases, the NLRB ordered substantial structural relief that went beyond rehiring or reinstating employees, requiring the reopening of a facility or the relocating of equipment that had been moved back to the original site where the closing took place. It is noteworthy that the courts of appeals reversed these broad remedial orders more often than they reversed findings that the employer committed an unfair labor practice. Bargaining orders were reversed on four occasions, new election orders once, and structural relief twice.[58]

This review of federal court decisions shows that plant closing cases have arisen with increasing frequency in recent years. Of the 89 decisions examined, 28 were issued in the 4 years before 1990. As Table 5 shows, more than twice as many (61) have been issued since 1990.

Table 5

U.S. Courts of Appeals Decisions in Plant Closing Cases

1986	1987	1988	1989	1990	1991	1992	1993
1	6	9	12	11	18	4	28

These annual figures reveal an overall increase in plant closing case decisions during the period under study. The decline in 1992 is counterbalanced by the large increase in 1993, suggesting that viewing the progression in 2-year increments may be more accurate. This view yields successive increments of 7, 21, 29, and 32 decisions issued. However, the volume of reported decisions and the limited time examined are not enough to conclude that the rate of cases involving the phenomena of plant closings and threats of plant closing that come before the federal appeals courts is dramatically increasing. (See tables in Appendix B for detailed data from federal courts cases.)

---

[58] This rate of reversal (14.8 percent, or 7 of 48 instances) is consistent with Professor Brudney's findings in his review of all court decisions on NLRB appeals that the courts reversed the Board more frequently on remedy issues than on liability issues. See James J. Brudney, "A Famous Victory: Collective Bargaining Protections and the Statutory Aging Process," 74 *North Carolina Law Review* 939 (1996).

Administrative Findings

NLRB Case Review

The Secretariat examined 319 NLRB decisions between 1990 and 1995 involving plant closings and threats of plant closing.[59] Of these decisions, 27 dealt with actual closings (either straightforward closings, or closings with reopenings); 82 addressed partial closings (refusals to hire or rehire union employees, subcontracting of union work, closing of a unit or department of the plant, major layoffs and transfers, and so on); and 210 decisions related to threats of closing.

Complaints numbered 275 in the context of a new organizing campaign in a non-union shop, while situations involving incumbent unions in established bargaining relationships arose on 44 occasions.

The NLRB found a violation by the employer in 283 of the 319 cases (89 percent). The Board found no violation in 29 cases and remanded the rest for further findings. The standard remedy, consisting of a cease-and-desist order and an order to post a notice, was delivered in virtually every case. Four additional remedies were frequently awarded: employers were ordered to bargain with the union on 83 occasions, new elections were ordered and/or election results were set aside in 42 cases, employers were ordered to make employees whole in 42 cases, and employers were ordered to reinstate groups of employees on 40 occasions.

Extraordinary remedies were also granted on a number of occasions. Employers were ordered to reinstate a department and/or reinstate subcontracted work in 14 cases, to restore the status quo in eight cases, and to reopen a facility in six cases. The opening and counting of ballots was ordered in four cases, and automatic certification was granted twice. A relocation order was made once, as was an order for the employer to pay the union the costs of the case. (See tables in Appendix C for detailed data from NLRB cases.)

Case Handling in NLRB Regional Offices

The foregoing review of NLRB decisions in plant closing cases reflects just a fraction of administrative treatment under U.S. labor law of plant closing effects on the right to organize. Unfair labor practice cases are filed in one of the NLRB's 33 regional offices around the country. Before such charges reach the level of a Board decision, they may be disposed of by withdrawal, dismissal, settlements, or a decision by an Administrative Law Judge (ALJ).

---

[59] Of the 319 cases, 30 were also part of the federal court case survey. This figure is not double counting. The Secretariat is looking overall at how such cases are handled at two different levels of the legal system, one dealing with court decisions on plant closing cases, and one dealing with Board decisions.

Only 2 percent of unfair labor practice charges against employers filed with the NLRB reach the stage of a hearing before an ALJ. One-fourth of these cases are settled after the hearing. The rest go forward to a decision by the NLRB. The earlier decision to dismiss the charge or issue a complaint rests with the Regional Director acting on behalf of the independent General Counsel, and the decision after trial is made by the independent ALJ. The Board hears the case as an appeal from the ALJ decision.[60]

There is no systematic record keeping or electronic access to NLRB cases that are treated below the level of full, published Board decisions. Faced with the impossibility of reviewing tens of thousands of case records in the Board's 33 regional offices, the Secretariat examined records covering a 4-year period (1992–1995) in two regional offices suggested by the NLRB as fairly reflective of Board experience nationally: Region 16 in Fort Worth, Texas, and Region 30 in Milwaukee, Wisconsin. These two selections also permit a comparison of experience in a "Sunbelt" area with low union density and a "Frostbelt" area with long-established unions.[61]

Of 24 unfair labor practice cases involving charges of plant closings or threats of plant closing that were received in the Fort Worth regional office in the 4-year review period, 9 were withdrawn or dismissed before a complaint was issued.[62] Of those that remained, 6 cases were settled before a complaint was issued.[63] Complaints were issued in 9 cases (finding "merit" in the charge, but not concluding whether a violation took place). Of these, 6 were settled after the complaint was issued. Trials before an ALJ were held in 3 cases.

---

[60] In its 1995 fiscal year, the NLRB closed 23,862 unfair labor practice cases involving charges against employers. In these cases, 8,175 charges were withdrawn, 6,213 were dismissed, and 8,870 were settled. A complaint was issued by the regional director in 3,271 cases, and 450 cases were decided by an ALJ. A total of 356 unfair labor practice cases against employers were closed by a Board decision. It must be noted that these are not necessarily the same cases. Many of the NLRB decisions involve cases filed in earlier years. However, tracking individual cases across years was not possible in the time frame of this report. In any event, the yearly case handling totals reflect Board experience over time.

[61] This phase of the research involved physical review of thousands of case files in the regional offices because files are not separate by subject matter to allow immediate access to plant closing or threat cases. The research also required assistance, which was graciously provided, by the staff of the Forth Worth and Milwaukee regional offices, both in obtaining case files and in further searching records for the ultimate disposition of the plant closing and threat cases.

[62] It is impossible to know the full reasons for withdrawal or dismissal of an unfair labor practice charge. Such action might indicate a case with weak evidence or one with strong evidence. It might indicate that the parties reached a substantive settlement without need for further Board involvement and agreed to withdraw the charge or to request the Board to dismiss the charge.

[63] Similarly, it is not possible to ascertain the relative merit of cases settled before dismissal or the motivations of the parties in deciding to settle the cases.

In the Milwaukee regional office, 43 charges were filed involving plant closings or threats of closing. Of these, 27 were withdrawn or dismissed before a complaint was issued. Of those that remained, 8 cases were settled before a complaint was issued. A complaint was issued in 7 cases, of which 3 were withdrawn or settled after the complaint. The other 4 were set for trial. (See Table 6 for statistics on plant closing cases in NLRB regional offices, 1992–1995.)

Table 6

Sample of NLRB Cases Filed in Regional Offices, 1992–1995
(Unfair Labor Practice Charges on Plant Closings/Threats of Plant Closing)

	Cases Filed	Withdrawn/ Dismissed	Settled Pre-Complaint	Complaint Issued	Settled Post-Complaint	To Trial ALJ
Fort Worth (Region 16)	24	9	8	9	6	3
Milwaukee (Region 30)	43	27	8	7	3	4
Total	67	36	16	16	9	7

These findings suggest that for every case involving plant closing or threat of plant closing that reached the stage of a trial before an ALJ, some 10 unfair labor practice cases were initiated at the regional level. Complaints were issued in almost 25 percent of the cases filed. This was twice the rate of complaint issuance for all other unfair labor practice charges against employers (see Table 1).

In the sample studied, 10 percent of all plant closing and plant closing threat cases filed, as well as over 40 percent of those in which a complaint was issued, advanced to trial before an ALJ. This is 10 times the rate of enforcement in other cases of unfair labor practice charges against employers.[64] While the sample of 2 regional offices out of 33 may not be sufficient to reach firm conclusions, these findings indicate that the NLRB is more likely to take such cases very seriously and to aggressively pursue cases involving plant closing and threats of plant closing to a litigated conclusion, prevailing in nearly 90 percent of such cases.

---

[64] To put this suggested, sample-based finding in perspective, it should be kept in mind that for all unfair labor practice charges filed before the NLRB, only 2 percent—not 10 percent—reach the level of an ALJ decision. That is, this is a relatively *modest* finding, one that confirms the importance of the sample research in the regional offices. Otherwise, one might use a factor of 50, not 10, to estimate the volume of plant closings and threats of closing for each case initiated that ultimately reaches the stage of a written decision.

Considering Tables 6 and 2 together with the incidence of cases decided by the NLRB, the following overall pattern emerges: of an average of 5,000 union election petitions filed per year, some 500–600 or 1 in 10, result in unfair labor practice charges that alleging plant closing or threats and that are filed with regional offices of the NLRB. Of these cases, 50–60 result in published Board decisions.

Survey Findings

To obtain information not available from published decisions or from NLRB case records, the Secretariat arranged for extensive, original survey research into plant closings and threats of plant closing in union organizing campaigns.[65] Researchers surveyed union representatives to examine why they decide to initiate, discontinue, or proceed with an organizing campaign, or to file or not file unfair labor practice charges in connection with their campaigns.

The survey covered the reported experience of U.S. union representatives in 525 organizing campaigns. Survey questionnaires were sent to union representatives who undertook to organize employees in workplaces with 50 or more employees in the potential bargaining unit over a 3-year period from January 1, 1993, to December 31, 1995.[66] In 149 of the campaigns, unions withdrew their petition for an election before an election took place. In 376 campaigns, the unions proceeded to an election. This is the largest comprehensive database on union organizing campaigns to date.

Key findings of the survey include the following:

- Plant closing threats were reported to have occurred in half of the sampled union organizing campaigns during the period studied.

- Threats were reported to have occurred frequently in industries more susceptible to plant closings such as manufacturing, trucking, and warehousing. In those sectors, the reported incidence of plant closing threats in organizing cam-

---

[65] In union organizing campaigns in which plant closings or threats of closing halt the campaign before it ever gets off the ground, a union may have no interest in filing charges, preferring to seek more fruitful organizing opportunities. Also, filing ULP charges requires supporting evidence in the form of sworn statements by workers, who may be reluctant to come forward when the campaign has been discontinued. For other practical reasons including litigation costs, litigation delays, staff organizers' time, staff attorneys' time, difficulty in obtaining witnesses and so on, many unions make a simple strategic decision to forego filing charges, hoping the campaign might be revived later.

[66] Recall that the review of federal court decisions covered a 7-year period, and the review of NLRB cases covered a 5-year period. Time and resource constraints required a telescoping of time periods examined as the volume of cases and organizing campaigns multiplied.

paigns surveyed was 62 percent, compared with 36 percent in relatively immo-
bile industries such as construction, health care, hotels, retail stores, and other
services.

- Where plant closing threats were reported, such threats were the most significant identified factor in a union's decision to withdraw its election petition.
Threats of closing were cited by 53 percent of respondents as the main reason
they withdrew petitions, followed by those reporting other threats and discharges (47 percent) and employer promises of improvements (38 percent).

- In surveyed campaigns where elections took place, the overall union win rate
when the employer reportedly threatened plant closing was 33 percent, compared with 47 percent in elections where no plant closing threats were reported
to have been made. The union election win rate in the total sample studied,
including elections where threats were reported to have been made and elections
with no threats reported, was 41 percent.

- The union election success rate in companies that reportedly have Canadian
locations (34 percent union success) or that reportedly trade with Canada (33
percent), as well as in companies with sites in Mexico or that trade with Mexico
(both 31 percent), was lower than the overall election win rate of 41 percent in
the sample.

- While no threats to move to Canada were reported by respondents, threats to
move to Mexico were cited in 15.5 percent of manufacturing sector campaigns
in which threats were reported to have occurred.

Note on Survey Results

In discussing survey results, the use of the term "threats" has to be clarified. Union
representatives responding to the survey might characterize as threats employer statements that, if they were tested in litigation, might be found to be lawful. The use of the
term "threat" in the survey and in this section does not imply any legal conclusion as
to whether what survey respondents characterized as a threat was lawful or unlawful,
unless it is clearly specified with reference to a final decision of an ALJ, the NLRB, or
a federal appeals court. Only a fraction of potentially unlawful closings or threats ever
reach the stage of a final, litigated conclusion.

Whether or not threats reported by respondents were lawful or unlawful is not
determinable here. However, respondents' perceptions are relevant to determining
how plant closings or threats of closing affect the right to organize. The design of the
questionnaire guarded against self-serving answers by union respondents, as is borne
out by the richness and variety of the data. Half of the respondents, for example,
reported no closings or threats in their campaigns.

Union respondents reported that they filed unfair labor practice charges in only one-third of the reported cases of threats and that a complaint was issued (indicating a preliminary finding of merit to the charge) in half of the cases filed. Unions and employers both have myriad reasons for not filing unfair labor practice charges or for settling cases without a final decision by an adjudicator. Those reasons cannot be connected to the lawfulness or unlawfulness of the alleged unfair labor practice. Settlements routinely contain a "non-admission" of liability clause that cannot be taken as conclusive whether a violation did or did not occur.

Similarly, the finding in the survey that plant closing threats reportedly occurred in half of the organizing campaigns in the sample cannot be seen as conclusive evidence that employers make unlawful threats in half of all union organizing campaigns. Union representatives reported what they perceived as threats, whether they were lawful or unlawful, in half of the campaigns in the sample, and accordingly took action to withdraw their petition or proceed to an election, with the results indicated.

Examples of Plant Closing Cases in the United States

A Lawful Prediction

At an Illinois restaurant where workers launched an organizing drive, the employer guaranteed that if the union came in he would be out of business within a year. In a taperecorded speech in a captive audience meeting, the owner stated *"If the union exists at [the company], [the company] will fail. The cancer will eat us up and we will fall by the wayside.... I am not making a threat. I am stating a fact.... I only know from my mind, from my pocketbook, how I stand on this."*

This statement was found by a U.S. Court of Appeals to be a lawful prediction that did not interfere with, restrain, or coerce employees.[67]

A Pre-Election Closing

A Georgia cardboard box manufacturer threatened to close the plant if the union won the election. In a tape-recorded speech on file with the NLRB Region 12 office in Jacksonville, Florida, the company president stated: *"There are people here who don't care whether [the company] survives or doesn't survive ... why kill this plant for the rest of the people who really care. ... There's plenty of small towns in Georgia for companies like ours ... and Alabama and Florida and North and South Carolina and Missouri and Texas and New Mexico...."*

Worker Question: *"So if we vote for the union, are you going to close the plant down?"*

President: *"I'm not going to fall into this trap. There are a lot of people who would love*

---

[67] See *NLRB v. Village IX, Inc.*, 723 F.2d 1360 (7th Cir. 1983).

Examples of Plant Closing Cases in the United States (continued)

me to say something like you just said. I won't do it.... Whether this company stays open or doesn't stay open, that will depend on economics...."

The company closed the plant 4 days before the NLRB representation election. The NLRB regional office issued a complaint that the company unlawfully threatened to close and then closed the plant because employees supported the union. The threats and the closing were among 66 separate unfair labor practice counts that also included individual discharges, mass layoffs, interrogation, surveillance, promise of benefits, other threats of reprisal, and other acts of interference, restraint, and coercion.

The company and the union settled the case after the trial took place. The company agreed to reopen the plant, rehire the workers with back pay, and recognize and bargain with the union.[68]

Effective Enforcement

At a Michigan auto parts manufacturer, the NLRB set aside an election where it found that the employer *"created and reinforced an overall atmosphere of fear among the employees that a union victory could result not only in loss of work and customers, but in plant closure itself."* Among the company's tactics was reference to a nearby plant that closed and moved to Mexico. The NLRB ruled that these threats were illegal, and ordered a new election. In a new election ordered by the Board, the union prevailed and was certified as the bargaining representative.[69]

Threatening to Move to Mexico (1)

An automotive parts manufacturer in Michigan responded to an organizing drive by the United Auto Workers (UAW) with a speech by the division president stating *"We are fortunate to have a growing operation in Mexico where we are able to produce when we become non-competitive here.... We are now trying to develop our plants to enable us to move product from one plant to another.... We cannot survive here if we continue to lose product ... even to our own plant in Mexico.... [In other locations] we have moved the work and closed the plant especially where light assembly or manual work was being done.... Don't let it happen here."*

Before the election the company displayed large "MEXICO TRANSFER JOB" signs on equipment placed on flatbed trailers in the employee parking lot. The union lost the representation election. In a decision issued July 17, 1996, the ALJ who heard the case ruled that the company's conduct was coercive, and ordered a new election.[70]

---

[68] See *Roblaw Industries, Inc., and International Brotherhood of Teamsters*, Complaint in Case No. 12-CA-17901 (1995), and Settlement Agreement (October 23, 1995) on file with NLRB Region 12.

[69] See *Contec Division, SPX Corp. and UAW*, 320 NLRB No. 52 (1995).

[70] See *ITT Automotive and United Auto Workers*, decision of Judge Marion C. Ladwig, NLRB Division of Judges, JD-79-96 (1996).

Examples of Plant Closing Cases in the United States (continued)

Threatening to Move to Mexico (2)

At an Illinois auto parts plant, a supervisor's comment to workers that *"I hope you guys are ready to pack up and move to Mexico"* did not violate the National Labor Relations Act, the U.S. Court of Appeals for the 7th Circuit ruled. The court decision reversed the NLRB's determination that the statement was an unlawful threat. The court ruled that the statement was a *"joke,"* not a threat.[71]

The Effects of Delay

A manufacturer of window coverings in New Jersey responded to an organizing campaign by the United Electrical, Radio, and Machine Workers (UE) by laying off the entire second shift, which was more than 40 percent of the workforce. The ALJ ruled that the layoff had legitimate business motivation. The NLRB reversed the ALJ decision. The Board found that this partial closing was motivated by anti-union animus. The federal court of appeals upheld the NLRB ruling, and workers were reinstated with back pay. However, during the more than 3 years' duration of the legal proceedings, the union's organizing impetus was dissipated. The workers never succeeded in forming a union.[72]

Sham Closing

A Texas foundry where employees were represented by the United Steelworkers Union closed its doors and ceased doing business under one corporate name, then reopened 3 days later under another name and hired new, non-union workers. The union filed an unfair labor practice charge and pursued it to a successful conclusion, including a Board order to rehire affected union members. The company then declared bankruptcy. Enforcement of the NLRB's order awaits a decision of the bankruptcy court.[73]

Converting Employees to "Independent Contractor" Status

A unionized Massachusetts wire and cable installation company converted employees to independent contractor status and cut off all salaries and fringe benefits under the collective bargaining agreement. Employees who protested were fired. The NLRB ordered the employer to reinstate the discharged employees and recognize and bargain with the union.[74]

---

[71] See *NLRB v. Champion Laboratories Inc.*, CA 7, No. 95-2433 (October 24, 1996).

[72] See *Hunter-Douglas, Inc. v. NLRB*, 804 F.2d 808 (1986).

[73] See *Texas Electric Steel Casting Co. and United Steelworkers*, decision of Judge James S. Jensen, NLRB Division of ALJs, JD (SF)-19-94.

[74] See *Cable-Masters, Inc., and Communications Workers of America*, 307 NLRB No. 139 (1992).

Examples of Plant Closing Cases in the United States (continued)

Converting Employees to "Temporary Manpower" Status

When workers at a Wisconsin plant launched an organizing campaign, management responded with a mass layoff of first-shift employees and a transfer of all employees from the employer's payroll to the payroll of a temporary manpower agency, telling workers that the transfer to temporary status was made *"to scare them off the union."* The NLRB found that the mass layoff was an unlawful act of discrimination and the transfer to temporary manpower status was an unlawful act of coercion. The Board ordered the company to cease discriminatory layoffs, restore employees to employment status with the company, and to recognize and bargain with the union. The union later obtained a collective bargaining agreement.[75]

A Threat to Withhold Investment

The plant manager of a large multi-national company (with extensive operations in Mexico) told workers in a West Virginia union-organizing campaign *"The company that supplies the investment dollars for our growth [is] watching what happens here.... We must learn to work together.... I'm afraid if we can't do that—we won't have a business here ten years from now.... If you choose [the union], we could be heading in the wrong direction...."* A company supervisor told a worker that if the union got in *"they would close the plant ... within 2 weeks."*

The NLRB found these statements to be unlawful, coercive threats of plant closing. In the same case, the NLRB also found the company guilty of unlawfully threatening loss of benefits, loss of wage increases, temporary layoffs, and other reprisals if the workers chose union representation. The Board set aside the election results (the union had lost the election) and ordered a new election.[76]

---

[75] See *America's Best Quality Coatings Corp. and Staff Right, Inc., Joint Employers, and United Electrical Workers,* 313 NLRB No. 52 (1993).

[76] See *General Electric Company and United Electrical, Radio, and Machine Workers of America (UE),* 321 NLRB No. 86 (1996).

CANADA

In a 10-year period from 1986 to 1995, 36 cases involving issues of anti-union closings and threats were decided by all of Canada's labor boards, labor commissioners, and labor tribunals combined.[77]

The plant closing and threats of plant closing cases arose in seven jurisdictions:

Federal .... 2 cases
Alberta .... 3 cases
British Columbia .... 17 cases
New Brunswick .... 2 cases
Ontario .... 8 cases
Quebec .... 1 case
Saskatchewan .... 3 cases

Manitoba, Newfoundland, Nova Scotia, and Prince Edward Island showed no plant closing cases.[78]

Notably, cases involving total or partial *closing* (25) exceed the number of cases involving a *threat* (11).[79] Moreover, all the Canadian cases (with the exception of one Quebec case)[80] were decided by the administrative labor authority of the relevant jurisdiction. None was decided by a court acting on an appeal from an administrative decision. This confirms that the civil courts rarely review or overturn a labor board or commissioner decision in Canada.

Of the 36 Canadian cases, 21 involved new union organizing or a first collective bargaining agreement and 15 arose in the context of an established bargaining relationship. In 15 of the 21 organizing/new union cases, the labor tribunals upheld un-

---

[77] These cases were obtained through Quicklaw (a legal database) searches, through review of the major Canadian texts touching on unfair labor practices, and through direct contact with the labor board and tribunals in each jurisdiction.

[78] The provincial differences noted here might also lend themselves to further research into, for example, why the three largest provinces—Quebec, British Columbia, and Ontario—range from the smallest number of reported cases to the greatest number, with one at the midpoint between the extremes.

[79] As shown above in U.S. cases, a sizeable majority (57 of 89 court cases, and 210 of 319 Board cases) involve threats rather than closings.

[80] Recall that in Quebec, the labor relations law is administered first by a Labor Commissioner of the provincial labor ministry. Appeals from commissioners' decisions go to the Labor Tribunal, a judicial branch entity. Thus, the single Quebec case is a court decision, as distinct from a labor board decision.

fair labor practice complaints involving plant closings or threats of plant closing. In 6 cases, the boards found no violation. In the 15 established union cases, the boards found violations 7 times, and no violation 8 times. That is, employers were found to be liable for unlawful conduct in 60 percent of the cases decided by an adjudicator.[81]

Remedies

The remedies most frequently awarded by labor relations boards were (1) reinstatement and/or compensation for employees,[82] and (2) cease-and-desist orders and/or declarations of breach of statute. Orders to post board decisions in the workplace or to mail them to employees were also made, though somewhat less frequently.

In addition to these normal remedies, many of the cases resulted in extraordinary remedies. Automatic certification was ordered in three cases involving extensive unfair labor practices by employers, and an order to resume negotiations was made once. Boards compelled employers to reimburse unions for the costs incurred in organizing on one occasion, and twice required employers to provide unions with access to employees for organizing purposes.

In contrast to the stronger remedy sometimes applied by the U.S. NLRB and the courts, no Canadian labor board has ordered an employer to permanently resume operations or reopen a plant.[83] Rather, the normal board response in a plant closing context was to provide monetary compensation to the employees and the union. On two occasions, however, boards did make orders involving an explicit return of work to the bargaining unit. First, a board ordered temporary resumption of operations for a period of 8 months, following an otherwise legitimate closing that had been advanced 8 months to punish a union.[84] Second, when an employer moved work from one operation to another, locking out its unionized employees, a board ordered that the work be returned to the unionized subsidiary.

---

[81] In U.S. cases reviewed for this report, employers were found liable for unlawful conduct in 94 percent of the federal court decisions and 89 percent of the NLRB decisions.

[82] On a number of occasions, reinstatement of an entire bargaining unit was ordered following the subcontracting or movement of a unit's work. Reinstatement was ordered in cases where layoffs of union members or organizers were related to the closing threat.

[83] While the decisions of several labor boards in Canada have suggested that they have the capacity to order an employer to resume operations, no board has actually done so, and many have expressed concern about the practicality of such an order.

[84] The employer was provided the option of not resuming operations but of maintaining the employees' wages and benefits as if they were employed throughout that 8-month period.

A cautionary note needs to be introduced here regarding comparisons of U.S. and Canadian findings. Although both systems apply the concept of unfair labor practices to deal with alleged plant closings or threats of plant closing, differences in legal definitions and administration, in the pace of new union organizing activity, and in the size of the labor force (Canada's is 10 times smaller) make strict comparisons difficult.

However, recognizing that comparisons between the two systems are inevitable, perhaps the most appropriate comparison using findings in this report may be the number of cases decided by labor boards per year relative to the number of union election petitions (in the United States) or union certification applications (in Canada) filed per year. In the United States, some 50–60 cases involving plant closings or threats of closing are decided each year by the NLRB. These cases arise in a context where 5,000 union election petitions are filed and 3,200 elections are held. In Canada, 3–4 cases are decided by the labor boards each year in a context where more than 2,600 certification applications are filed in the country's four major jurisdictions with most of the workforce, in the federal labor board, and in British Columbia, Ontario, and Quebec. (See Appendix D for detailed data from Canadian labor board cases.)

Examples of Plant Closing Cases In Canada

An Unlawful Threat

When some of the 134 employees at an airline ticket office in Toronto began organizing a union, a vice president of the U.S.-based company began holding mandatory "rap sessions" with small groups of workers. The official sent a letter to all employees that concluded by saying *"However ... I hope you will think very seriously before you take any action that will make your job a union job."*

The Canada Labour Relations Board (CLRB) noted that *"Any statement, action, comportment that indicates to employees the employer's desire not to have them join a union impresses on them that their action clearly goes against his wish, he who is ultimately responsible for their job security. Under such circumstances, what must an employee feel? How at ease were the 10 or 12 employees who were obliged to attend rap sessions?"*

The Board found that the overall letter to employees was unlawful interference with workers' organizing rights and that the concluding statement about *"thinking very seriously"* was unlawful intimidation.[85] The CLRB ordered the employer to mail to each employee another letter acknowledging that the CLRB had found the employer's earlier letter to be a violation of the Canada Labour Code, and to enclose a copy of the Board's decision.

---

[85] See *American Airlines, Inc. v. Brotherhood of Railway, Airline, and Steamship Clerks* (1981), 3 C.L.R.B.R. 90 (C.L.R.B., Foisy, Vice Chair).

Examples of Plant Closing Cases in Canada (continued)

Finding a Remedy for a "Runaway Shop"

A large Ontario manufacturing company relocated its operations from an urban center to several rural, non-unionized locations. The Ontario Labour Relations Board (OLRB) found that the action was motivated in part by a desire to escape the union and thus constituted an unfair labor practice. Significant employment was created at its new sites, complicating the problem of finding an appropriate remedy for the unlawful action. The OLRB directed the employer (1) to provide the employees of the closed plant with the right of first refusal for jobs at the new plants with no loss of seniority or fringe benefits, (2) to provide relocation allowances to employees who chose to move, (3) to provide the union with a list of employees at the new plants, (4) to provide the union with access to company bulletin boards at the new plants, and (5) to provide the union the opportunity to address the employees during working hours at the new plants. The Board also ordered the employer to reimburse the union for expenses incurred in organizing the new plants.[86]

Limits to Innovation in Remedies

In a maneuver characterized by the CLRB as "Machiavellianism," a Montreal bank closed one of its branches following union certification and transferred all accounts to another, unorganized branch office. The CLRB certified the union as the bargaining agent at the new branch and ordered that employees be permitted to attend union meetings during paid work time.

While upholding these aspects of the CLRB's order, the Supreme Court of Canada articulated an important limit: a remedial order must be *reasonably related* to the employer's breach of the statute. Thus, the Court quashed another part of the order requiring the employer to pay part of the savings gained from closing the unionized branch into a trust fund to promote the objectives of the statute. It also quashed an order to send a letter to all employees admitting violating their rights.[87]

Leaving the Province

Canada's primarily province-based labor law system raises problems of remedy when a plant closing and relocation occurs between provinces. After the first collective bargaining meeting following certification of a newly organized union, a British Columbia nursing home company closed its facility, terminated all of the employees, and shifted operations to another province.

---

[86] See *UEW, Local 504 v. Westinghouse Canada, Inc.* (1980), 80 C.L.L.C. 16,053 (O.L.R.B.); upheld on judicial review *Westinghouse Canada, Inc. v. UEW, Local 504* (1980), 80 C.L.L.C. 14,062 (Ont. Div. Ct.).

[87] See *National Bank of Canada v. Retail Clerks' International Union* (1984), 9 D.L.R. (4th) 10 (S.C.C.).

Examples of Plant Closing Cases in Canada (continued)

The British Columbia Labour Relations Board found anti-union animus an element in the closing. However, since the company had ceased operations in the province altogether, reinstatement was not a practical remedy. Instead, compensation equaling 2 months' pay was ordered for each employee (less any income earned during that 2-month period). Despite significant bargaining expenses to that point, the board refused to order the employer to reimburse the union.[88]

A Subcontracting Case

A Sudbury, Ontario, courier firm terminated all members of the proposed bargaining unit the day after a union seeking to represent its employees applied for certification. The company subcontracted all the work. The CLRB found that the employer failed to advance any convincing evidence that the subcontracting was undertaken solely for legitimate business concerns and that the timing of the move demonstrated anti-union animus. The Board distinguished this case from the general rule of not ordering an employer to reopen a closed business, since the employer continued to carry on the business in the same fashion in the same location. The Board ordered the employer to reinstate the employees with back pay and certified the union as the bargaining agent.[89]

A Closely Watched Current Case

The relative infrequency of anti-union closings and threats in Canada does not diminish the importance or the continuing timeliness of this issue in Canada. In a case being closely watched in Canadian and U.S. labor and management circles, a major U.S. company operating in Canada was found to have contravened the Ontario Labour Relations Act by a "subtle but extremely effective threat" to close if the employees unionized.

In a question-and-answer publication to employees shortly before the election in May 1996, the following questions were asked and answered by management (the questions were characterized by management as written questions from employees):

Q: There is an overwhelming concern that if the store unionizes, [the company] will close the store. Is this true?

A: It would be inappropriate for your company to comment on what it will or will not do if the store is unionized.

Q: Some people have said that if the store unionized it would be illegal for [the company] to close the store. Is that true?

---

[88] See *British Columbia Government and Service Employees' Union v. Humanacare Counselling*, unreported, November 30, 1995, (1995) B.C.L.R.B. 292–39.

[89] See *United Food and Commercial Workers, Local 175 v. Insurance Courier Services* (1993), 18 C.L.R.B.R. (2d) 286.

Examples of Plant Closing Cases in Canada (continued)

A: This statement is not factually correct. What would or would not be legal for your company to do following the store becoming unionized depends on the factual circumstances and the application of the law against those circumstances. It would be inappropriate for your company to comment or suggest what those factual circumstances might be.

Q: Can a union hurt this store? E.g., when it comes to renewing the store lease, will [the company] not renew and close its doors; therefore, we are out of a job? Please help clear this confusion for me and others. Thank you.

A. Whether or not a union would hurt this store is a matter for you to decide in your own mind. It would be inappropriate for your company to comment on what it will or will not do if the store is unionized.[90]

The same responses were given orally by top company managers who engaged employees in small group and one-on-one meetings in the days preceding the election. The union lost the election and filed unfair labor practice charges with the OLRB arguing that these statements and actions amounted to intimidation of employees by means of an unlawful plant closing threat.

The OLRB ruled in favor of the union in February 1997 and certified the union as the bargaining representative without requiring a second election. The OLRB found that, in the wake of the employer's actions, another vote would not likely reflect the true wishes of the employees in the bargaining unit. The Board also directed that the union be permitted to hold meetings with workers in the workplace during working hours without managers present, as long as such meetings did not disrupt operations. The company appealed the OLRB's decision.

---

[90] See *United Steelworkers of America and Wal-Mart Canada, Inc.*, Ontario Labour Relations Board, nos. 0387-96-R, 0453-96-U, February 10, 1997. See also Paul Waldie and Marina Strauss, "Windsor Wal-Mart Wins Right to Union: Firm Intimidated Staff, Board Rules," the *Globe and Mail*, February 11, 1997; Robyn Meredith, "Despite Election, a Wal-Mart Goes Union in Canada," the *New York Times*, February 18, 1997, at C3; "Wal-Mart Canadian Unit to Appeal Labor Ruling," the *Wall Street Journal*, March 28, 1997, at A13.

MEXICO

Administrative Findings

No data are available in public libraries or through electronic searches for decisions related to plant closings of Mexico's federal and state Conciliation and Arbitration Boards (CABs).[91] Decisions are maintained in CAB office files throughout the country and are available to parties involved in the case. Accordingly, Secretariat researchers examined, by hand, thousands of case files for the years 1991 through 1995 at the Federal CAB and at Local CABs of the states of Chihuahua and Nuevo Leon.[92] This review allowed researchers to obtain a quantitative sample of the avenues of recourse and of the procedures established by the Federal Labor Law (FLL) to deal with plant closings.

One such avenue is the "collective conflict of an economic nature," which is the procedure contained in Articles 900–919 of the FLL that employers are normally expected to follow before closing a plant.[93] Another avenue is "voluntary termination" whereby the employment relationship is terminated by mutual consent, which is embodied in a collective agreement to close the plant with specified severance pay and related benefits for workers.[94] Researchers also reviewed and reported on Supreme Court jurisprudence regarding such cases.

The Secretariat also reviewed data from the Mexican Social Security Institute (IMSS) for 1994 and 1995 as to the number of workers and firms dropped from the rolls, indicating the number of plant closings and their effects on workers.

---

[91] The Federal CAB publishes quarterly *La Gaceta Laboral*, which includes new legislation and significant FCAB decisions.

[92] In Mexico, the term "local" refers to state government. The examination of case files required the physical review of thousands of pages of records in CAB offices to extract those dealing with plant closing issues.

[93] The "collective conflict" procedure is not limited to plant closings. It applies to several common types of labor disputes in Mexico.

[94] Article 33 of the FLL provides that "any agreement or liquidation must be written and contain an account of the factual circumstances that motivates it and of the rights addressed in it. It shall be ratified by the CAB, which shall approve it as long as it contains no renunciation of the rights of the workers." Article 34 provides that such an agreement may not diminish benefits already accrued by the workers, and may not single out individual workers for differential treatment.

For the period between January 1991 and May 1996, Table 7 shows figures that emerged from the review of data from the Federal CAB and the state CABs of Chihuahua and Nuevo Leon.

Table 7

Mexican CAB Data on Collective Conflict Cases

	1991	1992	1993	1994	1995	1996 (through May)
Collective Conflicts of an Economic Nature	24	41	25	47	28	11 Total: 166
Collective Conflict Cases Involving Plant Closings	0	2	0	0	0	0 Total: 2

The Local CAB of Chihuahua handled only one plant closing case under collective conflict procedures in 1994, and one in 1995. The CAB of Nuevo Leon had no such cases.

Although these are just three among over 100 Federal and Local CABs, the results still indicate a negligible volume of plant closing cases under the "collective conflict of an economic nature" proceedings provided in Articles 892–899 and 900–919 of the FLL for such matters.

However, these cases occurred in a context of widespread plant closings. In 1994, the IMSS noted 3,214 workplaces dropped from the rolls. In 1995, 5,794 workplace reductions took place, affecting more than half a million workers covered by Social Security.[95] With so many plant closings taking place, the obvious question is why almost no "collective conflict" cases occurred. After all, this is the procedure in which unions could challenge a closing on grounds that it was motivated by anti-unionism, rather than by one of the permissible reasons for closing.

The answer appears to be found in data obtained by the Secretariat from the Federal CAB on the number of collective agreements made between workers and employers under voluntary, mutual consent provisions for termination of the employment relationship under Article 53 or Article 401 of the FLL. These agreements are submitted to the CAB for its review and approval. This information reveals that this voluntary termination avenue is used extensively for resolution of plant closing issues, rather than the collective conflict procedure.

---

[95] Information obtained from IMSS sources by Secretariat staff.

Table 8 indicates the volume of voluntary termination cases in federal private sector jurisdiction, 1991–1995.

Table 8

Mexican Federal CAB Approval of Collective Agreements for Termination, 1991–1995[a]

1991	1992	1993	1994	1995
169	307	203	238	194

Total: 1,111

[a] See "Estadísticas Laborales, 2do Semestre 1994," STPS, Subsecretario "B" at 92.

Analysis

Certain findings can be considered on the basis of the foregoing information:

1. Clear evidence demonstrates that the procedures created by the FLL for plant closings are not being used in the manner intended. In 5 years, only five cases arose in the CABs visited by Secretariat researchers, and those were ultimately resolved by an agreement between the parties rather than by a CAB order. Given the frequency of plant closings as derived from the Social Security Institute, the sample of CAB files reviewed by the Secretariat showed a massive difference between the total number of plant closings and the number of closings that proceed under the collective conflict provisions of the FLL.

2. The FLL procedures for plant closings contained in Articles 892–899 and 900–919 are long, burdensome, and technical. In contrast, the faster, more flexible procedures available under Article 53 or Article 401 for voluntary termination of the employment relationship permit workers and unions to negotiate directly with employers over favorable severance terms in plant closing cases. The preference for this avenue is confirmed in the number of collective agreements on termination of the employment relationship approved by the Federal CAB, more than 1,100 in the sample studied. Moreover, even when employers initiate collective conflict proceedings, workers can immediately suspend those proceedings by exercising their right to strike and seeking to negotiate a voluntary termination of the employment relationship. As yet another alternative, workers can file individual claims for *indemnización* under the unjustifiable discharge provisions of the law.

3. Significantly, the amount of severance pay available to workers under the collective procedures is less than that available under other procedures. Using the collective conflict mechanism, severance pay is 3 months' salary plus 12 days' pay per year of service. Under other procedures the 12 days' pay becomes 20 days' pay per year of service. This creates a powerful incentive for workers to avoid the collective conflict avenue in favor of the voluntary termination or unjustifiable discharge mechanisms, or to declare a strike and negotiate a strike settlement with the employer. Most notably, the voluntary, mutual consent mechanism permits workers to claim full salary from the date of closing to the date of a CAB order, in addition to their severance pay. All of these are lawful procedures before the same CAB that otherwise would hear the case under the collective conflict procedures.

4. Workers can usually obtain their severance pay more rapidly under the voluntary termination mechanism than under collective conflict procedures. Employers are usually more eager to reach a severance pay agreement than to let liability continue to mount under the collective conflict provisions of the labor law, which require lengthy hearings and expert testimony, and permit various appeals. Such agreements reached directly between the parties involved in the plant closing are submitted to the relevant CAB for validation, thus avoiding the need for costly, burdensome litigation and satisfying all parties' preference for a more rapid, practical resolution of the plant closing matter. The Secretariat's finding of 1,111 cases of voluntary collective termination of the employment relationship in the Federal CAB alone, which approved those termination agreements, confirms that this is a preferred avenue for reaching the same purpose of the rarely used collective conflict procedures, that of protecting workers' interests in plant closings.[96]

---

[96] For U.S. and Canadian readers of this report, the importance of severance pay in the Mexican system cannot be overstated. All workers are entitled to severance pay when they lose their jobs, unless they are discharged for one of the 15 specified acts of misconduct in Article 47 of the Federal Labor Law (falsifying an application, sabotage, insubordination, excessive absenteeism, etc.). There is no unemployment insurance system in Mexico, so the immediate provision of severance pay, in the highest possible amount, becomes of paramount interest to workers, both in individual discharge cases and in plant closings. In actual practice, negotiating over severance pay is the most common activity of labor lawyers in Mexico, first, because it is a statutory benefit for all workers so there is a high demand for legal assistance, and second, because workers usually prefer to get the best possible severance pay settlement now than to be tied up in legal proceedings for months or years before their case is decided by the CAB. Conscious of their own limited resources and time, the CABs themselves normally press the parties to reach a private settlement for severance pay. Workers' attorneys are entitled to a percentage of the total severance amount, which creates an incentive for them to get a settlement quickly but at the highest possible amount. In a general context of economic crisis where plant closings are frequent, workers realistically understand that using the "collective conflict" mechanism to try to keep a plant open is futile, so they turn instead to the "voluntary termination" route for faster resolution and higher severance pay.

Examples of Plant Closing Cases in Mexico

The following examples of plant closings and collective terminations of the employment relationship illustrate the methods of applying procedures for a "collective conflict of an economic nature" established by the Federal Labor Law (FLL). Secretariat researchers examined records of cases in the Federal Conciliation and Arbitration Board (CAB) and in the Local CAB of Chihuahua.[97]

Steel Bars of Mexico and National Union of Mine and Metallurgical Workers (Federal CAB)

The company initiated a collective conflict of an economic nature seeking CAB authorization under the "special proceedings" provision of the FLL (Articles 892–899) to close the plant for lack of raw material not imputable to the fault of the employer. The company asserted that its chief supplier for the past 27 years had ceased producing the necessary raw materials. The union took exception, arguing that alternative sources could be found or that the plant could use substitute materials to maintain production.

The union requested the CAB to order that the employment relationship remain in effect without alteration or suspension, that damages be paid to workers if the plant closed, that no reprisals be taken against the workers, and that a provisional lien be placed on the company's assets to satisfy potential claims. The CAB granted a preliminary order restraining the company from disposing of assets while the case proceeded.

After several months of legal proceedings, the union and the company settled the matter between themselves and requested the CAB to halt proceedings and close the file. As required when such a request is made by both parties, the CAB closed the case.

Volkswagen of Mexico and Independent Union of Automobile and Allied Industry Workers (Federal CAB)

In July 1992 the company halted operations and advised the Federal CAB of the collective termination of the employment relationship and of individual labor relations with all unionrepresented workers. The company sought CAB approval for such termination on grounds of *force majeure* not imputable to the employer. The employer also denied recognition to 14 employees for not having been duly recognized as employee representatives by the labor authorities.

The employer argued that the *force majeure* consisted of actions by workers intermittently stopping production and blocking entrance to the site. Management blamed the situation on labor strife based on internal union rivalries and argued that because the employer was prohibited by law from intervening in an internal union dispute and did not know how long the dispute would continue, *force majeure* was even more compelling. The company took action under Articles 53 and 434 of the FLL for approval of termination of the employment relationship and termination of the collective bargaining agreement, insisting that it took no position on the internal union dispute, which was for the workers alone to decide.

---

[97] Case files were reviewed by Dr. Juan Jose Ríos Estavillo as part of the empirical study noted earlier. The Secretariat also received anecdotal information on plant closings in newspaper articles on the subject, which are available along with other information from external consultants and contractors.

Examples of Plant Closing Cases in Mexico (continued)

Worker representatives argued that (1) the employer acted unconstitutionally by declaring termination without authorization by the CAB in violation of Article 435, (2) no work disruption had occurred except that attributable to the employer's failure to provide transportation as required under the contract, and (3) no internal conflict existed in the union.

After taking evidence and hearing arguments, the CAB ruled that (1) the employer could not avoid suspending work and that there was *force majeure* not imputable to the employer, (2) an internal union conflict existed, (3) the employer remained impartial in the internal conflict, (4) the internal union conflict gave rise to work stoppages giving legal cause for terminating individual contracts and the collective contract, (5) the employer should pay indemnization of 3 months' pay plus seniority-based pay on the condition that the union recognize the validity of the payments, and (6) the individual employment relationships and the collective contract be terminated.

Note: In August 1992, the union and the company reached an agreement, in talks joined by the Mexican Department of Labor and Social Welfare (STPS), to sign a new collective agreement and proceed to the re-engagement of workers under the terms of the new contract. In 1993 a different union sought title to the collective bargaining agreement at Volkswagen on the grounds that a majority of workers supported it as the workers' representative. This claim was found by the CAB not to conform to legal requirement for union registration. The case was closed on that basis.[98]

Anahuac Foundry and Plating, Inc. and Radical Union of Metal and Allied Workers (Federal CAB)

The company sought a ruling from the CAB through a collective conflict of an economic nature proceeding to terminate the individual contracts of union members. The company also sought termination of the collective employment relationship with the union on the grounds of failure to meet the costs of production. The company argued that it could not meet the cost of operations at its steel foundry.

However, the union had earlier declared and undertaken a strike, in which before the same CAB the union and the company reached an agreement for voluntary termination of individual and collective contracts with appropriate severance pay. The company thereupon dropped its case under the collective conflict of an economic nature provisions of the FLL, and the CAB closed the case.

---

[98] The Volkswagen affair was a *cause célèbre* in Mexico labor circles, giving rise to widespread commentary, analysis, and controversy. Many observers argued that the plant closing was an artificial device to eliminate militant unionists, thus interfering with their freedom of association. See, for example, Ludger Pries, "Volkswagen: Un Nudo Gordiano Resuelto?" 9 *Trabajo* 7 (1993). As indicated here, the labor authorities found that the closing was lawful.

Examples of Plant Closing Cases in Mexico (continued)

Balanced Seeds of Mexico, Inc. (Local CAB of Chihuahua)

The company invoked the special proceedings provisions in Articles 892–899 of the FLL for collective suspension of the employment relationship in the wake of an explosion that destroyed the plant and equipment for seed production. The company sought permission for a 2-year suspension of the employment relationship. The CAB approved the suspension under provisions that some workers would return to work during the suspension and others would receive appropriate severance pay, in view of the fact that automation in the new plant would require fewer workers.

Industrialized Concrete, Inc. (Local CAB of Chihuahua)

The company brought an action of collective conflict of an economic nature for temporary inability to meet costs. The company claimed lack of financial resources to operate the plant and impossibility of obtaining resources. Through CAB conciliation the parties agreed to terminate employment relations and close the plant with payment of 3 months' salary plus seniority pay and *pro rata* vacation and holiday pay.

The company's lack of cash led to non-compliance with the agreement, leading the workers to obtain a lien on the assets. At the time of the Secretariat's review, assets were being auctioned to satisfy the workers' claims under the agreement with the defunct firm.

PART FOUR

ECONOMIC AND SOCIAL CONTEXT

Worker displacement in general, as well as displacement caused by plant closings in particular, takes place constantly and has a number of causes.[99] Causes can include employer responses to economic concerns such as changes in factor prices, changes in market demand, import penetration, overcapacity, plants reaching the end of useful life, or new technology requiring new plant design, or they can include changes in public policy such as cutbacks in a heavily government-funded industry.

This study is not concerned directly with such natural market-driven or public policy reasons for plant closings. The focus of the study is the use of plant closings and threats of plant closing by employers to subvert the right of workers to form unions. However, it is important to establish a larger economic and social context for considering plant closings.

Data in this section also provide an indication of when displaced workers were forewarned of their displacement. The sudden closing of a plant, regardless of the reason, can create serious adjustment problems for individuals, communities, and government institutions. Therefore, the issue of the "suddenness" of a plant closing is a key consideration in this part.

DISPLACEMENT AND PLANT CLOSINGS IN THE UNITED STATES

Plant closings have had a significant effect on employment in the United States over the past 2 decades. This effect has become even more important in the 1990s. The Bureau of Labor Statistics (BLS) in its biennial Displaced Worker Survey (DWS) found that over the period January 1991 to December 1993, nearly 9.2 million workers were displaced (Table 9). From January 1993 to December 1995, more than 9.3 million workers were displaced, evidence of a continuing phenomenon (Table 10).

Although various causes were listed, the primary cause of worker dislocation according to the survey results was plant closings.[100] Close to 3.6 million workers (39 percent of all displaced workers) lost their jobs because of plant closings in the 3-year

---

[99] Displacement includes workers who lost their jobs because their plant or company closed or moved, their position or shift was abolished, or there was insufficient work.

[100] This term includes plant and company shutdowns as well as plants and companies moving to another location.

period covered by the first survey, and 3.4 million (36 percent of all displaced workers) in the 3-year period covered by the most recent survey. Of those displaced, non-unionized workers made up the majority of those displaced as a result of plant closings, totaling more than 3.0 million workers (86 percent of those displaced by plant closings)[101] from 1991–1993, and 2.9 million workers (86 percent of those displaced by plant closings) from 1993–1995.

Another recent survey conducted by BLS provides additional though less comprehensive data on displaced workers. The mass layoffs survey provided data for the fourth quarter of 1995 and the first quarter of 1996 and found that 270,598 and 232,713 workers were separated from their jobs in those two periods, respectively. Closure of work sites was responsible for 67,500 (25 percent) and 70,300 (25 percent) respectively of all workers laid off during that period. Unlike the DWS, the mass layoff survey covered layoffs of at least 31 days that involved 50 or more workers from the same establishment.

An important aspect of the effect of plant closings on workers in general is the ability of these workers to be reintegrated into the labor force. Social programs designed to provide a bridge for workers while they find new employment, or to provide training and readjustment services, are most helpful when they are able to respond in a timely way to dislocations. Therefore, dislocations that happen in a sudden and unplanned way can be more taxing on the social programs designed to assist workers.

The DWS found that nearly 2.0 million workers (55 percent) in the first survey period and 1.7 million workers (50 percent) in the second survey period were given no advance notice that they were to be displaced because of plant closings. Sudden plant closings make the adjustment process more difficult for individuals, families, and institutions charged with helping these workers reintegrate into the labor force. Of those who were given advance notice, only 611 thousand (40 percent) in the first period and 703 thousand (43 percent) in the second period were warned more than 2 months in advance. The existence of a union at the company being closed seemed to improve the likelihood of receiving advance notice. Approximately 182 thousand unionized workers (42 percent) in the first period and 154 thousand unionized workers (36 percent) in the second period were displaced because of plant closings with no advance notice; compared to nearly 1.8 million non-unionized workers (57 percent) and more than 1.5 million non-unionized workers (52 percent) who were displaced because of closings (Tables 9 and 10).

---

[101] This roughly mirrors the general rate of unionization in the United States.

Table 9

U.S. Workers Displaced Because of Plant Closings in the United States, January 1991–December 1993

(in 1,000s)

	Totals	Percentage	Union Total (percent)		Non-Union Total (percent)	
Displaced because of plant closing/move	3,597	100	432	(12)	3,097	(86)
Re-employed after closing	2,416	67	228	(52)	2,143	(69)
Unemployed after closing	664	18	109	(25)	540	(17)
Not in the labor force	517	14	95	(21)	414	(13)
Received advance notice	1,522	42	251	(58)	1,258	(40)
Less than 1 month	248	16	34	(13)	319	(25)
Between 1 and 2 months	519	34	77	(30)	437	(34)
More than 2 months	611	40	131	(52)	479	(38)
No advance notice	1,988	55	182	(42)	1,775	(57)

Source: U.S. Bureau of Labor Statistics, Current Population Survey, 1994. Revised, 1996.

Table 10

U.S. Workers Displaced Because of Plant Closings in the United States, January 1993–December 1995

(in 1,000s)

	Totals	Percentage	Union Total (percent)		Non-Union Total (percent)	
Displaced because of plant closing/move	3,404	100	421	(12)	2,948	(86)
Re-employed after closing	2,438	71	273	(64)	2,143	(72)
Unemployed after closing	459	13	62	(14)	396	(13)
Not in the labor force	507	14	86	(20)	409	(13)
Received advance notice	1,600	47	258	(61)	1,328	(45)
Less than 1 month	362	22	40	(15)	321	(24)
Between 1 and 2 months	464	29	65	(25)	396	(29)
More than 2 months	703	43	135	(52)	566	(42)
No advance notice	1,717	50	154	(36)	1,558	(52)

Source: U.S. Bureau of Labor Statistics, Current Population Survey, 1996.

Of those who were displaced because of plant closings, 2.4 million in the first pe-riod (67 percent) and 2.4 million in the second period (71 percent), were re-em-ployed. Approximately 664 thousand (27 percent) in the first period and 459 thou-sand (18 percent) in the second period were still looking for work. Approximately 517 thousand in the first period (21 percent) and 507 thousand in the second period (20 percent) had left the labor force, i.e., stopped looking for work, for a number of rea-sons. In the first survey period, approximately 1.1 million (47 percent) of those dis-placed by plant closings who found a new job received unemployment benefits (Table 11). That number was 1.0 million (41 percent) in the second survey period (Table 12).

Table 11

Unemployment Benefits of U.S. Workers Displaced Because of Plant Closings, January 1991–December 1993
(in 1,000s)

	Total	Percentage
Re-employed—Received UI (out of 2,416)	1,137	47
Exhausted benefits	340	29
Did not exhaust UI	767	67
Unemployed—Received UI (out of 664)	454	68
Exhausted benefits	191	42
Did not exhaust UI	258	56
Not in labor force—Received UI (out of 517)	252	48
Exhausted benefits	172	68
Did not exhaust UI	78	30

Source: U.S. Bureau of Labor Statistics, Current Population Survey, 1994.

Table 12

Unemployment Benefits of U.S. Workers Displaced Because of Plant Closings, January 1993–December 1995
(in 1,000s)

	Total	Percentage
Re-employed—Received UI (out of 2,438)	1,017	41
Exhausted benefits	388	38
Did not exhaust UI	591	58
Unemployed—Received UI (out of 459)	278	60
Exhausted benefits	108	38
Did not exhaust UI	170	61
Not in labor force—Received UI (out of 507)	212	41
Exhausted benefits	145	68
Did not exhaust UI	63	29

Source: U.S. Bureau of Labor Statistics, Current Population Survey, 1996.

A similar study of displaced workers in the decade of the 1980s was conducted by the U.S. Congressional Budget Office (CBO). That study found that approximately 73 percent of all workers displaced in the 1980s found new jobs.[102] However, almost half of those who were re-employed were paid less than they received at their old job. Whether they were re-employed at the time of the survey or not, most workers displaced in the 1980s experienced an extended period of unemployment, with an average duration of joblessness of 30 weeks. The average displacement from 1981–1990 was roughly 2.0 million per year, compared with an average of 3.0 million for the 1991–1993 period. Since questions on unionization were not added to the BLS survey until the 1994 survey, no data are available in the CBO study regarding whether unionized workers fared differently from non-unionized workers.

DISPLACEMENT AND PLANT CLOSINGS IN CANADA

Data recently released from the Canadian Survey of Labour and Income Dynamics (SLID) provide some insight into the displacement phenomena in Canada. The SLID was conducted in 1993 and provides information on displaced workers in Canada (Table 13).

Table 13

Job Separation in Canada, 1993–1997—Covered by a Collective Agreement

	Total	Unionized
Total Labor Force (ages 16–69)	18,073,000	4,742,900
Total Separations	4,649,800	n/a
Reason for job separation:		
Company moved	31,400	n/a
Company went out of business	246,200	25,000
Layoff/Business slowdown		
(not caused by seasonal conditions)	784,600	163,000

The SLID found that of the 4.6 million Canadian workers displaced from their jobs during the survey period, 1,062,200 (23 percent) had been displaced because their plants or companies moved, shut down, or had layoffs and business slowdowns.

---

[102] "Displaced Workers: Trends in the 1980's and Implications for the Future," Congressional Budget Office, Congress of the United States, February 1993.

The Canadian government also collected data similar to the above in the 1990 Labour Market Activity Survey (LMAS). According to a study by Statistics Canada, permanent layoffs have been above one million workers since 1981, during both peak and trough periods of the business cycle, suggesting displacement is acyclical.[103] During 1988–1990, the LMAS also found the following characteristics among displaced workers: most were non-unionized, young, working in low-wage jobs, and held their jobs for less than a year. The survey found mixed results with respect to how long displaced workers took to be reemployed and how much they earned in their new jobs. Half of the males displaced between 1988 and 1990 started new jobs within 12 weeks; however, 5 percent of males were unemployed for 1 year before starting a new job. The median period of joblessness for men was approximately 12 weeks. Nearly half of all displaced workers experienced losses in earnings in their new jobs.

An important finding of the survey that is relevant to this study is the difference between the rate of unionization among displaced workers and workers in the total labor force. As Table 14 illustrates, non-unionized workers were overrepresented among both men and women who were displaced in 1990. The LMAS did not address causality. However, it is an important factor in analyzing the effect of plant closings and displacement on unionization issues.

Table 14

Distribution of Displacement by Union Status in Canada, 1990

	Union Percentage	Non-Union Percentage
Men		
Displaced	28.3	65.4
Total workforce	29.7	54
Women		
Displaced	16.7	76.7
Total workforce	25.6	64.7

Source: Labour Market Activity Survey, 1990, Statistics Canada.

[103] Garnett Picot, Zhengxi Lin, & Wendy Piper, "Permanent Layoffs in Canada: Overview and Longitudinal Analysis," Business and Labour Market Analysis, Statistics Canada, May 1996.

DISPLACEMENT AND PLANT CLOSINGS IN MEXICO

Information from the Mexican Social Security Institute (IMSS) indicates that 5,794 workplaces were dropped from the registry in 1995, affecting more than 300,000 workers.[104] This reflects developments in the formal sector for firms that register with the Social Security system. No data are available on the total number of workers displaced in Mexico. The number of unemployed Mexican workers who left their job involuntarily is the closest estimate available. Those data are discussed next. Mexico has not undertaken a specific survey monitoring how displaced workers fare with regard to re-employment and earnings in a new job. Since there is no unemployment insurance program in Mexico, the length of time displaced Mexican workers spend unemployed is likely to be lower than that in the United States and Canada. However, no data are available to confirm this. Overall, duration of unemployment is much lower in Mexico compared with Canada and the United States, suggesting that the lack of unemployment benefits reduces the duration of joblessness.

ALTERNATE COMPARATIVE MEASURES OF DISPLACEMENT IN NORTH AMERICA

The only comparative data on displacement in the three countries come from unemployment statistics. As Table 15 illustrates, involuntary job losers make up between 40 and 70 percent of all unemployed workers in the three NAFTA countries. Canada seems to be hardest hit by involuntary job loss. These data reflect displacement at a very broad level, covering workers who lost their jobs involuntarily for a number of reasons, including plant closings.

---

[104] Information obtained from IMSS sources by Secretariat staff.

Table 15

Job Losses[a] in North America

(in 1,000s)

	1990	1991	1992	1993	1994	1995
Canada						
Total job losers	720.5	986.2	1,113.6	1,108.1	1,007.8	n/a
Percent of total unemployed	61.9	66.1	67.9	67.2	65.4	n/a
Mexico[b]						
Total urban job losers	123.2	129.4	153.2	192.5	227.0	513.0
Percent of urban unemployed	33.7	35.7	38.9	38.8	42.6	54.2
United States						
Total job losers	3,322.0	4,608.0	5,291.0	4,769.0	3,815.0	3,476.0
Percent of total unemployed	48.3	54.7	56.4	54.6	47.7	46.9

[a] This term includes only workers involuntarily unemployed who are not new entrants to the labor force.

[b] For Mexico, these figures represent only urban areas. Estimates are based on the National Urban Employment Survey, which covers 92 percent of the urbanized population and none of the non-urban population.

IMPACT OF PLANT CLOSINGS ON WORKERS

Workers who are displaced are often unemployed for long periods of time, and when they do find a new job, for most workers, it is at a lower wage. Workers also often lose health benefits when they are displaced, along with the seniority and other benefits that come with long tenure in a job. Given all these risks for workers, an employer faced with the possibility of a unionized workforce may effectively use the threat of closing a plant to discourage workers from forming a union.

The existence of a safety net to help workers who are displaced because of plant closings can be crucial to ease the adjustment burden for workers and help them to be reintegrated into the labor market. Although several federal, state, and provincial adjustment programs exist, many workers, for various reasons, never avail themselves of these programs. (Appendix E provides a discussion of labor market adjustment programs available to workers in each country.)

EARLY WARNING AND SUDDENNESS OF PLANT CLOSINGS

A key consideration for the adjustment of workers to plant closings is how much advance notice they were given to prepare for being displaced. The federal governments in Canada and the United States, as well as several provinces and several states, have recognized the importance of providing workers and communities with advance notice of a plant closing so that the adjustment process can occur more smoothly. Instead of requiring advance warning, Mexican law requires employers to obtain permission from the labor authorities to close plants (although the procedure is rarely used—see Part Three, Mexico findings).

Despite the fact that there is some evidence that such warning can be helpful in the adjustment process, most plant closings in the United States and Canada occur with no such notice, and the rapid adjustment costs are borne by workers, government institutions, and local communities. The following is a brief discussion of early-warning programs in the three countries.

United States

The Worker Adjustment and Retraining Notification Act (WARN) was enacted in 1988 to improve the adjustment prospects for displaced workers by providing workers and communities advance warning of impending dislocations. Under the WARN Act, certain firms are required to provide 60 days' advance notice to workers prior to a mass layoff or plant closing that will last more than 6 months and affect at least 50 workers.

In addition to the WARN Act, which is a federal requirement, numerous states have enacted advance warning legislation. Nine states enacted plant closing laws prior to the WARN Act enactment, and several others have since enacted such laws. The state requirements vary, with some exceeding the WARN Act 60-day requirement and others offering other improvements to the federal legislation.

Two exceptions to the WARN Act allow reduced notice requirements that are particularly relevant to this study. Given that the "intent" or "cause" of a plant closing is a key concern of this study, i.e., whether a plant closing was motivated by economic or anti-union reasons, exceptions to the WARN Act are useful to analyze.

The first exception is the so called "faltering company" exception, which applies only to plant closings. Under the Act, companies are allowed to provide less than the required 60-day notice in situations in which the announcement of a closing would adversely affect the company's ability to gain financing or new business that may keep the company afloat. Specifically, the exception applies if the company (1) is actively seeking capital or business at the time the 60-day notice would have been required, (2) possesses a realistic opportunity to obtain the financing or business sought, (3) has the ability to demonstrate that business sought would be sufficient to enable the employer to avoid or postpone the shutdown, and (4) believes in good faith that giving notice would preclude the employer from obtaining the needed capital or business.

A second important exception to the WARN Act's 60-day requirement is the "unforeseeable business circumstances" exception, applied to a sudden, unexpected action or condition outside the employer's control, such as the loss of a major contract, a strike at a major supplier of the employer, or a sudden dramatic economic downturn. Exceptions are also granted for temporary projects or facilities and strike or lockout situations.

Except for those employers who meet the requirements for the exceptions allowed under the Act, employers that do not provide the required 60-day notice are liable for monetary damages to employees who should have been notified under the Act. Such employees are eligible for damages including 1 day's pay plus benefits for each day that notice was not provided, for up to 60 days. In addition, employers are liable to the local government for damages of up to $500 a day for each day without notice.

A recent Supreme Court ruling reaffirmed the right of unions to file suit on behalf of employees to recover damages under the Act. This right had been questioned by some employers, who argued that only individual workers had standing to file these suits.[105]

A 1993 study by the U.S. General Accounting Office (GAO) and related academic research since then have highlighted some of the shortcomings of the WARN Act.[106] According to the GAO report, the WARN Act, in its current form, excludes 98 percent of American businesses and leaves 64 percent of U.S. workers unprotected against sudden plant closings and mass layoffs. The flaws result primarily from the Act's narrow requirements, which cover only the following: (1) businesses with a total workforce of 100 or more employees; (2) plant closings that affect 50 or more work-

---

[105] See *UFCW Local 751 v. Brown Group, Inc.*, ___ U.S. ___ (May 14, 1996).

[106] "Dislocated Workers: Worker Adjustment and Retraining Notification Act Not Meeting Its Goals" U.S. General Accounting Office, Washington D.C., February 1993; John Portz, "WARN and the States: Implementation of the Federal Plant Closing Law" (Paper presented to Annual Meeting, Midwest Political Science Association, 1992); see also Statement of Kary L. Moss, Executive Director, Sugar Law Center for Economic and Social Justice, to Senate Committee on Labor and Human Resources Subcommittee on Labor, July 26, 1994.

ers; (3) mass layoffs of 50 or more workers, where those workers represent at least one-third of the workforce at that site; (4) mass layoffs where 500 or more workers are affected; and (5) full-time workers (i.e., part-time workers are not covered). The 1993 GAO report found that more than 10,000 WARN Act notice violations have occurred since its enactment, but only some 100 lawsuits for WARN violations have been filed.

Canada

Employment Standards legislation in Canada provides for two types of employee entitlement in the event of mass termination resulting from plant closing. First, most jurisdictions stipulate that terminated employees are entitled to an increased period of notice (or pay in lieu of), as compared to the notice required for individual termina-tions.[107] Second, employees terminated as a result of plant closing in some jurisdic-tions are entitled to severance pay. At the federal level, the Canada Labour Code pro-vides for a group termination notice period of 16 weeks when 50 or more employees are terminated within a 4-week period, as well as severance pay for employees with at least 12 consecutive months of service. Not all provinces set the threshold number of employees at 50. In addition to employee entitlements, a number of jurisdictions com-pel the creation of joint committees, through which employers are to cooperate with employee representatives to search for alternative solutions to mass termination or to minimize the impact of terminations on employees.

When appropriate notice is not provided, Ontario law requires an employer to pay termination pay in the amount equal to the wages the employee would have earned during the period of notice, in addition to benefit contributions for this period. In Ontario, employers may be required to provide the following information: (1) the economic circumstances surrounding the intended terminations, (2) any consulta-tions that have occurred or that are planned with local communities or employees and their agents, (3) proposed adjustment measures and the number of employees ex-pected to benefit from each, and (4) a statistical profile of the affected employees. Similar, although less detailed, notice requirements are provided in British Columbia, Manitoba, Saskatchewan, and federal law. Table 16 summarizes Canadian notice requirements.

---

[107] H. W. Arthurs et al., *Labor Law and Industrial Relations in Canada*, Toronto: Butterworths, 1988.

Table 16

Canadian Advance Notice Requirements

Jurisdiction and Legislation	Number of Employees	Notice Required
Federal	50 or more, terminated within a period of 4 weeks, from the same establishment	16 weeks; notice in writing to Minister of Labour, Minister of HRD, trade union, and Employment Insurance Commission
British Columbia	50–100	8 weeks
	101–300	12 weeks
	more than 300, terminated within any 2-month period, from the same location	16 weeks; notice in writing to Minister of Labour, trade union, and each affected employee
Manitoba	50–100	10 weeks
	101–300	14 weeks
	more than 300, terminated within a period of 4 weeks	18 weeks; notice in writing to Minister of Labour, trade union, and affected employees
New Brunswick	10 or more, if they represent at least 25 percent of the employer's work force, terminated within a period of 4 weeks	6 weeks; notice in writing to the bargaining agent, to the Minister of Advanced Education and Labour, and to each affected employee
Newfoundland	50–199	8 weeks
	200–499	12 weeks
	500 or more, terminated within a period of 4 weeks	16 weeks; notice in writing to each employee whose employment is to be terminated and to the Minister of Environment and Labour
Northwest Territories	25–49	4 weeks
	50–99	8 weeks
	100–299	12 weeks
	300 or more, terminated within a period of 4 weeks	16 weeks; notice in writing to the labor standards officer
Nova Scotia	10–99	8 weeks
	100–299	12 weeks
	300 or more, terminated within a period of 4 weeks	16 weeks; notice in writing to each person whose employment is to be terminated; inform Minister of Labour
Ontario	50–199	8 weeks
	200–499	12 weeks
	500 or more, terminated within a period of 4 weeks	16 weeks; notice in writing to each person whose employment is to be terminated and Minister of Labour

Table 16

Canadian Advance Notice Requirements (continued)

Jurisdiction and Legislation	Number of Employees	Notice Required
Quebec	10–99	2 months
	100–299	3 months
	300 or more	4 months; notice in writing to the Minister of Manpower and Income Security
Saskatchewan	10–49	4 weeks
	50–99	8 weeks
	100 or more, terminated within a period of 4 weeks	12 weeks; notice to Minister of Labour, any affected employee, and trade union
Yukon Territory	25–49	4 weeks
	50–99	8 weeks
	100–299	12 weeks
	300 or more, terminated within a period of 4 weeks and to any individual affected	16 weeks; notice in writing to the Director of Employment Standards

PART FIVE

SUMMARY AND ISSUES FOR FUTURE CONSIDERATION

In each country party to the North American Agreement on Labor Cooperation (NAALC), labor authorities enforce laws to protect workers against interference with freedom of association and the right to organize, including when such interference involves the use of plant closings or threats of closing. However, results vary with the structure and administration of labor law among the countries.

Outright, sudden, total plant closing to forestall union organization is not a common occurrence. Most employers faced with a union organizing drive do not respond by totally closing the workplace. Some employers respond to a union organizing effort with partial closings through product line relocation, subcontracting or "outsourcing," partial layoffs, and the like. These too are exceptional cases.

Most plants or other work facilities involve investment, trained workers, existing supplier and customer links, and other features that complicate an immediate shutdown in response to a unionization drive. At the same time, new technology and new forms of work organization make it increasingly easy to close plants, in contrast to earlier decades when massive capital investments in huge facilities made closings more difficult.

More common than total or partial closings is the use of threats of closing to resist unionization. With new forms of capital mobility, information systems, communications technology, and similar developments in the economy, there is more frequent dislocation of work and workers. This makes threats of plant closing all the more convincing. The findings of this report suggest that plant closings and threats of plant closing can have adverse effects on workers' freedom of association and right to organize in the NAALC countries.

In the United States, labor law authorities effectively enforce the law with respect to determining violations and ordering remedies, including orders to reopen closed facilities and rehire affected workers. The General Counsel and the regional directors of the National Labor Relations Board (NLRB) actively prosecute plant closing and threat cases with a high level of success before the NLRB and the courts. However, while NLRB enforcement is effective in the cases it takes to a conclusion, many instances of plant closings or threats of closing that continue to occur never reach the stage of a final decision. Taking such cases to a litigated conclusion involves a lengthy, multi-stage process subject to numerous appeals that is often forgone by potential complainants.

In Canada, federal and provincial labor laws on union organizing have established rapid procedures for holding union elections where elections are held. A majority of provinces permit a "card-check" certification, without the need for an election. This minimizes the "campaign" aspects of union organizing where plant closings or threats of closing tend to arise.

Most unfair labor practice cases are heard relatively quickly in a single-stage proceeding by the relevant labor board or commissioner. Moreover, labor board decisions in Canada normally are not appealable to the civil courts and are generally accepted by all sides as final. In general, legal doctrines, administrative procedures and effective enforcement appear to have a significant effect on the phenomenon of anti-union plant closings and threats of closing in Canada.

In Mexico, the labor law system and the union organizing system are fundamentally different from those of the United States and Canada. Several features of Mexican labor law prevent issues of plant closings or threats of closing from arising under Mexican law as they arise in Canadian and U.S. law.

The certification process of union formation, accompanied by a campaign that gives rise to plant closings or threats of plant closing to influence an election, does not exist in Mexico. Unions are normally formed without elections or election campaigns. Employers in the formal sector tend to accept the existence of unions as an inevitable component of Mexico's labor relations system. Generally speaking, most workplaces likely to be unionized—medium and large firms in the formal sector—are already unionized, so new organizing efforts are limited in number. Most organizing that occurs is what is called "raiding" or "poaching" in the United States and Canada, where one union seeks to displace another as the collective bargaining agent at an already unionized workplace.

While there are many plant closings in Mexico, discriminatory anti-union closings are not discernible in records of cases where the collective conflict legal procedure for plant closings is used. Virtually no cases arise in which a union challenges a plant closing by alleging anti-union motivation. In contrast, many cases arise in which the union grants mutual consent to the closing to obtain the best possible severance terms. Moreover, threats that are susceptible to an unfair labor practice charge and a test of proof in litigation in the United States or Canada are not unlawful in themselves in Mexico. Therefore, plant closing threats are not susceptible to research through review of administrative and judicial records.

Nonetheless, two very significant findings emerged in the review of Mexican administrative data. The first was that the legal process created to deal with plant closings and to test the employer's motivation for closing the plant—which would enable unions to challenge the closing—is virtually never used by Mexican companies and unions.

The second finding was closely related to the first. A great number of workplace closings in Mexico follow an alternative legal route wherein the union consents to the closing. Using the "mutual consent" clause of the Federal Labor Law obviates a "collective conflict of an economic nature" and the legal process meant to resolve it. Both of these findings, and the fact that they would not typically be expected in Canada or the United States, illustrate the extent of legal differences in the Mexican labor relations system.

ISSUES FOR FUTURE CONSIDERATION

1. Improving Information on the Administration of Labor Laws

Governments could seek to improve the quality and accessibility of administrative data in the three NAALC countries, which is essential for examination of the effectiveness of labor laws.

The information compiled for this report presents a partial picture, demonstrating the need for more empirical information about labor law administration in NAALC countries. For example, enhanced methods for capturing standardized information on the disposition of cases from decentralized labor law authorities—the NLRB regional offices in the United States, the State CABs and State labor departments in Mexico, the provincial labor boards and labor ministries in Canada—could develop a sharper national picture of labor law administration. Analysis would also require careful disaggregation of data to adjust for population differences, industrial sector differences, union density differences, and other related information. Each country's federal and subfederal labor agencies are best capable of designing administrative data systems in each of their jurisdictions, but with a national and trinational coordination, a high level of comparability of the effectiveness of labor law enforcement might be achieved.

2. Identifying Possible Further Research

Subjects for consideration by labor researchers in the three NAALC countries for further treatment of matters raised in this report include the following:

- review of the records of more or all of the remaining 31 regional offices of the NLRB to see if the pattern perceived in the sample of two offices is reflected in other offices;
- in-depth examination of cases in which labor boards in Canada and the United States ordered remedies to be imposed, in order to study their effectiveness;
- a survey of Canadian and Mexican unions for comparison with U.S. survey data used in this study;

- further study of Federal and State CAB records in Mexico to see whether the procedure for voluntary termination of the employment relationship (which appears to be a common avenue for plant closings) coincides with other procedures, such as those for disputes over title to collective agreements, or correlates to better severance arrangements, or has other effects, which may shed more light on possible effects of closings on the freedom of association;

- examination of alternative routes for dealing with plant closings in Mexico, such as strike declarations or individual claims of unjustified dismissal, that would indicate whether unions have developed strategies for using these procedures to obtain favorable severance terms; and

- more analysis of the implications of the current labor market environment and the restructured "new economy" for labor laws that protect the freedom of association and the right to organize.

3. Linking to National and International Labor Relations Initiatives

Consideration can be given as to whether this report can serve as a bridge to other national and international initiatives in the labor relations field, through special meetings, conferences, studies, and so on, to promote awareness of the issues involved in the report and to relate them to current concerns in each country.

For example, the issues in this report could be considered in light of the "New Labor Culture" agreement recently developed in Mexico, which contains *Principles of Ethics in Labor Relations.* The principles establish a code of conduct between unions and employers based on "strict adherence to ethical and juridical principles in the exercise of legal representation."

In Canada, the theme of this report could be examined in relation to major labor law reforms initiated by various jurisdictions over the past several years, including the current federal reform of Part 1 of the Canada Labour Code.

The United States has seen much attention devoted to the development of *Model Business Principles* proposed by the Clinton administration, and other national or international codes of conduct developed by companies, by labor-management groups, and by non-governmental organizations, which could be related to the issues in this report.

All three NAALC countries are members of the Organization for Economic Co-operation and Development (OECD), which has adopted, with the concurrence of employer and trade union advisory committees, the OECD *Guidelines for Multinational Enterprises*,[108] and of the International Labor Organization (ILO), which has adopted the ILO *Tripartite Declaration of Principles Concerning Multinational Enterprises and Social Policy*.[109] Both these instruments deal with issues raised in this report, and could enhance trinational, tripartite discussions in the NAALC context.

---

[108] Section 8 of the OECD Guidelines states that employers should, "while employees are exercising a right to organize, not threaten to utilize a capacity to transfer the whole or part of an operating unit from the country concerned ... to hinder the exercise of a right to organize."

[109] Paragraph 52 of the ILO Declaration calls on multinational enterprises not to threaten to transfer all or part of their operations to other locations "with a view to undermining ... the workers' exercise of their right to organize."

MINISTERIAL CONSULTATIONS— SUBMISSION 9501 (SPRINT CASE) AGREEMENTS ON IMPLEMENTATION

The Secretary of Labor of the United States, and the Secretary of Labor and Social Welfare of Mexico, in accord with the provisions of the North American Agreement on Labor Cooperation, have agreed to carry out consultations regarding labor law related with the effects of the sudden closing of a plant on the principle of freedom of association and the right of workers to organize. Both governments lend the greatest importance to such issues, and therefore have reached the following agreement:

1. The Secretary of Labor of the United States agrees to continue to keep the Secretary of Labor and Social Welfare of Mexico fully informed of developments related to submission 9501 (Sprint case) as appeals are considered under the United States legal system. The Department of Labor of the United States will present an appropriate report to the Secretariat of Labor and Social Welfare of Mexico within 120 days of final adjudication of the case by United States competent authorities.

2. The Secretaries of Labor of the United States and Mexico, after consultations with the Minister of Labour of Canada, will instruct the trinational Labor Secretariat, located in Dallas, Texas, to conduct a study on the effects of the sudden closing of a plant on the principle of freedom of association and the right of workers to organize in the three countries.

    ○ The study shall be completed within 180 days.

3. The U.S. Department of Labor will organize and conduct a public forum in San Francisco, California to allow interested parties an opportunity to convey to the public their concerns on the effects of the sudden closing of a plant on the principle of freedom of association and the right of workers to organize. Mexican and Canadian tripartite delegations will be invited to attend.

    ○ The forum shall take place within 120 days.

    ○ The proceedings of this event shall be recorded by the U.S. Department of Labor.

4. The outcome of each of the agreed actions shall be promptly made available to the public. The Secretary of Labor of the United States and the Secretary of Labor and Social Welfare of Mexico shall decide on the form and timing of the public announcements.

5. Completion dates are effective from the date of the agreement.

The aforementioned is agreed to and becomes effective on FEB 1 3 1996 _____ 1996.

Robert B. Reich
Secretary of Labor
United States of America

Javier Bonilla
Secretario del Trabajo y
Previsión Social
México

The Government of Canada endorses the agreements on implementation reached by the United States and Mexico in the Ministerial Consultations and agrees to participate, as appropriate, in the follow-up activities it contains.

Alfonso Gagliano
Minister of Labour
Canada

U.S. FEDERAL COURT DECISION DATA

(89 cases decided by U.S. Courts of Appeals on issues of plant closing and threats of plant closing)

Time Period: 1986–1993

By Type of Complaint

Type of Conduct Complained of[a]	Sub-Categories of Conduct	Number of Charges	
Closures	Straightforward closures	5	(6%)[b]
	Closures with later reopenings (nonunion)	10	(11%)
	SUBTOTAL	15	(17%)
Partial Closures	Refusal to hire/rehire union employees	6	(7%)
	Subcontracting out of union work	5	(6%)
	Closure of unit or department, or substantial reduction in work	7	(8%)
	SUBTOTAL	18	(20%)
Threats		56	(63%)
	TOTAL	89	

[a] Cases in which both a threat and an actual closure (either partial or total) occurred have only been included in the "closure" category. Thus, the category "threats" includes only cases where no closure actually occurred.

[b] Percentages of total number of cases may not add up to 100 percent because of rounding. This total includes one case where *all* employees had been dismissed.

Table B.2

By Disposition of Complaint (where NLRB found that an unfair labor practice occurred)

Nature of ULP violations[a]		Cases Explicitly Coded as Such[b]		Cases that Appear to Fall Within Category		Total of Preceding 2 Columns	
8(a)(1)	Upheld	34	(92%)[c]	28	(100%)	62	(95%)
	Rejected	3	(8%)	0	(0%)	3	(5%)
	Remanded re: result[d]	0	(0%)	0	(0%)	0	(0%)
8(a)(3)	Upheld	16	(94%)	20	(95%)	36	(95%)
	Rejected	0	(0%)	1	(5%)	1	(3%)
	Remanded re: result	1	(6%)	0	(0%)	1	(3%)

[a] Neither 8(a)(5) (failure to bargain) nor illegal lock-out cases were included in the analysis. In cases where both a threat of closing and an actual closing occurred, those issues are in separate categories here, in contrast to their combining in Table B.1. (See note a *supra* in Table B.1.)

[b] This includes cases that, although not explicitly coded as 8(a)(1), implied an 8(a)(1) coding (such as cases that involved threat *and other 8(a)(l)* violations). However, it does not include cases that stated "other 8(a)(1) and 8(a)(3) violations."

[c] Percentages are of each particular type of complaint.

[d] As contrasted with cases remanded regarding specific remedies.

Table B.3

By Remedy Awarded (by the NLRB, and affirmed by the Court of Appeals)

Remedy[a]	Number of Times Awarded[b]	
Reinstatement, job offer, or recall	47	(53%)
Make whole	26	(29%)
Back pay	27	(30%)
Cease-and-desist order	77	(87%)
Return subcontracted work to bargaining unit	2	(2%)
Reopen/resume operations	5	(6%)
Restore status quo	2	(2%)
Apply terms of last collective agreement	3	(3%)
Post notice	66	(74%)
President of company publicly read notice	1	(1%)
Gissel bargaining order or order to bargain with an existing union	25	(28%)
Vacate election results and/or order a new election	12	(13%)
Expunge anti-union by-law	1	(1%)
Remand (in whole or in part) to Board for remedy	7	(8%)

[a] Many of the cases involved other unfair labor practice (ULP) complaints, in addition to those related to plant closures and/or threats. There is no way of ascertaining which remedies were specifically designed to deal with ULPs that are related to plant closing without an in-depth analysis of each case opinion, not possible within the Secretariat's time frame.

[b] Percentages are of total number of cases; percentages may not add up to 100 percent because of rounding and because of multiple remedies being awarded in individual cases.

Table B.4

New Organizing v. Existing Unions

Status of Relationship	Sub-Status	Number of Cases	
New organizing		70	(79%)
Existing union	Successor/alter ego employer	14	(16%)
	Same employer	5	(6%)

Table B.5

Successful and Unsuccessful Complaints, by Status of Bargaining Relationship

Status	Sub-Status	No. of Cases	Successful Complaints		Unsuccessful Complaints[a]	
New organizing		70	67	(96%)	3	(4%)
Existing union	Successor/ alter ego employer	14	14	(100%)	0	(0%)
	Same employer	5	3	(60%)	2	(40%)

[a] This category includes both cases that were rejected and cases that were remanded with respect to disposition.

Table B.6

Chronological Progression of Complaints

1986	1987	1988	1989	1990	1991	1992	1993	Total
1	6	9	12	11	18	4	28	89

Table B.7

Particular Unions Involved

International Brotherhood of Teamsters (IBT)—17	United Electrical Workers (UE)—3	Woodworkers—2
United Food and Commercial Workers (UFCW)—13	Allied Clothing and Textile Workers Union (ACTWU)—3	Laborers—2
United Auto Workers (UAW)—9	United Mine Workers of America (UMWA)—2	Glass, Plastic, & Allied—2
United Steel Workers of America (USWA)—6	International Association of Machinists (IAM)—2	Other AFL-CIO—13
International Brotherhood of Electrical Workers (IBEW)—5	HERE—2	Unaffiliated—3
GCIU—3	OCAW—2	

Table B.8

Geographic Location of Employers in 89 Cases Studied[a]

Michigan—10 cases	New Jersey—7 cases	Kentucky—5 cases
Ohio—9 cases	California—6 cases	Indiana—4 cases
Pennsylvania—7 cases	Tennessee—5 cases	West Virginia—4 cases
New York—7 cases		

[a] Remaining 25 cases spread among 15 other states.

U.S. NATIONAL LABOR RELATIONS BOARD DECISION DATA

(319 cases decided by NLRB on plant closing and threats of plant closing)

Time Period: 1990–1995

Table C.1

By Type of Complaint

Type of Conduct Complained of[a]	Sub-Categories of Conduct	Number of Charges	
Closures	Straightforward closures	15	(50%)[b]
	Closures with later reopenings (nonunion)	15	(50%)
	SUBTOTAL	30	(9%)
Partial Closures	Refusal to hire/rehire union employees	7	(9%)
	Subcontracting out of union work	23	(29%)
	Closure of unit or department, or substantial reduction in work	49	(62%)
	SUBTOTAL	79	(25%)
Total and Partial Closures Combined		109	(34%)
Threats		210	(66%)
	TOTAL	319	

[a] Only cases in which both a threat and an actual closure (either partial or total) occurred have been included in the "closure" category. Thus, the category "threats" includes only cases where no closure actually occurred.

[b] Percentages of total number of cases; percentages may not add up to 100 percent because of rounding.

Table C.2

By Disposition of Complaint

Complaint		1990 (23)[a]	1991 (71)	1992 (77)	1993 (53)	1994 (38)	1995 (57)	Total (319)
ULP	Upheld	14 (70%)[b]	45 (90%)	52 (95%)	31 (89%)	24 (96%)	46 (82%)	212 (88%)
	Rejected	5 (25%)	3 (6%)	2 (4%)	4 (11%)	0 (0%)	9 (16%)	23 (10%)
	Remanded	1 (5%)	2 (4%)	1 (2%)	0 (3%)	1 (4%)	1 (2%)	6 (2%)
	SUBTOTAL	20	50	55	35	25	56	241 (76%)
Objections	Upheld	3 (75%)	20 (95%)	20 (91%)	17 (94%)	12 (92%)	0 (0%)	72 (91%)
	Rejected	1 (25%)	1 (5%)	1 (5%)	1 (6%)	1 (8%)	1 (100%)	6 (7%)
	Remanded	0 (0%)	0 (0%)	1 (5%)	0 (0%)	0 (0%)	0 (0%)	1 (1%)
	SUBTOTAL	4	21	22	18	13	1	79 (25%)
Total Cases	Upheld	16 (70%)	65 (92%)	72 (94%)	48 (91%)	36 (95%)	46 (81%)	283 (89%)
	Rejected	6 (26%)	4 (6%)	3 (4%)	5 (9%)	1 (3%)	10 (18%)	29 (9%)
	Remanded	1 (4%)	2 (3%)	2 (3%)	0 (0%)	1 (3%)	1 (%)	7 (2%)
	TOTAL	23[c]	71	77	53	38	57	319[d]

[a] The total number of cases from each year is provided in parentheses.

[b] Percentages are of each particular type of complaint (e.g., 70 percent of ULP complaints in 1990 were upheld); percentages may not add up to 100 percent because of rounding.

[c] The total of 23 cases is less than the sum of ULP (20) and Objections (4) cases, as one case was included under both categories.

[d] The total of 319 is 1 less than the sum of the subtotals (241 + 79 = 320) because of the dual categorization mentioned in the preceding footnote.

Table C.3

By Remedy Awarded[a]

Remedy	1990 (23)		1991 (71)		1992 (77)		1993 (53)		1994 (38)		1995 (57)		Total (319)	
Make whole	4	(17%)	8	(11%)	10	(13%)	7	(13%)	6	(16%)	7	(12%)	42	(13%)
Reinstate employees[b]	3	(13%)	7	(10%)	10	(13%)	10	(19%)	5	(13%)	5	(9%)	40	(13%)
Reinstate department and/or subcontracted work	0	(0%)	5	(7%)	1	(1%)	3	(6%)	0	(0%)	5	(9%)	14	(4%)
Reopen	1	(4%)	0	(0%)	2	(3%)	2	(4%)	0	(0%)	1	(2%)	6	(2%)
Relocate	0	(0%)	0	(0%)	1	(1%)	0	(0%)	0	(0%)	0	(0%)	1	(0%)
Restore status quo[c]	1	(4%)	0	(0%)	3	(4%)	1	(2%)	2	(5%)	1	(2%)	8	(3%)
Bargaining order	5	(22%)	14	(20%)	25	(32%)	18	(34%)	9	(24%)	12	(21%)	83	(26%)
New election/set aside election	0	(0%)	16	(23%)	10	(13%)	8	(15%)	6	(16%)	2	(4%)	42	(13%)
Open and count ballots	0	(0%)	1	(1%)	1	(1%)	0	(0%)	1	(3%)	1	(2%)	4	(1%)
Certification	0	(0%)	0	(0%)	1	(1%)	1	(2%)	0	(0%)	0	(0%)	2	(0%)
Pay union costs of case	0	(0%)	0	(0%)	0	(0%)	0	(0%)	0	(0%)	1	(2%)	1	(0%)

[a] Almost every case contained a standard cease-and-desist and posting remedy.

[b] This includes only reinstatements where at least 10 percent of the bargaining unit had been laid off or discharged. This does not include reinstatements for individuals (or small groups) such as union organizers who had been laid off.

[c] In addition to express orders of status quo ante, this category includes orders to restore terms of earlier collective bargaining agreements and orders to rescind unilateral changes.

Table C.4

New Organizing v. Existing Unions

Status of Relationship	1990 (23)		1991 (71)		1992 (77)		1993 (53)		1994 (38)		1995 (57)		Total (319)	
New organizing	17	(74%)	61	(86%)	66	(86%)	45	(85%)	32	(84%)	51	(89%)	272	(85%)
Existing union	6	(26%)	10	(14%)	11	(14%)	8	(15%)	6	(16%)	3	(5%)	44	(14%)

Table C.5

Successful and Unsuccessful Complaints, by Status of Bargaining Relationship

Status	No. of Cases	Successful Complaints		Unsuccessful Complaints[a]		Remanded Complaints	
New organizing	272	245	(90%)	21	(8%)	6	(2%)
Existing union	44	37	(84%)	7	(16%)	0	(0%)
Unclear	3	1	(33%)	1	(33%)	1	(0%)
Total	319	283	(89%)	29	(9%)	7	(2%)

[a] This category includes both cases that were rejected and cases that were remanded with respect to disposition.

Table C.6

By Chronological Progression of Complaints

1990	1991	1992	1993	1994	1995	Total
23	71	77	53	38	57	319

\

CANADIAN LABOUR BOARD DECISION DATA

(36 cases decided by labour boards in Canada on plant closing and threats of plant closing)

Time Period: 1986–1995

By Type of Complaint

Type of Conduct Complained of	CA[a] (2)	BC (17)	AB (3)	SK (3)	ON (8)	PQ (1)	NB (2)	Total (36)
Actual closure	1 (50%)[b]	9 (53%)		2 (67%)	3 (38%)		1 (50%)	16
Partial closure or contracting out	1 (50%)	5 (29%)		1 (33%)	2 (25%)			9
Threats of closure		3 (18%)	3 (100%)		3 (38%)	1 (100%)	1 (50%)	11

[a] The total number of cases summarized from each jurisdiction is provided in parentheses.

[b] Percentage of total number of cases; percentages may not add up to 100 percent because of rounding.

By Disposition of Complaint

Complaint		CA (2)	BC (17)	AB (3)	SK (3)	ON (8)	PQ (1)	NB (2)	Total[a] (36)
Unfair labor practice	Upheld	2 (100%)[b]	8 (47%)	2 (67%)	2 (67%)	4 (57%)	1 (100%)	1 (50%)	20
	Rejected		9 (53%)	1 (33%)	1 (33%)	3 (43%)		1 (50%)	15
Breach of duty to bargain in good faith	Upheld	1 (100%)			1 (50%)	2 (50%)			4
	Rejected		2 (100%)		1 (50%)	2 (50%)			5
Illegal lockout	Upheld		1 (100%)						1
	Rejected								0

[a] The total in this column is greater than the number of cases (36) because multiple complaints were made in individual cases.

[b] Percentages are of each particular type of complaint (e.g., 40 percent of unfair labor practice complaints were upheld by the British Columbia Board).

Table D.3

By Remedy Awarded

Remedy[a]	CA (2)	BC (17)	AB (3)	SK (3)	ON (8)	PQ (1)	NB (2)	Total[b] (36)
Reinstatement and/or compensation for employees	1 (50%)[c]	7 (41%)		2 (67%)	4 (50%)			14
Cease-and-desist order/declaration of breach of statute	1 (50%)	5 (29%)	1 (33%)		2 (25%)		1 (50%)	10
Return of work to bargaining unit, either at present or new location, either mandatory or as one option for employer				1 (33%)	1 (13%)			2
Order to resume negotiations	1 (50%)							1
Order concerning access to employees for union		1 (6%)			1 (13%)			2
Reimbursement of costs of organization of bargaining		1 (6%)						1
Letter dictated by Board								0
Creation of trust fund for union								0
Posting/mailing of decision		1 (6%)	1 (33%)		2 (25%)		1 (50%)	5
Automatic certification or refusal to decertify	1 (50%)	2 (12%)						3
Tribunal to remain seized re: remedy	1 (50%)	1 (6%)			1 (13%)	1 (100%)		4
No remedy (no violation)		5 (29%)	1 (33%)	1 (33%)	3 (38%)		1 (50%)	11

[a] Many of the cases involved other ULP complaints, in addition to those related to plant closures and/or threats. There is no way of ascertaining which remedies were specifically designed to deal with the ULPs related to plant closing. Thus, the numbers are likely inflated.

[b] As with the preceding table, the total of this column is greater than the number of cases (36) because of multiple remedies being awarded in individual cases.

[c] Percentages are of total number of cases; percentages may not add up to 100 percent because of rounding and because multiple remedies were awarded in individual cases.

Table D.4

New Organizing v. Existing Unions

Mature Relationship	New Organization					Unknown
12 (33%)	21 (58%)					3 (8%)
	Organizing	Applied for cert.	Newly certified	1st CA negot.	1st CA reached	
	11 (52%)	2 (10%)	6 (29%)	1 (5%)	1 (5%)	

Table D.5

Successful and Unsuccessful Complaints, by Status of Bargaining Relationship

Status	Sub-status	No. Cases	Successful Complaints		Unsuccessful Complaints	
New organization						
	Organizing	11	9	(82%)	2	(18%)
	Applied for cert.	2	2	(100%)	0	(0%)
	Newly certified	6	3	(50%)	3	(50%)
	1st CA negot.	1	0	(0%)	1	(100%)
	1st CA reached	1	1	(100%)	0	(0%)
	SUBTOTAL	21	15	(71%)	6	(29%)
Mature		12	5	(42%)	7	(58%)
Unknown		3	2	(67%)	1	(33%)
	TOTAL	36	22	(61%)	14	(39%)

Table D.6

Chronological Progression of Complaints

1986	1987	1988	1989	1990	1991	1992	1993	1994	1995	Total
3	3	4	0	7	1	3	7	3	5	36

Table D.7

Particular Unions Involved[a]

RWDSU (Sask)—3	(*Retail, Wholesale, and Department Store*)
USWA—3	(*Steelworkers*)
IWA—3	(*Woodworkers*)
UFCW—2	(*Food and Commercial Workers*)
IBT—2	(*Teamsters*)
UAJAPPI—2	(*Plumbers and Pipefitters*)
CUPE—2	(*Public Employees*) (also, BCGEU—1) (*British Columbia Government Employees*)
GCIU—2	(*Graphic Communications*)

[a] Only unions that were involved with more than one case are included in this list.

LABOR MARKET ADJUSTMENT PROGRAMS

ADJUSTMENT PROGRAMS IN THE UNITED STATES

States Unemployment Insurance

The most widely used and accessible program in the United States is the federal and state Unemployment Insurance (UI) program, established by the Social Security Act of 1935. The UI program provides displaced workers with income assistance in the form of weekly cash benefits. The amount of benefits varies among states, with the average weekly benefit equal to 40 percent of the worker's previous wage. Most states provide benefits up to 26 weeks, with the possibility of extension in exceptional circumstances. Funding for the program has increased steadily as the number of dislocations has increased.

In exceptional circumstances, as when a state experiences an unusually high rate of unemployment, the Extended Benefit (EB) program provides up to an additional 13 weeks of benefits to eligible workers. Almost all wage and salary workers are covered by the UI program. Railroad workers, veterans, and civilian federal employees are covered by separate federal programs. In 1990, $17 billion was dispersed in payments. That number grew to an estimated $24 billion in 1996. (See Table E.1.)

Table E.1

Estimated UI Program Activity for Fiscal Year 1996

Civilian unemployment rate	5.7 percent
Number of workers covered	112 million
Average duration of benefits	14 weeks
Number of recipients	9 million
Average weekly benefit	$182
Total benefits paid	$24 billion

Source: U.S. Department of Labor, March 1996.

Most unemployed workers in the United States do not receive UI benefits, in part because of the sometimes restrictive eligibility criteria. Only half of all employed workers in the 1980s were eligible for benefits, as UI does not cover new entrants, re-entrants, or voluntary job leavers. Other criticisms of the UI program include the fact (1) that the program pays only limited attention to helping workers find new jobs; (2) that it does not include training; and (3) that it is not sensitive to difficulties that individual workers might experience, such as age, family status, education level, or location.[110]

The Economic Dislocation and Worker Adjustment Assistance Program

Another important labor market adjustment program is Title III of the Job Training Partnership Act (JTPA). As amended by the Economic Dislocation and Worker Adjustment Act of 1988 (EDWAA), the Act provides states with federal funding to deliver training and related adjustment services to displaced workers. Under the program, each state is required to respond rapidly to large displacements of workers, including plant closures. Under the program, these workers are eligible for job search assistance, retraining, and income maintenance. Workers who have lost their jobs and are unlikely to return to their previous industry or occupation are eligible for the program.

EDWAA provides several services:

- Rapid response—Each state receives notices of plant closures and mass layoffs covered under the Worker Adjustment and Retraining Notification (WARN) Act and responds with on-site services to displaced workers. States may also help set up labor-management committees at the workplace and coordinate efforts to avoid dislocations.

- Retraining services—Displaced workers receive one or more of the following: occupational skills, on-the-job training, basic and remedial education, entrepreneurial training, and literacy/language training.

- Readjustment services—Readjustment includes outreach and intake, testing and counseling, labor market information, job search and placement, supportive services such as child care and transportation allowances, and relocation assistance.

- Needs-related payments—Workers who have exhausted their UI benefits may receive special payments while they complete training programs.

- Certificates of continuing eligibility—Workers are allowed to defer the start of training or to obtain their own training.

---

[110] See, for example, Howard Rosen, "Training: Who Gets It; Does It Work?" Competitiveness Policy Council Working Paper, March 1996.

Of EDWAA's budget, 80 percent is allotted by formulas to the states. The remaining 20 percent is retained by the Secretary of Labor for discretionary projects involving workers affected by plant closings and mass layoffs and other special projects.

The JTPA was amended twice in 1990 to assist workers displaced by the effects of two new pieces of legislation, the Clean Air Act and the Defense Economic Adjustment, Diversification, Conversion, and Stabilization Act. The funds for all of these programs are used primarily to provide training and job search assistance to eligible workers.

Relatively few EDWAA participants have received income support beyond their UI benefits (26 weeks or less), and therefore few have participated in long-term training programs. The most common criticism of the program is its relatively low participation rate: less than 20 percent of displaced workers use the program. (See Table E.2.)

Table E.2

JTPA Title III Analysis, Program Year 1993

Total participants	306,340
Total terminations	164,850
Total entered employment	112,210
Average hourly wage at dislocation	$7.90
Average hourly wage at termination	$9.40
Average weeks of participation	39
WARN notices received	2,690

Source: Employment and Training Administration,
U.S. Department of Labor, 1995.

Trade Adjustment Assistance

A program targeted to one of the many causes of displacement is Trade Adjustment Assistance (TAA), which is designed to assist workers who are displaced or whose hours of work or wages are reduced as a result of increased imports. TAA provides several benefits to assist displaced workers, including training, job search allowances, relocation allowances, and other re-employment services. Special income payments, called trade readjustment allowances (TRA), may be provided to workers who have exhausted their UI benefits but who are still enrolled in a training program.

Certified workers can receive benefits for up to 2 years from the date of dislocation. To be eligible, workers must be displaced or put on a reduced work schedule (hours of work reduced to 80 percent or less of workers' average weekly hours and wages reduced to 80 percent or less of worker's average weekly wage). Services are administered by state-designated agencies.

The program has undergone several changes since its inception in 1962. It started as a program to provide income maintenance along with training benefits for workers affected by trade liberalization. The eligibility requirements have since been changed several times in an attempt to make the program more accessible to affected workers. In its current form, TAA's primary function is to provide income support to trade-affected workers. The training and job search components of the program have diminished significantly.

The program was funded at $179 million for benefits and $98 million for training in fiscal year 1995. (See Table E.3.)

Table E.3

TAA Program Analysis, 1995

Applicants for reemployment services	43,440
Placed directly in jobs	11,620
Entered training	27,600
Relocated	1,529
Income support (TRA) applications	52,297
Received TRA benefits	27,900
Average weekly benefit	$192.63

Source: U.S. Department of Labor, Employment, and Training Administration, 1996.

NAFTA Transitional Adjustment Assistance Program

The North American Free Trade Agreement Transitional Adjustment Assistance (NAFTA–TAA) program is a special program designed specifically for employees affected by the NAFTA. The program provides benefits to workers who are displaced because of increased imports from Mexico or Canada or by the relocation of a U.S. plant to one of those countries. The program combines elements of the EDWAA and TAA programs to provide rapid response to the threat of unemployment along with income maintenance and training opportunities. Workers in companies indirectly affected by NAFTA, such as suppliers of affected firms, are also eligible. Farmers are also eligible for benefits if they worked at least 8 weeks during the previous year. Under the program, each state where a petition is filed makes a preliminary determination of eligibility, and then the Department of Labor makes a final determination within 30 days of the state's finding. The NAFTA–TAA program combines many of the best elements of EDWAA and TAA into a comprehensive program that includes rapid response and basic readjustment services, employment services, training, income support, job search allowances, and relocation allowances.

To date, 936 workplaces employing 116,418 workers have been certified as having lost employment as a result of NAFTA-related trade. Of these workers eligible for NAFTA–TAA benefits, 4,566 applied for assistance in 1995. (See Table E.4.)

Table E.4

NAFTA-TAA Program Analysis, 1995

Applicants for reemployment services	4,566
Entered training	2,300
Relocations	105
Income support (TRA) applications	3,313
Received TRA benefits	1,600
Average weekly benefits	$192.16

Source: U.S. Department of Labor, Employment and Training Administration, 1997.

Health Benefits Under the Consolidated Omnibus Budget Reconciliation Act

In the United States, most full-time workers have health insurance through group coverage provided by their employer. Before 1986, displaced workers lost health insurance when they lost their job. With the passage of the Consolidated Omnibus Budget Reconciliation Act (COBRA) in 1986, these workers were allowed to continue in the health insurance plan by paying the premium themselves at group coverage rates for a limited period of time. Under the law, health care insurance companies must allow displaced workers the opportunity to choose to continue their coverage. Since employers normally pay a significant portion of the health insurance premium for employed workers, continued COBRA coverage is much more expensive for those workers who choose it, because they must pay the entire premium, plus a small administration fee. However, coverage under COBRA at group insurance rates is usually less expensive than health coverage at individual rates. The COBRA obligation covers employers with 20 or more workers.

ADJUSTMENT PROGRAMS IN CANADA

Like the United States, Canada has myriad labor market adjustment programs for unemployed and displaced workers. The basic income support program was Unemployment Insurance (UI). With recent changes in Canadian law (see below) the program is now called Employment Insurance (EI).[111] Several other programs target displaced workers specifically or try to improve the skills of workers to ease their adjustment and reintegration into the labor force.

Employment Insurance

Canadian workers who lose their jobs are eligible for the federal EI program. While many EI recipients use only the income support portion of the program to sustain them until they find a new job, many others require training to upgrade their skills so that they can find a new job. Developmental Uses programs provide a comprehensive framework of training for unemployed workers, including job search assistance, counseling, job placement, and skills training. Approximately 530,000 workers used the program in 1993. The Work Sharing program allows workers to continue to receive part of their EI benefits while sharing a work week with another worker. The Job Creation program continues benefits for workers doing community projects. Both help ease the adjustment process for displaced workers.

Self-Employment Assistance

Under EI, funding is provided for individuals who wish to start their own businesses. Participants receive EI benefits in addition to supplementary allowances while they implement their business plan. Counseling, training, and other support is also provided while participants make the transition to self-employment. A review of the program prepared as a briefing paper for the 1995 G–7 meeting showed that participants in the program had fewer UI claims and received fewer paid weeks of UI benefits in the 3 years after the program than in the same period before they entered the program. Participants also improved earnings compared to preprogram earnings and compared with non-participants.

Work Sharing

The Work Sharing program enables employers to avoid layoffs by shortening the work week, thus paying reduced wages. Workers benefit by not being entirely separated from their jobs and not suffering as much of a reduction in earnings. The EI program pays regular benefits for the days not worked. Workers can often use these

---

[111] The terms EI and UI are used interchangeably in this section, both refer to insurance provided to unemployed workers either under the old Unemployment Insurance system, or under the new Employment Insurance system.

paid days off to acquire training or to search for another full-time job. A review of the program found that participants in the program were more likely to be employed than those who did not participate in the program.

Job Creation

Workers in this program receive EI benefits while working on community projects. It is designed to help unemployed workers get back into the workforce and learn some new skills so that the transition to a regular job will be easier.

New Labor Market Adjustment Proposal

Canadian unemployment, training, and adjustment programs are currently in a process of major reform. In May 1996, a new labor market proposal was sent by the federal government to the provinces offering them more jurisdiction over unemployment programs. Under the new proposal, provinces would have authority and funding to provide services such as wage subsidies, income supplements, support for self-employment, and partnerships for job creation. The new proposal would also give provinces the option of taking over services currently provided by the federal government, such as screening and employment counseling and labor market placement. The federal government would withdraw from labor market training as soon as provinces wished, but in no longer than 3 years. The new legislation took effect July 1, 1996, and provinces can begin signing agreements with the federal government.

These agreements will implement the following set of labor market policies for unemployed Canadians:

- Targeted wage subsidies: wages will be subsidized for workers hired by employers who will provide on-the-job training and the possibility of a permanent job.
- Targeted earnings supplements: provided to assist individuals re-entering the labor force.
- Self-employment assistance: financial and other assistance will be provided to individuals wishing to start their own businesses.
- Job creation partnerships: provincial and community plans and priorities for dealing with displaced and unemployed workers will be a more central part of the approach.
- Skills loans and grants: funding will be provided directly to qualified individuals, who will decide on their own what kind of training they need. Grants and loans will be provided for tuition, books, and other expenses related to acquiring training.

Under the new plan, the federal government has already or will soon withdraw from existing programs, including the purchase of training from public and private sources, cooperative education for college students, workplace-based training, and project-based training.

Funding for the new measure will come from the EI account (approximately $2 billion). The federal government would continue to be responsible for managing the EI account and for delivering insurance benefits (approximately $12.3 billion in 1996–1997).

Industrial Adjustment Services

One of the most important adjustment programs that will not be affected by the new labor market proposal is Industrial Adjustment Services (IAS), which targets laid-off workers for assistance. The IAS is a committee-based program that brings together employers, workers, and community groups to try to better manage the worker adjustment process. When a potential adjustment problem exists, IAS representatives approach the parties involved (usually the workers and employer representatives) to create an IAS committee to address the adjustment. If the parties agree, a committee is established with equal representation from employers and employees and other interested parties. The committee develops a strategy for addressing the adjustment problem. The outcome can include three types of agreements: firm-level agreements, which address individual plant closures and similar changes that could cause adjustment pressures; association agreements, which deal with adjustment problems of a more general nature affecting several firms in a given industry or occupation; and community agreements, which try to address regional adjustment pressures brought about by major plant closures, and similar localized events.

The program will fund up to 50 percent of the cost of an Industrial Adjustment Committee (up to $200,000). For nonprofit associations and special hardship cases, the federal contribution can cover up to 100 percent of the cost (up to $100,000) and up to $500,000 over 3 years for agreements with associations.

According to a review of the program by the Ekos Consulting Group, the IAS is less effective than the general programs.[112] The Ekos study found that IAS participants spend more time in job search, possibly explaining the longer periods of unemployment. The major weakness of the IAS, according to the Ekos study, is that many workers involved in the program say that while the program is good for identifying adjustment problems and devising action plans for resolution of those problems, the committee system is not effective at implementing the solutions. More important,

---

[112] "Industrial Adjustment Services Program Evaluation," Ekos Research Associates, Inc., for Employment and Immigration Canada, Ottawa, November 1993.

according to the study, workers participating in the IAS process tended to suffer larger income losses and longer unemployment periods than those in the general population.

Program for Older Worker Adjustment

A Canadian adjustment program that deviates from the general approach, the Program for Older Worker Adjustment (POWA), was implemented in 1988 to replace the benefits provided to laid-off older workers under the Labour Adjustment Benefits Act (LABA). Although POWA did not have industry or regional requirements like the LABA, the qualifying criteria were still difficult to meet. The criteria related to the size of the layoff relative to the local labor force, the proportion of older workers affected, and the likelihood that workers will not become re-employed. Annuities are purchased for qualifying workers and benefits are paid by the institution to the worker. Benefits are payable only after UI benefits have been exhausted.

Sector Councils

The Employment Programs and Services Framework was introduced in 1991 to improve adjustment services available to displaced and other unemployed workers. Human Resources Development Canada (HRDC) sponsors Sector Councils that offer adjustment assistance on a sectoral basis. The largest and most active has been the Canadian Steel Trade and Employment Congress (CSTEC), which has tried to address the adjustment problems faced by the extreme downsizing of the Canadian mining and primary metals industries. The CSTEC approach focused more on retraining workers than on providing job search assistance. CSTEC-assisted workers experienced higher re-employment levels and higher earnings than those who participated in other programs or in no program at all.

Earnings Supplementation Project

HRDC introduced a pilot income supplement project in March 1995 to see whether such an approach would improve re-employment possibilities for displaced Canadian workers. The earnings of participants are supplemented by 75 percent of the difference between their old job and their new job, up to a maximum weekly supplement of $250. The idea is to get displaced workers back into a job quickly to improve their chances of being reintegrated in the workforce.

Mexican Adjustment Programs[113]

In 1995, the Mexican economy suffered the most severe economic crisis since the 1930s, and the adjustment to it had a serious impact on employment. In response to this situation, training and support programs directed toward unemployed workers were reinforced, special incentives to promote the incorporation of the unemployed population into the workforce were established, and emergency and temporary employment programs were launched.

Mexico has no unemployment insurance system such as in the United States or Canada. However, a series of instruments and active placement policies exist, such as PROBECAT (discussed below), that offer training and supplemental income during that training to a portion of the unemployed population. Workers can also be aided during adjustment periods by continued benefits provided under the Mexican Social Security system described below.

In addition, Mexican law normally requires a substantial severance payment (*indemnización*) to be paid to workers affected by plant closings. Severance pay can amount to 3 months' salary plus 12 days' pay for each year of service, depending on the circumstances of the displacement. Workers are entitled to free legal assistance from the Labor Ombudsman Office (*Procuraduría Federal de la Defensa del Trabajo*), an organism coordinated by the Secretariat of Labor and Social Welfare, to settle disputes over severance pay and other labor matters.

National Employment Service

The Mexican National Employment Service (*Servicio Nacional de Empleo*—SNE) was created in 1978 to promote the placement of workers. It has been the primary link between employers and job seekers (unemployed and underemployed)[114] through a network that comprises 99 offices located in 84 Mexican cities.

In 1987, the actions of the SNE were strengthened with a substantial increase in resources allocated to the Human Resource Training Program (*Programa de Calidad de la Mano de Obra*—PCMO) by the federal government, with partial funding from the World Bank. The activities of the SNE were further advanced from 1993–1997 with the Labor Market Modernization Program (*Programa de Modernización del Mercado Laboral*—PMMT). For 1997–2001, a new program will be inaugurated with financial support from the Inter-American Development Bank (IDB).

---

[113] Source: Programa Nacional de Desarrollo 1995–2000, Programa de Empleo, Capacitación y Defensa de los Derechos Laborales 1995–2000, Informe de Avance de Ejecución del Plan Nacional de Desarrollo 1995, Informe de Labores de la Secretaría del Trabajo y Previsión Social 1995–1996.

[114] This includes employed workers looking for a better, different, or additional job.

In 1996, the SNE received 992,397 applications; posted 337,716 vacancies; referred 321,480 candidates; placed at least 127,151 workers; and promoted the training of over 500,000 applicants.

PROBECAT

PROBECAT (*Programa de Becas de Capacitación para Trabajadores Desempleados*) is a training scholarship program established by the SNE in 1984 to provide grants that aid unemployed and underemployed workers as they adapt their knowledge, abilities, and skills to the requirements of the labor market and employers' demands. This program has become the most important retraining program for unemployed workers in Mexico and one of the most important active labor market policies. From 1984 to 1995, PROBECAT trained 1,054,231 workers through 99 local SNE offices. In 1996, 544,026 grants were awarded.

Training periods last between 1 and 6 months (3 months on average), and participants receive a monthly stipend equal to the minimum wage plus medical and transportation expenses. General eligibility criteria include the number of economic dependents, prior work experience, level of basic education, and recent unemployment. Additional requirements include age (16–55) and registration at a local employment office.

The majority of program participants enroll in classroom training, primarily in short-term vocational courses offered through contracts with local private and public institutions. Courses are organized to respond to the needs of the local labor market and are designed to address local shortages of workers with particular skills. Those needs are determined through systematic communication with employers and their organizations.

Currently, PROBECAT includes the following subprograms:

Classroom Training Program

This skills training program is divided into theoretical and practical training. The above-mentioned eligibility criteria apply for participation in this program, except for the age requirement (participants must be at least 18 years old). The courses are held at facilities used for vocational and technical education. Besides the scholarship, a stipend for transportation is provided.

On-the-Job Training Program

This joint government-private sector program consists of on-the-job training under special agreements between STPS and firms seeking large numbers (15 or more) of new workers. PROBECAT provides a scholarship. The company pays for training costs (trainer salary and material) and provides facilities for the training, transportation, and compensation insurance for the participants. Employers are committed to hire 70 percent of the participants. Eligibility criteria mentioned above apply to participants.

Local Employment Initiatives

This scholarship program is provided to small groups of underemployed workers living in the poorest areas of the country by involving them in local productive projects and by improving infrastructure of highly marginalized communities.

Self-Employment

This program is similar to the classroom training program but is more flexible in terms of age (16 years old and up). Higher performing students are provided with a tool package to help them to set up their own business.

School-Industry Link

This program is also a joint private/governmental program, but it is focused on small groups of participants, with small enterprises. Training is aimed at very specific needs of the companies involved.

Health Care Training

This program provides targeted training for traditional health care workers living in the poorest areas to improve health care conditions in the area. Courses are mainly designed to train midwives, nurse assistants, and other health care workers.

PROBECAT was evaluated by the World Bank, which found that (1) participants on average tended to find jobs more quickly than workers not participating in the program; (2) workers were more likely to be employed 3 and 6 months after training; (3) training increases the monthly earnings of male trainees increased with training (but this effect varied by level of schooling); and (4) in general, monetary benefits of training outweighed the cost of the program.[115]

---

[115] Ana Revenga, Michelle Riboud and Hong Tan, "The Impact of Mexico's Retraining Program on Employment and Wages," World Bank, WPS 1013 (1992).

The World Bank analysis stated that

> although the Mexican retraining program has proven to be effective, several issues need to be considered before such programs are replicated on a large scale in other countries:
>
> (1) As the impact of the program depends on the characteristics of the unemployed, it appears essential to analyze the structure and characteristics of unemployment prior to implementing any training program.
>
> (2) Results and cost-effectiveness of the program also appear to be sensitive to other factors such as the length of the program and the overall state of the labor market. In the case of Mexico, the program may have been helped by the fact that unemployment remained moderate and employment fairly stable during the program implementation period.
>
> (3) For the above reasons, implementation of these types of training programs should be gradual, and accompanied by a strong monitoring and evaluation system.

CIMO

In 1992, the PCMO became the Integral Quality and Modernization Program (*Programa de Calidad Integral y Modernización*—CIMO). CIMO provides incentives for small and medium-sized firms to train their workers and raise productivity.[116] The program operates through 60 Training Promotion Units and provides integrated business consultant services, contacts with other institutions, and training for active workers in small- and medium-sized businesses. The program provides technical and financial support for a limited period to encourage the development of training programs, enhancement of productivity, and access to industrial and market information.

The program is jointly funded by the federal government (including World Bank loans), organizations of entrepreneurs, and participating firms. In 1996, 549,095 workers participated in the program.

PROSSE

The Essential Social Services Program (*Programa de Servicios Sociales Esenciales*—PROSSE) is a multi-faceted social program partially funded by the World Bank and the IDB. One of the primary components of the program is a retraining and employment-creation program. From 1995–1996, retraining stipends were awarded to several hundred thousand workers participating in PROBECAT.

---

[116] Secretaría del Trabajo y Prevision Social, "El Mercado de Trabajo en México, 1970–1992."

A second component of PROSSE is the Short-Term Employment Program (*Programa Emergente de Empleo Temporal*—PEET) that provides employment related to infrastructure development projects in low-income areas. Projects must provide public benefits such as construction and maintenance of rural roads, spot road improvements, cleaning of drainage canals, garbage removal, reforestation, and conservation programs for soil and water.

Workers earn 80 percent of the minimum wage in the program. Expenditures were US$283 million in 1995, and the 1996 budget increased to US$418.2 million. The program is partially funded by loans from the World Bank.

In 1996, under the Temporary Employment Program, managed by the Ministry of Social Development (*Secretaría de Desarrollo Social*—SEDESOL), 751,717 jobs were created in highly marginated rural areas with elevated levels of poverty.

With the Emergency Program to Lessen the Drought Effects in northern Mexico, in 1996, the National Water Commission promoted the rehabilitation of wells and channels in 19 different districts, paying 2,718,544 days' wages that benefited 113,950 families.

In collaboration with this program and under the Emergency Employment Program, the Ministry of Communications and Transportation invested 383 million pesos on roads, paying 20.4 million days' wages.

Social Security

Article 118 of the Social Security Law guarantees that a worker can continue to receive medical assistance for up to 8 weeks after termination of employment, at no cost to the employee. This insurance covers general and specialist care, surgery, maternity care, hospitalization or care in convalescent homes, medicines, laboratory services, dental care, and eye care.

The Program to Reinforce the Unity Agreement to Overcome the Economic Emergency (*Programa de Acción para Reforzar el Acuerdo de Unidad para Superar la Emergencia Económica*—PARAUSSE) implemented on March 9, 1995, and extended the coverage period after termination of employment to 6 months until December 1995. The new Social Security Law[117] that will come into effect in July 1997 reinstates the 2-month coverage period.

Displaced workers 60 years of age or older are allowed to take early retirement benefits at a reduced rate, providing 95 percent of the old-age pension as an unemployment benefit for up to 2 years (the normal retirement age is 65). Old-age benefit amounts are based on multiples of the minimum wage of the Federal District, ranging

---

[117] Ley del Seguro Social, Instituto Mexicano del Seguro Social, 1997.

from one to six times the minimum wage.

Other Available Income Support

Displaced workers age 60 or older may withdraw their funds from their individual retirement accounts (*Sistema de Ahorro para el Retiro*—SAR).[118] The same elderly workers may also withdraw their credited funds from the national housing fund (INFONAVIT, a subsidized housing program for workers).

Workers up to 60 years of age can withdraw up to 10 percent of their SAR funds during periods of unemployment one time, at intervals of 5 years. Displaced workers liable for monthly payments to the national housing fund may obtain a suspension of payments without penalty for up to 1 year, but only once. If after 1 year the worker is still unemployed and has a balance in his or her SAR, transfers can be made from this fund for INFONAVIT monthly payments.

---

[118] SAR is an integrated retirement system for all workers registered in the Mexican Social Security Institute (Instituto Mexicano del Seguro Social—IMSS) and in the Social Security System to Public Employees (Instituto de Seguridad y Servicios Sociales de los Trabajadores del Estado—ISSSTE). Workers receive a deposit equivalent to 2 percent of their monthly salary in a personal bank account paid by the employer. Those deposits are not taxed and will pay a real annual rate no less than 2 percent.

TRANSCRIPT OF PUBLIC FORUM

UNITED STATES DEPARTMENT OF LABOR

BUREAU OF INTERNATIONAL LABOR AFFAIRS

PUBLIC FORUM

Tuesday, February 27, 1996

9:30 a.m.

Moderator: Joaquin F. Otero
Deputy Under Secretary of Labor
for International Labor Affairs
U.S. Department of Labor

Ana Hotel
50 Third Street
San Francisco, California

AGENDA

Closing

PROCEEDINGS

9:40 a.m.

MR. ZEE: Before we have the formal start of today's program, I would like to make some comments on some procedural details which I hope will make the meeting go by a little more smoothly.

First, you will notice that there is interpretation equipment at all the tables. Channel 4 is English and Channel 3 is Spanish. Of course, if you don't understand English, you don't know that Channel 3 is Spanish, but Channel 4 is English, Channel 3 is Spanish.

There are a variety of materials at the table in the back as you come in. I think most people have taken those materials. They are for you and please feel free to take as many as you want.

If you need something, I will be around throughout the course of the meeting. Please let me know and I will help get those materials for you.

There is a section on the side here reserved for the media and I ask only that the reporters not do any interviews in this room during the course of the meeting. There will be plenty of opportunity during the break at lunchtime. And also if you have an interview scheduled with somebody during the course of this meeting, please just do it outside the room. And there's also a mult box set up if any reporters require the mult box and that's at the back of the room also.

All the speakers, by the way, will come up to this podium, there will be no speakers or questions or comments from the floor, so we do ask that the speakers sit at these first two tables up here to minimize the time traveling back and forth and to help us expedite today's program.

I believe that's all I have. If you have any questions, as I said, I will be around. And with that, I am going to turn the meeting over to Deputy Under Secretary for International Affairs Jack Otero and he will chair today's program.

Thank you.

MR. OTERO: Thank you, Bob.

Good morning ladies and gentlemen.

Muy buenos dias, senoras y senores. Bienvenidos a todos.

My task today is to chair this public forum on behalf of Secretary of Labor Robert Reich. I would like first of all to identify those at the head table with me for your benefit.

First, to my extreme right is Mr. Warren Edmondson, who represents the Human Resources Department in Canada and he is the leader of the tripartite Canadian delegation which involves government, unions and management representatives.

To his left is the representative of the Mexican Government, Dr. Luis Miguel Dias, from the Ministry of Labor and Social Welfare of Mexico. He, too, is leading a tripartite delegation composed of union, management and government.

To my immediate right is Mrs. Irasema Garza, who is the Secretary of the United States National Administrative Office, which is the first line agency set up at each government's level for the purpose of implementing the North American Agreement on Labor Cooperation.

And to my left is Mr. Bart Widom, who is from the Solicitor's Office of the Department of Labor. He is my legal advisor and both he and Mrs. Garza will be assisting me should there be any question for technical or legal questions which I may be not able to answer on my own.

I would like to thank all of you today for being here promptly and at the outset I should also say that I am delighted to see such a large number of people present as well as to see so many faces in the audience which are familiar to me.

We also have headsets for simultaneous interpretation. I ask each and every one of you to please not inadvertently take them out of the room, leave them in your place when you go out to lunch and when the meeting is concluded today because they do not belong to the Department of Labor, they have been rented for the purpose of this meeting.

The public forum that we are conducting today is being conducted pursuant to the North American Agreement on Labor Cooperation which is in the vernacular known as the labor side agreement to the NAFTA trade agreement.

As you know, the NAFTA agreement itself is supplemented by an agreement on the protection for the environment and an agreement on the protection of workers' rights. But this forum is specifically conducted today as a result of a ministerial consultations implementation agreement on Case 95-01. This agreement was reached by Secretary of Labor Robert Reich and Mexican Secretary of Labor Javier Bonilla on December 15, 1995. And I would like to say in passing that the agreement was endorsed and signed by the government of Canada through the Labor Minister, Luzian Robilliar.

This public forum presents an opportunity for public debate on the freedom of association and the right to organize, principles on which the three NAFTA signatory countries place the highest of importance.

Ministerial consultations were held on Submission 95-01 under Article 22 of the Labor Supplemental Agreement following the Mexican National Administrative Office issuance of a public report on May 31, 1995. Submission 95-01 was filed with the Mexican NAO on February 9, 1995 by the Telephone Workers Union of Mexico. The submission alleged that the Sprint Corporation closed its facility known as La Conexion Familiar, a Spanish-language telemarketing subsidiary in San Francisco, in

July of 1994 just one week prior to a scheduled union representation election, thereby dismissing over 200 employees and denying them the right to freedom of association and the right to organize.

Mexico's public report on this submission requested ministerial consultations to address the effect of sudden closure of a workplace on the workers' freedom of association and the right to organize in the United States of America.

The agreement negotiated by the United States and Mexico during these ministerial consultations recognizes the importance of this issue and provides several action items, one of which is, and I quote, "that within 120 days of the agreement the United States Department of Labor will organize and conduct a public forum in San Francisco, California to allow interested parties an opportunity to convey to the public their concerns on the effect of the sudden closure of a plant on the principle of the freedom of association and the right of workers to organize."

That, ladies and gentlemen, is why we are all here today. Notice of today's forum was published in the Federal Register on January 25, 1996. In that notice, advance registration procedures for all presentations were outlined with the intent of ensuring an orderly process and allowing sufficient opportunity for all interested parties to participate within the time allowed each speaker.

This is a one-day event, scheduled to end today no later than six p.m. We will have a break for lunch at approximately 12:30 and we will return to work at two p.m.

The published guidelines allow me as chairman of this event today to allow each speaker no more than 10 minutes and I ask each speaker to be mindful of this requirement so as not to encroach on someone else's right to speak.

Only those people who have registered in advance with our office will be permitted to speak today. We have compiled a list with the names of persons who wish to speak and who registered timely with the United States Department of Labor. That list containing the names of persons speaking today is available at the table located at the rear of this room.

If you have registered to speak, please locate your name on the list because to the extent possible I will try to follow the order in that list and will call your name accordingly.

I request again your cooperation and assistance in conducting an orderly proceeding so that all those who have registered can make an oral presentation and have the opportunity to do so without any encumbrances. To this end, I request that all oral presentations be limited to the issue before us today, Submission 95-01, and the general objective of the forum is to analyze the effect of the sudden plant closures in the United States have on workers' rights to organize and on the freedom of association.

After each presentation, I will have the discretion to question the presenters if appropriate or necessary. There will be no questions from the audience to the presenters. At any time during the forum I will have the leeway of calling a recess if I deem it appropriate.

In addition to the recording of today's proceedings, written statements which have been submitted to the United States National Administrative Office will be included in the public record of this forum. The complete record of these proceedings will be available to the public upon request.

I would like to thank all of you in advance for your cooperation in ensuring the orderly process of these proceedings and I would like also to announce to the presenters that it is their choice to address this audience either in English or in Spanish as we have simultaneous interpretation provided for this event.

Having said that, it is my pleasure at this point, first of all, to recognize the leader of the Mexican delegation and invite him to make a few remarks, Dr. Luis Miguel Diaz from Mexico.

DR. DIAZ: First of all, I would like to thank the Department of Labor for organizing this event and I would like to express my appreciation to the local authorities for having us here.

(THROUGH TRANSLATOR)

My presentation will be a short one and it will focus on three points. They are, number one, a new way of focusing on the worker; number two, the North American Agreement on Labor Cooperation as a venue for cooperation; and, third, I would like to highlight the situation of labor in the framework of labor relations between the United States, Mexico and Canada.

Regarding the first point, in recent years the subject of labor and labor conditions as opposed to the original approach taken has been focused in a more broad manner. Workers are approached as human beings and working conditions now take into account their economic situation, productivity of companies and the well-being of nations. On the other hand, the worker is considered in the light of his environment and work environment. This theory focusing on the worker as an economic being and as a generator of wealth and environment is relatively new.

The topic is clearly identified as one of the typical topics in the globalization we are experiencing and has been dealt with by the ILO, the WTO, the Organization for Economic Development, OECD, and by the United States, Canada and Mexico within the Organization of American States. However, within this debate the North American Agreement on Labor Cooperation seems to have taken the fore since it is an agreement which along with NAFTA and along with the environment cooperation agreement is an international agreement binding for the three countries.

The preamble of the NAFTA agreement says that one of its objectives is the well-being of workers. The preamble of the North American Agreement on Labor Cooperation in several ways insists on this purpose. And, finally, article first of the cooperation agreement refers to the objective of raising the standard of living of workers within an international context, within a context of creation of jobs and the expansion of workers' rights.

Now I'll turn to the second point and with your permission I would like to highlight five specific aspects of the cooperation agreement which brings us here.

The first aspect is that the agreement is based on a tenet which is a respect for labor legislation in each of our three countries. Article 2 says that all mechanisms set forth are based on this principle by virtue of which in each country the corresponding labor authorities are the only ones acting in the matter. This agreement does not aim to and, as Article 42nd would say, this agreement cannot be interpreted as substituting authorities from one country to the other.

The second point has to do with one of the objectives of Article 1 which says that the countries undertake to find transparency in the implementation of labor laws. The three countries want to discuss all matters openly and we want all elements of society to participate in this debate and this is why at this forum we are showing that we are taking seriously this obligation.

The other point has to do with the establishment of national administrative offices. Dr. Otero referred to this. And this means that in order to comply with the agreement the three countries established three offices which aim to serve as points of contact among themselves or with local and state organizations in the three countries and then to establish contact with a labor secretariat created by three countries. It is an institution created by the three countries with equal composition from Canada, Mexico and the United States. It is based in Dallas, Texas.

The other point I wanted to highlight is that the North American Agreement on Labor Cooperation, breaking with an internationalist tradition, does not set forth new rights nor new obligations for the parties in a substantive way. The basic concern of the three countries was to seek ways to effectively implement our laws which result from our traditions, our idiosyncrasies and our aspirations.

So the reason we are here, the specific reason we are here is to discuss the principle of freedom of association and organization which is contemplated in our national laws and which we have specified as common principles. This is not a new right. It is not a new right but we would like for this right to be more effective.

And, finally, on the North American Agreement on Labor Cooperation, I wanted to say and underscore that this is an international instrument and if we are to analyze it in keeping with international law, it is a perfect law. It is a perfect law because the document itself sets forth a series of requirements so that sanctions may be applied and penalties maybe applied. It is not merely a declaration of principles of good will, of political will, it is a legal instrument which is binding and so non-compliance can be corrected through penalties.

147

The last point I wanted to make was that the area of labor is something which the United States and Mexico have focused on and have reached an understanding to address problems. It is a way to detect possible irregularities and problems, to analyze them and to expose them to the public so that our authorities can be more effective.

A second point that I wanted to underscore is that the composition of this forum breaking with the traditional pattern is not just a forum of government entities. No. We have tripartite delegations with us representing different sectors of our societies, so the representation of what we are, what we want to be, is very broad to the extent that we are represented here in a tripartite way, and I would even say four parties because we have invited sectors of our society which are not representative of governments or companies or workers, they represent society at large.

And, finally, I wanted to end by saying that through me the Secretary of Labor of Mexico, Secretary Bonilla, believes that this forum is a demonstration of the fact that there is communication to address problems, there is political will present and we are expecting concrete results.

Thank you very much.

MR. OTERO: Thank you, Dr. Diaz.

I now would like to introduce Mr. Warren Edmondson, Director General of the Federal Mediation and Conciliation Services, Human Resources Development, Canada, representing the government of Canada.

MR. EDMONDSON: Thanks very much, Jack. And it's always a pleasure when traveling from Canada to visit our neighbors in the south not only to renew acquaintances but also to escape some of the colder climates that we become exposed to at this time of year.

As a partner to this North American Agreement on Labor Cooperation, we're certainly pleased to be here to participate in this public forum dealing with a very important subject, the subject of freedom of association and rights of workers to organize. These issues, of course, and this process, the process for the resolution of complaints under the North American Agreement are of considerable importance to us in Canada, not only to the government of Canada and to the provincial governments but also to our trade unions and our employers, so we look forward to today's proceedings.

We certainly hope that our participation here in this forum will further contribute to improving the dialogue that exists between business, labor and government in our three countries and will further assist us in our efforts in achieving the objectives of the North American Agreement.

Accompanying me today from back east, northeast, are Mr. Dick Martin from the Canadian Labour Congress, which is the largest Canadian central labor organization in Canada, Dick is seated over here at the left, and Mr. Larry Bertuzzi, a practicing labor lawyer from Toronto who has had considerable experience in representing companies in many jurisdictions in Canada and also in the United States. Both of them are experienced labor relations practitioners and I understand that they have been scheduled to speak later on today on the subjects at hand and I look forward to hearing their views.

I can certainly assure you from my experience in dealing with them that neither one of them is shy and if they happen to agree or disagree with anything that I happen to say today that I'm sure they will do so and will certainly give you their perspective on the Canadian experience in dealing with labor law.

Those of you who are familiar with Canadian labor law know that the constitutional jurisdiction for labor law in our country is divided between the federal government and our provincial governments. Each jurisdiction has its own labor laws, protecting workers' health and safety, basic employment standards, equity laws and laws providing, of course, the right to organize unions and laws governing the process of collective bargaining.

Although there may be some differences, and some of them significant, between these respective laws in our country and also in the way in which they are administered, fundamentally they are all based on the U.S. Wagner Act model. And those of you, of course, in this room who are familiar with labor law will know the model well.

They all recognize in the statute, in the respective statutes, the fundamental right of workers to organize and become members of trade unions of their choice, whether they be local unions, national unions or international unions. This, of course, is consistent with the basic rights and freedoms of association found in our Canadian Charter of Rights and Freedoms as well as in Convention 87 of the International Labor Organization which has been ratified by Canada.

Our Federal Minister of Labour, Mr. Gagliano, who asked me to bring his greetings to this group, is the minister responsible for the Federal Canada Labour Code. Part 1 of that code is the part that establishes a framework for collective bargaining for federally regulated industries and these industries include industries such as airlines, telecommunications, railroads, longshoring, grain handling and many of the major infrastructure industries in Canada. Although I think about 10 percent of the workforce is governed by the federal labor law, the law, as I said, applies to a number of significant industries.

This part of the code was recently reviewed by an independent task force which submitted its report to the minister on January 31st of this year. The report contains a number of important recommendations and underscores once again the value of our system of collective bargaining as an effective instrument in Canada of both social and economic policy, which is a particularly important statement, I think, as we move into the 21st century.

To quote from the report of the task force chaired by a Mr. Andrew Simms who was the former chair of the Alberta, one of our provinces, labor boards, he states, "Canada must continue to facilitate means by which individuals can express themselves through democratic intermediary groups. Free collective bargaining is an important example."

He goes on to add, "It is not only the absence of rights and freedoms that can lead to the growth of disorder, but also and perhaps more importantly the sense of injustice that results from the inability to secure these rights and freedoms."

It's worth noting that during that process of the task force process that with the assistance of government key labor and management representatives in the industries affected by this legislation met jointly to discuss a number of the issues included in the terms of reference of the task force. The fact that they were able to reach consensus on a significant number of points I believe is an indication of their mutual respect, their ability to work together and as well an indication of their faith in the system of collective bargaining and their mutual interest in designing a system that works for them. That's not all to say that there is peace and harmony between labor and management in every situation in Canada, but I think it's an important indication of their ability to work together.

I should point out that the percentage of unionized workers in Canada remains relatively constant at approximately 37 percent of our workforce, despite the significant impact of changes in government policies such as deregulation, privatization, and the pressures of worldwide competition on Canadian companies and workers in recent years.

Wage increases in Canada remain relatively low at an average of about 1.4 percent while inflation is running at 2.1 in an environment of, again, relatively high unemployment within our country of 9.6 percent.

Discussions at collective bargaining tables like here in the United States have generally focused on the need for concessions, as many companies attempt to remain competitive or to increase profits.

Companies have attempted to reduce labor costs by seeking lower wages, seeking reorganized and more flexible workforces, and attempting to increase productivity by introducing new technology.

Governments also who are faced with large debts and deficits are finding it necessary to adopt some of the strategies of the private sector in their efforts to balance their budgets.

And yet the number of work stoppages in Canada, perhaps understandably, are at an alltime low. Last year, 982,000 person days were lost due to work stoppages, compared to 3.5 million days in 1990.

However, in this difficult environment, organized labor in Canada has managed to hold its own. As I said, it remains at about 35 percent, 37 percent.

Canada's laws, and in particular its labor laws, and the efficiency of its arm's length labor boards which are responsible for determination of bargaining unit structures, for the investigation of unfair labor practice complaints, for the certification of trade unions and their respective jurisdictions, I believe may be in a large part accountable for the ability of trade unions in Canada to organize and maintain their membership in this complex environment.

For example, when we examine the experience of labor boards in our three largest jurisdictions, the provinces of Ontario, Quebec and British Columbia, the statistics are revealing.

In Ontario, in 1993–'94, the numbers indicate that there were 11,066 applications for union certification filed with the Ontario Labour Relations Board, of which 829 were granted, 102 were dismissed and 204 were withdrawn. Most importantly, the median time taken by the board to grant certification was 22 calendar days. During that same period, there were only 110 applications for decertification, 53 of which were granted and 26 were dismissed.

In the province of Quebec for the year '94–'95, relatively similar numbers: 854 applications with 555 granted, 87 dismissed.

Again, similar in the province of British Columbia. In the province of British Columbia, the average time taken to grant an application is 27 days.

I will confess that our federal labor board, those of you who want to take the time to read the report of the task force, will note that it is not quite as efficient. I'm sure that will probably improve as a result of the recommendations that Mr. Simms has made.

While certainly Canada's system of industrial relations is far from perfect, and we've seen the pendulum swing in various provinces on various occasions, I think both labor and management would not find too much argument with the fact that in general our labor laws are being enforced. Not only are they being enforced, but I think they might also agree that they are being enforced fairly, effectively and efficiently.

In a highly competitive global marketplace where the rate of technological change is accelerating at a breathtaking pace, there is much speculation about the future of work. We find apparently competing interests between the quest for corporate survival and profitability on one hand and the pursuit of meaningful work and improved standards of living for workers and the protection of worker rights on the part of trade unions on the other.

These competing interests are not irreconcilable, but rather need to be balanced, not only through a fair and effectively administered legislative framework but also through changing attitudes, I believe, on the part of labor and management in our countries, through cooperation, through good faith, mutual trust, which unfortunately we can't legislate.

While many companies and unions in Canada take their traditional adversarial stances and appear to want to do battle at almost every occasion, there are currently many Canadian success stories in industries such as telecommunications, steel, manufacturing and others where organized labor and management are working together to find innovative and creative ways to advance their mutual interests.

They have recognized the competitive advantage and the benefit to both social partners to be gained by tapping the resources of a well trained, well motivated, empowered and represented workforce.

I believe that effective labor laws efficiently administered will allow us to move to the next dimension and perhaps change the traditional paradigm and enable labor and management as we move into the 21st century to work more effectively together to the mutual benefit of all three countries and workers in Canada, the U.S. and Mexico.

In closing, let me simply say that we are here to listen. We are here to learn. And I look forward to the day's proceedings and hearing the views of the various speakers.

Thank you very much.

MR. OTERO: Thank you very much, Mr. Edmondson.

And now that we have completed the introductory statements by the three countries signatory to the North American Agreement on Labor Cooperation, we will move on with the forum itself.

I would like to ask the presenters to please come to the podium to make their presentations. And, again, I ask all of the presenters to be mindful of the time allotted.

The first presenter this morning is Mr. Francisco Hernandez Juarez, President of the Telephone Workers Union of the Republic of Mexico.

Mr. Hernandez, please.

MR. HERNANDEZ: (THROUGH TRANSLATOR)

Thank you very much. Good morning.

Ladies and gentlemen, my name is Francisco Hernandez Juarez, as you have just heard, Secretary General of the Telephone Workers Union.

I would like to point out that the organization that I represent has approximately 50,000 affiliates throughout the country. Actually, we are represented in 31 of the 32 states that make up the Mexican Republic.

First of all, I would like to express my great appreciation to the representatives of the Labor Department of the United States and Canada, as far as the Labor Department goes, for having hosted this meeting.

Secondly, I would like to point out that I am here not only because of the fact that the Telephone Workers Union of Mexico is responsible for having initiated this whole procedure within the framework of the North American Agreement on Labor Cooperation, I am also here and above all because in my entity as a unionist, I believe and I trust in solidarity of workers and as a worker and as a union leader in a globalized and complex work of intertwined economies that are interdependent, I wish to trust in the aquitative dialogue, in bargaining, in negotiation, in justice and laws and institutions as being the best instruments to improve the relationship between management and workers and to conciliate their problems.

I would also like to point out that the decision to initiate these procedures to its ultimate consequences was not a coincidence, nor the result of a personal decision. It was the unanimous decision of our national congress celebrated in January of '95 in which we affirmed the commitment that we have with the alliance that we have with the workers union of telecommunications from the United States and Canada in February of 1992, as well as our participation in the international trade unions for postal workers and communication workers.

In the case of La Conexion Familiar, it was a particular concern for us, not only the fact that certain laws were being violated in such an obvious manner, but that there was also a racist aggression and also that this was not by just a small fraction of a systematic aggression towards labor organization on behalf of Sprint with whom Telefonos de Mexico has a strategic alliance.

I would like to make as a complementary observation the following. Through a high executive of Telefonos de Mexico, it was tried to convince me not to speak this day, precisely because it would demerit the presence of Sprint in its alliance with Telefonos de Mexico.

I pointed it out to this executive that that would mean that Sprint meant to change its attitude in the situation of La Conexion Familiar but he told me that he could not assure that it would happen. Therefore, I answered that I could not therefore not attend this meeting.

Since this violation of the rules were published, we want justice to be carried out towards the people from La Conexion Familiar but also we want to send a clear message, not only to Sprint but to all telecommunications companies in the region, the continent, throughout the world, about what workers and trade unions are willing to do if they stand together to defend each other and to make progress as far as our rights go, in spite of the aggressions and offenses that have taken place against workers' rights. These affect not only the workers but the companies themselves, even though this might not seem too evident for the general public.

We wish that this is a message of the defense of basic human rights because labor rights and trade union rights are part of human rights. We would also like to appeal to the transnational companies, to multi-nationalist companies, that they should keep open this dialogue with trade workers, with trade unions all over the world regardless of their nationality.

We wish that the multi-national companies should understand that progress is not necessarily something that is in conflict with the right of workers, with the assurance of their working place. If companies such as Sprint are willing to do everything in their power in order to prevent trade unions to exist, then trade unions would have no other option than to carry out whatever is necessary to accomplish the contrary. And if we had the same despotic attitude the company has shown, then we would also have to plan our fight in a confrontational way.

This absurd confrontational scenario is not desirable for anybody, but should it happen, it would be a responsibility of the companies. It would be their responsibility. We wish also that through this we can appeal to our governments that through modernization and regional global integration some policies and strategies would be developed that would promote a more balanced working environment, a fair working environment and therefore better for everybody involved.

We trust that this North American Agreement on Labor Cooperation be an instrument that is sufficient and enough to comply with all these expectations but we also trust in the fact that for the same reason it could be the basis for a more specific and more functional regulation that could defend workers' rights.

Through the IPCTT, we have defended a code of behavior for multi-national companies. Through this code, companies should recognize trade unions and their representatives, depending on the country they come from. In the same way, they cannot wander from one place to the other trying to avoid the recognition of trade unions, nor will they be able to interfere in the initiatives of the workers, such as happened in La Conexion Familiar.

I am convinced that the colleague Morton Bahr is also going to talk about this and in advance I would like to express that we coincide with his opinions and we are willing and determined to go on in our joint struggle.

To conclude, I would like to make one final remark. It is definitely the first time in which a Mexican trade union initiates a legal action to support labor struggle for the American workers. This is for us an incredible engagement and commitment that we undertake. We believe that the conditions to act in such a manner will be more favorable in the future because within the Mexican labor movement, there are important changes taking place and in which we communication workers are taking part of.

This redefines the traditional patterns of international labor organization, in order to be able to believe in justice and that this is not only an idea but a real possibility, that it is based on unity and solidarity amongst all workers.

MR. OTERO: Thank you very much, Mr. Hernandez Juarez.

I now invite to the podium Mr. Morton Bahr, the president of the Communications Workers of America and a member of the Executive Council of the AFL-CIO.

MR. BAHR: Good morning.

MR. OTERO: Good morning.

MR. BAHR: I am Morton Bahr, the president of the Communications Workers of America. CWA represents about 600,000 workers, primarily in the telecommunications and information industries.

I want to commend the Secretaries of Labor of the United States, Mexico, and Canada for their decision to hold this public forum on Sprint's sudden shutdown of La Conexion Familiar.

We were stunned when Sprint fired all of the workers within one week before they were scheduled to vote in a union election. This forum will help expose and we hope stop the use of sudden plant closing and other legal and illegal anti-union behavior which prevent workers from exercising their right to organize.

I also want to thank Deputy Under Secretary Jack Otero for presiding over this forum and giving the discharged Sprint workers the opportunity to finally be heard.

Finally, on behalf of the workers of LCF, I want to thank the Mexican Telephone Workers Union, STRM, and its president, Francisco Hernandez Juarez, for taking up the cause of the LCF workers and filing a formal complaint under the provisions of the North American Agreement on Labor Cooperation.

I will submit for the record my complete written statement and attached exhibits. In this testimony I lay out in greater detail CWA's relationship with Sprint, Sprint's anti-union philosophy, and an overview of the events which occurred at LCF. Today, given our limited time, I will focus on the importance of this forum and the recommendations we wish to present to the governments which have convened it.

The decision to hold this forum is a breakthrough for workers in Canada, Mexico and the United States who want to improve their working conditions and their standard of living by joining together to form a union. The forum has focused public attention on one of the worst cases of corporate abuse of workers' rights and on the use by companies of a sudden plant or office closing to prevent their workers from organizing. Sprint's action epitomizes decades of increased attacks by corporations on workers' rights.

This forum has focused attention also on the inability of U.S. labor laws to protect workers' rights and the inability of the United States Government to enforce its own laws.

The National Labor Relations Act is broken and our enforcement mechanisms are ineffective. We must act now to fix them. We hope this forum will contribute to efforts here and abroad to educate the public and our elected officials that meaningful reforms are needed if we want workers to organize and to bargain for a better life.

This public forum is important too because it demonstrates that the NAFTA labor side agreements provide another vehicle to hold Sprint and other companies who violate workers' rights accountable for their actions.

As our country's integration into global economy deepens, we must look to trade agreements to establish an international code of conduct towards workers and their elected representatives. Foreign companies want access to the lucrative U.S. market and U.S. companies want to leverage their financial, technological and managerial to penetrate markets outside the U.S.

Companies on all sides want to increase opportunities for international trade and investment. Governments must balance these opportunities with the responsibilities of creating good jobs and respecting the rights of workers to organize and bargain collectively.

The Preamble and Annex 1 of the NAALC contain all the necessary objectives: the right to organize, the right to collective bargaining, the need to create employment opportunities, improve working conditions and raise living standards and the need to "protect, enhance and enforce basic workers' rights."

What is missing are effective remedies for violations of these objectives and prompt enforcement of these remedies. Under the current provisions of the NAFTA labor agreement, companies do not face any risks for blatantly violating the agreement. Yet there is nothing that companies understand better than risk. They manage for it every day of the year.

In the current political environment, where trade agreements are drawing more criticism, the governments of the U.S., Mexico, and Canada are in a unique position to tell these companies in no uncertain terms that more trade agreements will never fly unless there are improved protections for workers, their jobs and their rights. The agreements must provide meaningful penalties for violation of these rights.

Today we are recommending that the North American Agreement on Labor Cooperation be amended to include an international code of conduct for enterprises operating in the three countries which are parties to the NAFTA agreement.

CWA together other telephone unions affiliated with our international trade secretariat, PTTI, propose a code of conduct which in summary would require companies:

(1) To disclose to employees and their elected representatives company plans for investment, employment levels, technological change, and movement of work.

(2) To meet annually with all their unions to discuss organizational rights, equal employment opportunities, safety and health, and education and training.

(3) To not interfere in worker organizational efforts where they conduct business.

(4) To recognize a union when the workers show the appropriate level of support.

(5) To not shift work from one nation to another to avoid a union.

The full text of the code of conduct is in my written statement.

In my written statement, we also make three recommendations to the government of the United States. I will summarize them here.

(1) We need meaningful penalties to deter companies from illegally interfering with their workers' right to organize. In the Sprint case, the violations were astounding yet the remedy was a mere notice to employees who have already been thrown out of work that the company will not do it again. This only added insult to injury.

(2) We advocate a change in the law which would deter companies from using the subterfuge of alleged business considerations to close a plant to avoid a union and prevent a first contract. Under current law, injunctive relief is heavily weighted toward the employer and has been awarded by the courts in only a few cases. We recommend that if a union has filed for an election or if an election has been won by a union but a first contract has not been reached, a company which is considering a shutdown for business reasons (a) must open its books to the employees and the union representatives and (b) must prove its business case to an independent arbitrator before it can shut a facility down.

(3) The Federal Government can refrain from doing business with major labor law violators. Defense contractors who have defrauded the taxpayer have had their right to bid on new contracts suspended. The U.S. Government should extend this practice to companies which have been found to have committed major violations of labor law.

Above all else, this forum is very important because it gives the Sprint workers their first real opportunity to tell the story of what happened at LCF. This is a story of a company, the Sprint corporation, the third largest long distance telephone company in the United States, that tells its managers that their main job is not to provide for quality telephone service, but to keep the union out at all costs. It's in their handbook.

It is a story of more than 200 workers, mostly Latino women, who had the courage and determination to withstand the threats, the coercion, and the spying by management to stand up for their rights. They got within 1 week of accomplishing the unprecedented feat of forming a union at Sprint's long distance division.

This is also the story of how a company used every trick in the book to try to stop these workers and in so doing committed over 50 violations of law.

It is also the story of a management which suddenly realized they were about to lose their first union election and decided to shut the place down.

It is the story of a senior Sprint executive, the vice president of labor relations, who fabricated evidence submitted to a government agency to make it appear that the closure was done for business reasons.

It is the case of a company which not only shut down a facility, suddenly and brutally in 1 day, to prevent these workers from voting in the union election, but did it in a way which sent a chilling message to all of its other employees that unionization is off limits.

You will hear today from the Sprint workers themselves who will describe for you in vivid detail the poor working conditions at this company, the energy and spirit of their organizing efforts, the anti-union campaign launched by Sprint against their drive, and the residual long-term effects of the shutdown on their lives.

You'll hear from many others about the international repercussions, the outrage in the Latino community, the concern among elected officials that current law is incapable of protecting workers in the public interest, and the extent to which Sprint's actions have been commonplace in the private sector.

The workers of LCF are still waiting for a remedy in the legal case which is outstanding against Sprint. More than 2 years will have passed when the National Labor Relations Board finally issues its order. And it will be years more before all appeals are exhausted. This situation is simply unacceptable.

That is why this public forum is so important, not only to the workers of LCF but to others who will face similar circumstances in the future. Sprint must be reminded again and again that CWA and all those who have stood up for the rights of these workers will never give up this fight until Sprint provides them with meaningful remedies, including compensation and job opportunities at other Sprint locations.

We know that in spite of the chilling effect of the LCF closing on other Sprint workers and the continued fear and intimidation by Sprint management Sprint workers will again stand up and seek to be recognized.

These workers in Sprint need to know that when that time comes the world will be watching and fair-minded people will be ready to act against any attempt by Sprint to interfere with its workers' rights.

This forum gives the Sprint workers new hope that when that time comes the federal government and their elected representatives will have fixed our system of labor laws and be ready to enforce them.

The workers are not asking for handouts or entitlements. They are simply asking the government to level the playing field so they can stand up for their rights without the fear of reprisals from their employers. They should be able to organize into a union without the fear of losing their jobs.

We hope the testimony presented in this forum and the 6-month study by the international labor secretariat will cause the governments of Canada, Mexico, and the United States to take the necessary measures to strengthen the NAFTA agreement to prevent the recurrence of the travesty suffered by the Sprint workers.

Thank you.

MR. OTERO: Thank you, Mr. Bahr.

I would like to now invite the next presenter, Professor Roberto L. Corrada, Assistant Professor of Law at the University of Denver, Denver, Colorado, who has registered to speak on behalf of Sprint Inc.

Professor Corrada, please.

PROFESSOR CORRADA: Good morning. My name is Roberto Corrada. I am an assistant professor of law at the University of Denver, College of Law, Denver Colorado. I have been teaching labor and employment law courses and courses in contract law and administrative law at the law school since 1990.

In December 1995, I was asked by Sprint Corporation to conduct an independent review of the regulatory activity undertaken and the two opinions that have been issued in a labor dispute involving La Conexion Familiar, LCF, a business entity that had been affiliated with Sprint. The questions posed to me were (1) whether the National Labor Relations Board's actions in this matter demonstrate enforcement of the National Labor Relations Act, NLRA, the United States labor law implicated by the dispute, and (2) whether the two opinions in this matter have applied the appropriate NLRA standard in deciding the dispute.

My conclusion based on a review of the decisions as well the enforcement activity undertaken by the NLRB in this matter is that United States labor laws involving the NLRA have been enforced and the proper standards applied.

In this testimony, I will first talk briefly about the origin and acceptability of the standard, the *Wright Line* test applied by the district court judge deciding whether to issue a 10(j) injunction in the case and the administrative law judge deciding the merits of the case.

Next, I will assess the regulatory activity undertaken by the NLRB in this matter and finally I will discuss the two opinions, the district court opinion and the administrative law judge's opinion that have been issued in this case.

First, with respect to the standard applied, this matter implicates the NLRA, the United States labor law that governs relations between unions and management in the private sector.

MR. OTERO: Professor Corrada, they want you to slow down so that the translation can take place. Take your time.

PROFESSOR CORRADA: Excuse me. Maybe I had a little bit too much coffee this morning.

In particular, it involves a dispute under Section 8(a)(3) of the Act, which establishes at its core that it is an unfair labor practice for an employer to discriminate in regard to hire or tenure of employment or any term or condition of employment, to encourage or discourage membership in any labor organization.

Administrative Law Judge Wacknov and District Court Judge Walker both applied the NLRB's *Wright Line* standard in deciding the claims of the parties involving Section 8(a)(3) of the Act. The NLRB general counsel also argued for application of the *Wright Line* standard in this case.

The standard was announced by the National Labor Relations Board some 16 years ago in its 1980 decision in *Wright Line* and was upheld by the United States Supreme Court in its 1983 decision in *NLRB v. Transportation Management Corporation* as a reasonable interpretation of the requirements of Section 8(a)(3).

The *Wright Line* standard may well represent the best approach to deciding who should prevail when legitimate but competing interests of labor and management must be reconciled under Section 8(a)(3). According to the Board, a dual-motive case is presented under Section 8(a)(3) when there is evidence of employer reaction to union organizing activity but there is also believable competing evidence that an employer has acted pursuant to a legitimate business reason. This existence of both a good and a bad reason for the employer's action requires further inquiry into the role played by each motive.

In *Wright Line*, the NLRB adopted a standard that was used by the United States Supreme Court in *Mt. Healthy v. Doyle* to decide a constitutional rights dispute between a school board and a teacher. The Supreme Court stated that a rule of causation which focuses solely on whether protected conduct played a part, substantial or otherwise, in a decision not to rehire could place an employee in a better position as a result of the exercise of constitutionally protected conduct than he would have occupied had he done nothing.

Most importantly, according to the court, the constitutional principle at stake is sufficiently vindicated if such an employee is place in no worse position than if he had not engaged in the conduct.

Following the Supreme Court's analysis in *Mt. Healthy*, the *Wright Line* test announced by the NLRB places the initial burden on the Board's general counsel to make a prima facie showing sufficient to support the inference that protected conduct was a motivating factor in the employer's decision. Once this is established, the burden will shift to the employer to demonstrate that the same action would have taken place even in the absence of protected conduct.

The *Wright Line* test is a well-reasoned standard for governing dual-motive cases, is consistent with the legislative history of the NLRA and fairly accommodates the legitimate competing interests of labor and of management under the Act.

The *Wright Line* standard has been broadly accepted and indeed has become a fixture in United States labor and employment law. Since the Supreme Court's affirmance of the *Wright Line* standard in 1983, it has been faithfully applied in scores of Section 8(a)(3) cases, yielding results in favor of both unions as well as employers.

The NLRB has applied the *Wright Line* standard to partial closing cases similar to the LCF case on a number of cases. For example, the *C.M. Breyer Corporation* case in 1993, *Cub Branch Mining* in 1990, and the *Redwood Empire* case in 1989.

Moreover, the test has been used in cases involving employer action impinging constitutional rights, as in the *Mt. Healthy* case, and in non-employment cases involving dual motives where constitutional freedoms are implicated, as in the *Arlington Heights* case.

The test has also become an important standard in employment discrimination law in the United States. In 1989, the Supreme Court issued its decision in *Price Waterhouse v. Hopkins* in which it applied the *Mt. Healthy Wright Line* test to dual-motive cases brought under Title 7 of the Civil Rights Act of 1964 which protects against discrimination based on race, color, sex, national origin, and religion.

Let me now turn to the application of the *Wright Line* standard in the matter involving La Conexion Familiar, LCF. I will discuess first the NLRB's enforcement activity in the case, then the district court decision involving the 10(j) injunction and, finally, the administrative law judge's decision on the merits of the case.

In conducting my review of the NLRB's enforcement activity and the decisions by District Court Judge Walker and ALJ Wacknov, I have examined the written opinions as well as the briefs filed by both parties. This opinion is limited to a review of the written materials in this matter. I have not personally reviewed the documents filed with the ALJ or the district court and have relied on the characterizations made of them in the written ALJ and district court decisions and in the briefs filed by the parties. In addition, there can be no effective review of ALJ credibility determinations by persons like myself who have not personally listened to witness testimony.

Given all of that, with respect to the NLRB's enforcement activity, it is my considered opinion that the level of enforcement activity undertaken by the Board in this matter has been extraordinary. It is not common, for example, for the NLRB to seek a Section 10(j) injunction in a labor dispute. General Counsel Fred Feinstein stated in October of 1995 that, "The Board is filing more 10(j) cases although they still represent only about 3 percent of the total number of unfair labor practice complaints issued."

In addition to the NLRB 10(j) filing, the NLRB's general counsel's office has proceeded aggressively to enforce the NLRA in this matter. The NLRB general counsel's brief in this case filed with the ALJ is in excess of 250 pages in length, detailing a large amount of evidence and testimony. The brief is impressive with respect to the way it has organized the evidence and with respect to the way that it argues that the evidence should be assessed under the *Wright Line* standard.

When the brief is considered alongside the NLRB's decision to seek a 10(j) injunction in the case it is more than fair to conclude that the Board's efforts in LCF have been above average in quality and extensive in scope.

As I mentioned before, the NLRB regional director, as part of its enforcement of the NLRA in this case, filed a petition in federal district court for the issuance of a

10(j) injunction. In the 9th Circuit, district courts must weigh the likelihood of success on the merits against the possibility of irreparable injury, mindful both of public interest and a federal court deference to NLRB decisions.

In assessing whether the Board was likely to prevail or merely had a fair chance of success on the merits, the district court properly chose to apply the *Wright Line* test. The district court first analyzed the Board's evidence to determine whether a prima facie case had been presented. Based on the hearsay nature of the Board's evidence as well as the position of the persons making the allegations against respondent and the context in which alleged threatening statements were made, the district court characterized the Board's chances at a prima facie case as fair at best.

The district court nevertheless and in line with the *Wright Line* requirements shifted its focus to analyze the quality of the respondent's evidence supporting its action as motivated by legitimate business reasons. Ultimately the district court was persuaded by the extent of the evidence presented by the employer that showed substantial losses by LCF. Rather than a projected profit of 7.9 million, LCF's actual earnings in January and February of '94 projected a year-end loss of 3.9 million.

In addition, between January and March 1994, the evidence showed that LCF lost 10,000 customers and that the churn rate, which is the percentage loss of customer base, was greater than 20 percent higher than projected.

The district court went on to weigh the hardships of an injunction on the parties and found that since the facility had already been closed for a time, the hardship of reopening would fall squarely on Sprint without much gain to the workers involved, many of whom were by that time unreachable or had already secured new employment. Thus, having failed to meet the burdens for a 10(j) injunction, the district court refused to grant preliminary relief.

Although the circumstances are certainly unfortunate, in my opinion it is hard to find fault with the district court's opinion. The court followed the standards for 10(j) injunctions in the 9th Circuit to the letter, engaging in a step-by-step approach to each requirement. Thus, in my opinion, the district court evaluated the evidence on both sides and applied the burden shifting analysis of *Wright Line* in an appropriate manner.

A hearing was held on the merits of the LCF case in San Francisco during November and December of 1994. The hearing was presided by Gerald Wacknov, an administrative law judge in the NLRB's division of judges. At the outset, I find it striking and significant that both the district court deciding the Section 10(j) matter and the ALJ deciding the merits of the case both viewed the evidence in a similar fashion. The fact that two independent decision makers reviewing much of the same general evidence have reached similar conclusions with respect to such evidence tends to corroborate and lend credence to the view that the *Wright Line* standard was properly invoked and appropriately applied.

The ALJ applied the *Wright Line* standard in deciding the dispute between management and labor. In my view, this standard was appropriately applied given the quality of the evidence presented by both management and labor. It is precisely when there is good evidence on both sides of a dispute that the *Wright Line* standard is appropriate invoked. There is nothing in the opinion that is unusual or remarkable compared with other ALJ decisions that I have reviewed that apply the *Wright Line* standard in a dispute of this nature.

A review of the record evidence shows a sufficient amount of evidence to make out a prima facie case under a *Wright Line* analysis. However, the record also shows substantial evidence to conclude that the employer met its burden of proving that LCF would have been closed for legitimate financial reasons.

The employer's evidence concerning a $12 million variance in forecasts versus outlook for LCF in 1994 and the employer's evidence concerning the future of LCF given competition by MCI and AT&T was persuasive, tending to support the ALJ's conclusion that the employer's burden under *Wright Line* was met.

Based on the very detailed findings of facts set out in over 30 pages of the ALJ's decision, I can fairly conclude that the ALJ reached a reasonable decision under the *Wright Line* approach.

Thank you.

MR. OTERO: Thank you, Professor Corrada.

The chair is advised that one of the registered speakers, Mr. Calvin McDaniels, is unable to be present with us this morning. Should Mr. McDaniels appear in the hall later today, we will allow him the opportunity to make his presentation.

At this time, we will call the next person that registered in sequence.

I would like to invite to the podium Ms. Dora Vogel, who is a former employee of La Conexion Familiar.

MS. VOGEL: Buenos Dias.

MR. OTERO: Good morning.

MS. VOGEL: (UNTRANSLATED TESTIMONY IN SPANISH.)

(THROUGH TRANSLATOR) ... terrible conditions under which we had to work. I had to know how to sell the service and I could reach my quota that we had to fulfill. The manager told us that we would fill our quota, we would get a commission and continuously we were being reminded how much more we could make with this commission. Sometimes the sales quota would go up. If we would manage to sell 15 sales, then the quota immediately went up to 18. It was never important to see how many sales we made. We never got the commission, even though we would ask when are we going to get this commission. They always had a reason or an excuse why we were not being paid that commission for our quota.

We could not speak amongst ourselves. We were told to continue working, that we had to keep making call after call after call. The pressure to sell was enormous and constantly we were being watched to see what we were doing. We were allowed to go to the bathroom at lunchtime or during our rest periods. We had to ask for a special permission to go to the bathroom if it wasn't done during our rest period. Sometimes we would ask for permission and they would tell us that we would have to wait until the regular time to go to the toilet.

Whenever we had the meetings with our supervisors, we were told that we should not drink too much water so that we didn't have to go to the bathroom all the time. Since we were on the phone constantly, we got very thirsty, but we didn't have any water to drink. There was a water fountain for everybody, for the 130 telemarketers, and this was broken. It didn't work. Most of us would bring our own water.

About the first of May, the manager announced that the work schedule was going to change. That very same day we were told what was going to be our next schedule. We had two schedules. Monday to Fridays we worked from 12:30 to 9:00 and Tuesdays and Saturdays we worked from 10:00 to 5:00 p.m. My schedule was changed for Tuesday and for Saturday. I was very frightened because I could not work on Saturdays because I had to take care of the children. My mother-in-law would look after my two children during the week. My baby was barely 4 months old and I knew that my mother-in-law could not take care of them on Saturdays because she worked on Saturdays.

So therefore other workers and myself went to talk to the manager about this problem, but we were told that this schedule would not be changed, that we had to work according to the days that were given to us. For me, this meant more expenses because I had to pay somebody to baby sit my children on Saturdays.

Also, besides the tensions that we felt all the time because we had to make so many calls to make our quota, we also had the tension that we were going to be fired any moment.

One day, one of the colleagues was called to the manager's office. She's here. I saw her. She used to sit in front of me. All of us who sat around here were waiting anxiously to find out what had happened to her, what had the manager said to her. A while later, she came back with the manager. The manager was shouting at her, saying that she couldn't take anything out of her desk and that she had to leave immediately. The manager told her that he was going to call the security guard so that he would see and escort her out of the office. This is what they would do always with any worker who was being dismissed.

My colleague said that the guard would have to bodily carry her out because she was not going to be escorted out. All this was going on around me. I got very nervous but I looked around and then I broke out in tears. I started to cry. Others started to cry also. I just could not hold back my tears. Somebody came and helped me to the bathroom. They gave me a little bit of water. And I couldn't believe that somebody could be so shabbily treated in front of all the colleagues and all the other workers. Everybody heard and saw what was going on.

When I found out about the union, I felt a little better. I was a little calmer. I felt that we needed a union in order to improve our working conditions. When somebody asked me to sign up, I did so immediately and I even asked around and took the petition around for others to sign to.

At the beginning of June, we all used union T-shirts to show our solidarity. And even though we were also nervous because we didn't want to so openly show our support of the union, nevertheless we felt pretty good about wearing our T-shirts because we saw that the majority was supporting the union.

Then I heard rumors that if I went into the union the office would close, but I didn't believe it because why on earth would they close? They were selling very well. We knew that the business was going very well because we were the ones that were making the calls that were bringing in the sales. I felt that many of the workers were in unions and I figured that Sprint would then pay us better.

The supervisors tried to show us that sales were very low. During a meeting they had different graphs where they showed us that sales were off, but we knew better than that.

On the 14th of July, the day that they announced the closing down of the facility, I heard somebody saying that the office would be closed and I saw that there was a lot going on and I suspected that something was up.

When they made the announcement, we were all taken by surprise. I thought that I would call my husband, but then I figured how upset he was going to be because I was really being the only breadwinner in my family. My husband could not work. He had hurt his wrist. There was no money. How were we going to pay our rent? How were we going to purchase food? What was going to happen to the children?

After the office closed down, it was very tough. My husband went back to work even though he still was in pain. His wrist had not healed completely. And to this day, he hurts because it was never healed properly.

We borrowed from other members of the family in order to continue living. Catholic Charities paid our rent one month. The food that we got from the union helped us to put some food on the table. It took us 1 year in order to be able to get on our feet economically once again.

I will never be able to forget the way they made us work, the promises they gave us that they never came through and all the pain and suffering that was brought about only because they did not want a union.

Thank you.

MR. OTERO: Thank you, Ms. Vogel.

Mr. Federico Anaya, president of the Law Firm of Anaya Valdepena, Management Attorneys and Consultants, who are also counsel to the Confederation of Chambers of Commerce and Industry of Mexico.

Mr. Anaya.

MR. ANAYA: (THROUGH TRANSLATOR)

Thank you very much. Good morning.

I would like to compliment Mrs. Vogel for her outstanding presentation. Certainly we are all fired up after listening to her so that we can look after and try to resolve these type of problems that affect humanity.

I would like to divide my talk in three parts. First of all, I would like to talk about some legal aspects. Number two, I want to talk about some commercial aspects and the third part will talk about the labor relations.

In the first place, I would like to tell you that the world is full of contracts. The contracts are accords and agreements of goodwill. Let's give an example. Let's say I come out of the university. I have just graduated as a lawyer and I don't have any clientele. I don't have any clients. I must have clients. In order to have the clients, I must be able to demonstrate that I am capable and I am professional. The title alone is not going to bring me clients.

We can also say that if I open up a business or a store the fact that I am just opened up for business is not going to bring clients to buy my wares and we can think the same about a union.

A union has to be formed because the laws of international says so. This is laws all over the world. But setting up a union per se does not mean that it is automatically a collective automatization and I am not trying to justify in any way the attitude of certain companies. I am not justifying it. But as I was saying, we need the goodwill of the person who is going to make a collective contract with workers. We cannot do anything against anybody's will.

It is so much so that at least in my country there is a very clear standard that determines the following. When a union tries to have a collective contract, they have to follow a certain procedure and this procedure is a document has to be written, officially sent to the National Board of Arbitration and the threat by the union is that they will shut down the company if this contract is not signed. What does the company do? What is the defense of the company?

The company either signs the contract or it doesn't want to sign the contract for other reasons and does not go before—what can happen is that they will have to pay off the workers. But if these workers are fired unduly, the law protects the workers that belong to a union and when there is a dismissal of such grand magnitude, the companies also have to pay indemnization, which means paying 3 months' salary if the conflict is not resolved.

Therefore, it is very clearly set forth that when the companies make use of their right not to have this collective contract they have to then pay damages and severance pay. In other words, they get penalized and they have to pay off all of the workers that are dismissed.

When a company is made up this company has a whole series of factors that are very specific to them and the company has to select vendors, personnel, the bank they are going to work with and also, why not say so, the company has the right to, let's say, lean toward certain factors that are going to make the company successful and to make things easier for the company. When there are great dark clouds in the sky, the company takes evasive action, just like a pilot does when he goes to a higher altitude or a lower altitude to avoid the bad weather that lies ahead. This, I think, occurs to everybody who is head of any company.

Now, regarding the third point that I mentioned, I would like to say to all of you that in my modest opinion nobody can discuss the fact that the workers don't have a right to unionize and nobody has to say anything against—nobody can say anything against that the companies can also do something to protect themselves. Nobody can do that. So the value of the union value is parallel to the company whether it's going to select or not select or sign or not sign a contract with this or that union, which maybe will bring on problems later on.

I would like to insist on the fact that at this forum we are not just addressing an individual case. We are talking about the prospects for understanding between unionized employees and a group of companies which also have the right to carry out their program and I say this because there are assembly lines, there are organized services, financial services, commercial services, there are systems such as these, so the workers have the need to continue their associations. They exist as a need to defend the needs of organized employees.

What are these interests or needs? There are basically two: just wages and also just and fair working conditions that have to do with benefits and hygiene conditions and so on.

The businessman invests capital for a profit and when the economic conditions are adverse, for example, the price of materials does not allow him to be competitive in the market or when banks withdraw financial support, fear regarding a new and unknown trade union, and this happens to everybody when we don't know what's happening, a trade union which is coming about of which you know only that it is being created, it is sending a red flag regarding a risk. You don't know what will happen with a nascent or new trade union. You don't know the intentions of this group. It's not the same thing with a trade union that has been in existence for a time and the businessman knows what this trade union does day by day.

So you have to see what's happening. There are trade unions that would increase the risk factor for companies. This is not a problem regarding the law but a problem regarding attitudes and as Warren Edmondson said when he addressed the forum, you cannot legislate attitude, you cannot legislate goodwill, the desire to understand each other. This comes out of the quality of human beings and the quality of trade unions and companies. When companies seek only profits and they forget, as I told a son of mine, the best thing you have in your company is your workers and you should deal with them as though they were your best customers. When you forget this, problems crop up.

This social phenomenon, the establishment of a new trade union, makes every businessman think whether it is not better not to deal with this trade union because he doesn't know whether this trade union will be something he cannot control. He ignores whether his authority will be undermined. There is this fear installed. You don't know whether there will be a lack of discipline, a lack of respect and whether down the road this will mean that the company will go bankrupt or that productivity will go down, that you don't work so hard because in any event the employee will feel exploited, whether the trade union would be an enemy of the company or whether the trade union leaders are going to ask for special perks and benefits.

That is why if the trade union is known, is a known quantity, if it is famous for being a professional and authentic, an objective and a modern trade union, these risk factors go down to the extent that the trade union has shown that it has goodwill, that it wants to get involved in the company's decision making, that it shows respect for management, that it promotes order and hygiene and good working conditions, and that it has concerns in terms of reducing waste for the company, that it wants to participate to increase productivity through training of workers, that it seeks friendly resolution of conflict without resorting to strikes, that it wants to improve the environment, the overall working environment, in the company and that it wants to bring up ideas that may lead to higher competitiveness for the company and increase profits which may be distributed among workers.

This is a good-quality merchandise which you always buy. When companies and trade unions change their positions radically and get, closer collective bargaining will always be an instrument of goodwill and peace and you will have balance and justice in labor relations.

MR. OTERO: Thank you.

The chair wishes to correct the record. I failed upon introducing Mr. Anaya to underscore that he represents part of the tripartite delegation from Mexico, representing the employers' side.

At this juncture in the proceedings, I think it is fair that the chair express deep appreciation to all the presenters for the extraordinary discipline that you have shown in observing my admonition. Some of you have not used the 10 minutes that is allocated to you and in balance, we are doing very well on time. I want to thank you very much for this. We have also had a presenter that did not appear this morning, so we are doing well time-wise, but I want to signify my appreciation for your discipline and for your cooperation with the chair in ensuring the orderly process of these proceedings.

I would like to ask also if Mr. John Zucker from Congressman Tom Lantos' office is in the audience. If he is, please stand up. Okay. Thank you very much. I don't see Mr. Zucker.

Now, I will like to call to the podium the next presenter, Maria Blanco, Associate Director of the Women's Employment Rights Clinic at Golden Gate University School of Law.

Ms. Blanco.

MS. BLANCO: Thank you.

MR. OTERO: Thank you. Good morning.

MS. BLANCO: Good morning. Good morning. My name is Maria Blanco and, as indicated, I am an associate professor of law at Golden Gate University School of Law here in San Francisco, a couple of blocks over.

Together with the director of the clinic, Marcy Seville, who is also here, and our clinic students, our clinic represents currently over 60 La Conexion Familiar employees who were denied California unemployment benefits after they were fired from La Conexion Familiar. Our lawsuit is a challenge to the California Unemployment Insurance Appeals Board decision that workers who had received offset payments, in other words, payments because Sprint closed its plant in violation of the notification law, the Board decided that they could not simultaneously receive unemployment benefits.

I am very honored to be here at this forum which is really historic and one of a kind and I think that given the globalization of labor and capital that others have talked about today it's no coincidence that the first case of this kind brought in the United States under the labor agreement is one in California involving Latino workers.

It brings together many of the elements that many of us working in the labor movement and unemployment issues and immigrant worker issues in California have been seeing develop over the years.

The purpose of my testimony here today is to describe how the sector of the United States workforce represented by the more than 200 employees fired from La

Conexion Familiar is often unable to enjoy or assert the labor rights they are entitled to theoretically under state and federal labor laws. When I say this sector of the workforce, I am referring to fairly recent immigrant workers who are at the bottom of the economic ladder here in California and other parts of the country.

As you will hear today and have already heard, the workers at La Conexion Familiar were primarily Latinas, non-English speaking and, for the most part, unskilled. For many, this was their first full-time permanent job. Many of us in San Francisco thought a company like La Conexion Familiar represented the welcome possibility that the very consumers targeted by companies attempting to capture the Spanish-speaking market might also result in good jobs for those consumers. This would have been a welcome change from the concentration of immigrant workers in low-paying, dead-end jobs which in spite of the anti-immigrant clamor heard in many quarters these days few other workers are willing to perform.

Initially, the employees, and you will probably hear this today, of La Conexion Familiar felt fortunate beyond all their dreams when they got their jobs. With Sprint, they thought they had the unique opportunity to work at above the minimum wage and to be employed at jobs where their native language was an asset and not a drawback.

Yet the job also had problems. Very big problems. The hours, the speed-up, as Ms. Vogel testified today, the lack of breaks. Non-payment of wages. Non-payment of commissions. So the workers who felt so fortunate to have this job had the courage, or some would say the nerve, to assert their right to decent working conditions through seeking to join a union, their right under United States labor laws.

Unfortunately, as highlighted by the complaint filed by Mexico, United States labor relations law has failed them and for these highly vulnerable workers, the failure has occurred on several fronts, not just the National Labor Relations Act that we have heard about today.

For example, and I'll start with the National Labor Relations Act. You will hear substantial testimony today about the circumstances surrounding Sprint's closure, how the company sales were growing, how employees told that the workforce was going to grow. That is until over 50 percent of the workers indicated their support for representation by the Communications Workers of America.

Despite the decision by the National Labor Relations Board judge that Sprint's transfer was purely economic, the workers, the Union, many experts and non-experts and many people here today who followed this case very closely are convinced and know that the company's move was nothing but good old-time illegal union busting.

To the workers of La Conexion Familiar, the protections of Section 8 and Section 8(a)(3) of the National Labor Relations Act proved meaningless. And the fact remains that La Conexion Familiar ex-employees will never see a remedy for Sprint's illegal actions and this forum is not a remedy. We are glad we are here, but it is not.

Even if back pay were ever awarded, this would not compensate for the lost jobs, for the havoc created for the workers who faced this job loss, and for their then having to be thrust in a labor market where they face the triple barrier of being unskilled immigrant women of color with very few chances of employment in a city like San Francisco.

Violation of federal plant closure laws. La Conexion Familiar employees were also treated to a clear violation of federal law that required Sprint to give 60 days' notice to its employees before plant closure. This protection is set forth in the Worker Adjustment Retraining and Notification Act, known as WARN by many of us, which was passed in Congress in 1989. Thus, Sprint compounded its unfair labor practice with a violation of the WARN Act. The purpose of this long-fought-for provision is to give employees time to retrain, adjust, and seek work when informed that their place of employment is about to close. No workers have ever needed notice to retrain and prepare more than those of La Conexion Familiar.

Often knowing minimal English and with few economic resources, the sudden closure threw their lives and that of their families into complete turmoil. I know you are going to hear more about that this afternoon.

Denial of California unemployment benefits, perhaps the part of this that I am the most familiar with. The process of applying and obtaining unemployment benefits should have been relatively simple for the ex-employees of La Conexion Familiar. Instead, their attempt to obtain this basic safety net turned out to be a nightmare. As a result of the California Department of Unemployment's decision that any penalties paid by Sprint for its violation of the WARN Act made the workers ineligible for unemployment benefits, the fired workers went months without unemployment. Even more incredible, the fired employees had penalties imposed upon them by the Unemployment Insurance Department that accused them of lying on their application when they stated that the plant closure fines they received were not wages. Thus the fired employees face two sets of unemployment hearings: one to determine their eligibility to benefits and another to prove that they had not made false statements and not be assessed penalties.

Failure to receive wages under California wage and hour laws. Among the working conditions at Sprint La Conexion Familiar which fueled the unionization drive was the employer's failure to consistently pay overtime penalties and commissions, as required by California law and regulations. To resolve this breach in the law, the workers turned to traditional federal labor law remedies, the National Labor Relations Act and the Section 7 right to join unions and pursue collective bargaining.

When the plant closure effectively eliminated that avenue of resolution for the wage claims, the employees were left to individually file wage claims. Next month, more than a year and a half after La Conexion Familiar closed, many of the claims for unpaid wages will finally go to a hearing before California's labor commissioner. With no union to help them, the ex-employees, many of them non-English speaking and from countries with no comparable laws, face this complex wage claim process alone. Fortunately, here in San Francisco La Rasa Central Legal has stepped forward to help with the wage claim and is representing many of the workers.

Thus, 2 years after Sprint's sudden closure of La Conexion Familiar in order to avoid collective bargaining, the majority of the workers are still unemployed, still engaged in complex legal proceedings to recover partial unemployment benefits, still trying to recover unpaid wages which Sprint owes them, and the NLRA case is winding its way through the legal process.

It should come as no surprise, then, that in the eyes of many of La Conexion Familiar workers the United States system of labor laws has not worked. Wage laws, unemployment laws, labor relations law, plant closure notification laws, all failed in this case example. It is not an exaggeration to say that many believe that their attempt at unionization and collective bargaining fared no better here in the United States' system of labor relations than in other countries where labor rights are considered to be notably less than in the United States.

For now, they are left with serious doubts about the true right to freely associate and it may be a long time before they recover their faith in our legal system.

Thank you.

MR. OTERO: Ms. Blanco, before you depart, first of all, would it be possible for us to have a copy of your statement?

MS. BLANCO: Yes. I brought some copies.

MR. OTERO: And, secondly, I did not quite follow the sequence of your presentation. I was distracted, so I apologize.

MS. BLANCO: Perhaps it was me.

MR. OTERO: From the sequence of the WARN Act and the role of the California state unemployment insurance, would you please repeat that for the record, please?

MS. BLANCO: Sure. Do you want me to explain or to read it?

When Sprint closed without giving the 60 days' notice required under the law, what it did was it gave the employees what are called offset payments. What an employee is allowed to do when a plant closes without notice is take the employer to court. That's the remedy. You take the employer to court for violation of the notice requirement and then you can get 60 days' salary because you didn't have the advance notice.

Some employers rather than go to court anticipate that they're going to lose in court and they offset that and they give it to the fired employees at the time that they fire them.

The employees in this case received those offset payments and as a result when they applied for unemployment benefits and they filled out the section that says have you received any wages they said no because these are not wages. This is a penalty which actually you have to normally go to court to obtain. And the unemployment appeals board in California has decided that they are wages and we are currently appealing that decision and arguing that those payments are really a fine meant to enforce the plant closure law and they should not be considered wages.

MR. OTERO: The California state board has interpreted that that 60-day payment was wages.

MS. BLANCO: Exactly.

MR. OTERO: I see. Okay. That's the portion that I had not quite understood before.

MS. BLANCO: Okay. Thank you.

MR. OTERO: Thank you very much, Ms. Blanco.

The chair now calls to the podium Ms. Liliette Jiron, a former employee of La Conexion Familiar.

Ms. Jiron?

MS. JIRON: Good morning.

MR. OTERO: Good morning.

MS. JIRON: Hello. My name is Liliette Jiron.

MR. OTERO: Do you want a glass of water?

MS. JIRON: A tissue would do.

MR. OTERO: A tissue? I don't have a tissue.

(Pause)

MS. JIRON: Thank you.

My introduction to Sprint's anti-union tactics of threats and intimidation began on my job interview. I applied for a telemarketer position at Sprint La Conexion Familiar in the spring of 1994. During my interview, I was told the Union was trying to organize at LCF but the troublemakers would get fired eventually. I was told I should have no part of them. I was told that some people who worked at LCF were ungrateful. My interviewer said that these people don't deserve a job this good because they don't speak any English. He continued to say they should be happy to have this job.

Although the tension in the workplace frightened me, I desperately needed the job so when it was offered I said yes.

I had been out of work for 6 months. My fiancé was our sole supporter. Our bills were piling up and we were unable to pay rent —

MR. OTERO: Take your time, Ms. Jiron. Take your time to compose yourself. There is no hurry.

MS. JIRON: We were unable to pay rent on our apartment. We had to move with my two children into a studio apartment. This job was an opportunity to make some money to help pay the rent, buy food, diapers, and clothing for my children.

Within 3 weeks of arriving at LCF, I was asked to spy on my co-workers. As I was on probation for my first 90 days, I felt I had no choice but to do as asked. I couldn't lose this job. My supervisor asked me to search through my co-workers drawers after hours to see if anyone in my group was hiding union materials in their desks. I was also asked to talk with my co-workers and find out who was the leader of union supporters in my group.

During break, my supervisor would ask me what I had learned about my co-workers' involvement with CWA. I was hired along with four other women. Two of them signed their names to the union petition. My group supervisor told me to talk with them and try to get them to take their names off the petition. I was told they would find a reason to fire any new person who signed the petition. They said it would be easy as we were still on probation. There was a constant fear that we would be fired if we supported the Union.

About 10 days after I started working at Sprint, they fired someone at her work-station right in front of everyone. They told her to get her things and get out. I don't know why she was fired but I felt even more threatened. I couldn't believe that they would fire someone like that in front of everyone. It made me want to stay away from the union supporters.

But I understood why my co-workers wanted to form a union. We had problems getting paid. Also we had a commission program. I never received a commission check. They kept changing the rules on the number of sales we needed. Every super-visor had a different quota. At one group meeting I asked about the commission pro-gram. I was yelled at and made to feel stupid for asking the question.

We were not allowed to go to the bathroom until our break time. Also, we were on the phone all day and our throats got dry and sore. They told us not to drink a lot of water so we wouldn't need the bathroom breaks.

On payday, we had to wait until our supervisor wanted to give us the paychecks. She said she didn't want to give them to us at lunchtime because we would go to the bank and take longer lunch. We were under such tight control all the time. They just didn't respect us.

One day when they were remodeling the floor above us, horrible fumes came through the vents. People were coughing. I got a rash on my arms, but they wouldn't let us leave. Finally, after 2 hours we were told we could go home.

We all knew we needed a union but the frightened and intimidated many of us. We were too afraid to say it publicly. They kept telling us if we voted for the Union, the office would close down and their threats to close the office came true.

A week before our chance to vote in the union election we were called in the conference room. It was just before lunch. They locked all the doors. There were security guards at each exit. They told us LCF was closing that day. They said we had until 4 p.m. to clear our stuff. As we left, we were each personally searched and they went through our belongings.

For me, everything fell apart that day. I couldn't face being out of work. I started abusing alcohol. I was so depressed. I fought with my fiancé and I yelled at my children. It was hard for me to get out of bed. I didn't want to do anything. I felt so helpless.

Financially, we were having a hard time. I was too depressed to look for work and the bills were piling up. I was unable to pay for my car insurance, so it was eventually canceled but I still had to drive so I did and I got caught. I had to spend 5 hours in jail for driving without insurance and a license.

It took me a year to finally make sense of everything and to start to get myself together. I thank my fiancé for seeing me through this. I got another job through the unemployment with an Internet provider. Next month I celebrate my year anniversary at this job.

After a very tough year, I am happy. My fiancé and I are still saving money hoping to buy a home.

But my experience at Sprint changed everything for me. I will always carry around the fear of being fired and I will remember the threats to close if we voted for the Union. And I will remember the day that they did what they said. And to think all we wanted was a union.

Thank you.

MR. OTERO: Thank you, Ms. Jiron.

We had two no-shows this morning which added to the cooperation of all the presenters have made the morning session go faster than we had anticipated.

I wonder if I could perhaps call someone who is scheduled to be here this afternoon, have one more speaker, and then we will recess until the afternoon session to allow the interpreters an opportunity to have a longer rest. They have been doing an excellent job and we have not given them the opportunity to rest.

So I wonder if Mr. Sergio Tapia is in the audience and I wonder if he would mind speaking now rather than later. Is that okay?

Let me introduce formally Mr. Sergio Tapia, who is with the Consultants Associates in Monterrey, Mexico. Mr. Tapia is a management consultant and we invite him to come to the podium.

MR. TAPIA: (THROUGH TRANSLATOR) Thank you very much, Mr. Otero. I thank you for this opportunity to speak to you.

Actually, I had brought with me the paper I wanted to submit to this forum this afternoon. However, I believe it's not worthwhile. I think that I will present in a somewhat different format and I am modifying it or I am adapting it to what I have heard so far.

With due respect, I think it sounds like an encounter between the good guys and the bad guys. Naturally, the presentation of working conditions in such a dramatic manner under which—or the dramatic way in which the workers have presented how they were working at Sprint make us believe that they are the good ones and also the presentation or the introduction that was given to this forum recognizing, of course, the sacred right to unionization of workers not only in this country but in the three countries represented here and also in most parts of the world and, of course, that leads us to admit it is a real situation. The press, the media, are present and this also gives recognition to the good guys, only the poor management I think in this case is very poorly represented. The manager of the company, I think, was under shock and did not want to attend. The attorney who submitted the case and who explained the legal resolutions already left—I can see that he already returned but, I mean, he only received applause by three people, I counted them very discretely.

Mr. Anaya, who represents an important section of the Mexican management, also received only very little recognition on behalf of the forum but, of course, I believe this is rather natural considering this intense participation and attendance on behalf of representatives of the workers.

Considering all these circumstances, I can only adhere to the good guys and recognize, of course, the sacred right of workers to form a union. I don't think that any rational person in this day and age denies that. Of course I recognize the success Mr. Hernandez Juarez has had in directing his trade union and the success he has had achieved for his union. It is very impressive what successes have been achieved also on behalf of other union leaders throughout the world. This dramatic representation of the Sprint case really motivates us, really fills us with emotion, feelings of empathy towards workers. I can think of other dramatic and emotional cases that have been shown on the big screen. For example, the case of Norma Rae, there's a great movie by Dépardieu called *Termination* about the workers in Europe and simply the kind of epilogue I would like to talk about in the last part of my presentation.

I want to make the following reflection. Social justice traditionally tends to create a balance between opposed rights or opposing rights. Also traditionally workers' rights have been considered weaker or more vulnerable than the rights of its counterpart or the complement which is the employer, the management. However, in recent years, this situation has tended to revert and has created situations in which workers' rights exceed sometimes those of the management, recognizing that these circumstances, of course, vary from one region to the other or from one industrial sector to the other. For example, we could say that labor rights of the agricultural worker in California are weaker than those of the steelworker in Pittsburgh or that the labor rights of the workers, for example, in the state Chiapas are weaker than those of the workers in general in the State of California.

Therefore, we need to be very cautious in studying case by case and not making generalizations and saying that the workers' rights are in general more vulnerable or weaker.

I believe that workers have the right to unionize if they so wish, but I also defend the right of the employer to close a plant if it's not cost-efficient or if it's strategically convenient for his business. I also believe that this forum in a certain way cannot really resolve the controversy that is being presented here. It is a controversy that the United States through its legitimately represented agencies and through its laws that have also been approved in this country have resolved.

Unfortunately in this case, for the employer—of course I believe that the workers have the right to unionize, that is something that the forum needs to recognize, but also the forum needs to recognize that the employer has the right to create successful businesses.

I believe that by recognizing these rights this forum will have fulfilled its commitment with specific cases with such as Sprint's case in this country or Sony which will soon be admitted to Mr. Otero and maybe some other people of this forum in Monterrey, my hometown, will be resolved according to the laws of each country and according to the circumstances of each specific case.

Thank you very much and I know that I will not get a lot of applause.

MR. OTERO: Thank you, Mr. Tapia.

Your presentation gives the chair the opportunity to wrap up this morning's session by underscoring two or three points that I think are germane.

The intent of this forum was never to put in question the process of law that has been pursued through the National Labor Relations Board. That is a process that speaks for itself. A decision was made by the judge. The Union is appealing. The general counsel of the National Labor Relations Board is appealing that process. It's there on its own.

The reason we are here today is because we have a duty under the North American Agreement on Labor Cooperation to examine the question of labor law and its application in the three NAFTA countries. Mexico, the United States, and Canada pay the greatest of importance to the principle of freedom of association and the right to strike and we want to underscore by this forum and by a number of other activities how sacred we, the three countries, the three governments, believe that such freedom is.

We had hoped through this forum, and we still have this afternoon plus a number of other activities, to try to examine in more detail and an in-depth analysis of the impact that the sudden closure of plants and factories have on that very principle of freedom of association.

Naturally the forum is generated as a result of the case that was filed with the Mexico NAO pursuant to the Sprint case and that's what gave rise to this forum, but we hope that in the process of this discussion, as well as in the study that we have commissioned through the Labor Secretariat in Dallas that we will be able to examine cases other than just the case of Sprint, other instances in the United States, in Mexico, and in Canada where similar sudden closures may have an impact on that very basic freedom which is embodied in Convention 98 of the ILO.

And so it is in that context that we hope that these discussions as well as the study of the Labor Secretariat will enable us to examine in more detail what impact the incidents have on that freedom of association, which is one of the main components of our labor agreement on cooperation between the three countries.

So I thank you, Mr. Tapia, for giving me the opportunity to make this clarification just before we break for lunch.

Let me suggest that we will have a little longer period of recess than we had anticipated. We will not come back here until 2:00 this afternoon, but I will ask you if you will kindly be here before 2:00 so that we can proceed on time precisely at 2:00.

This forum is now recessed for lunch. Thank you very much.

(Whereupon, the forum was recessed, to be reconvened this same day, Tuesday, February 27, 1996, at 2:00 p.m.)

AFTERNOON SESSION

2:00 p.m.

MR. OTERO: Good afternoon, ladies and gentlemen.

Muy buenos tardes a todos, señoras y señores.

I ask that you take your seats, as we are about to begin the second session of this public forum today.

I would like to announce that in view of the fact that we have received word that some of the registered speakers are unable to come to present the testimony, we are going to have a little more time this afternoon than I had anticipated and I also have a special request from the interpreters.

This morning, some of the speakers because of the pressure of having to give their speech in 10 minutes, they spoke too rapidly, thereby making it difficult for the interpreters to properly translate and enunciate every word.

So this afternoon, I am taking the liberty as chair to expand the period of each speaker from 10 to 12 minutes, given the fact that we have some vacancies in the speaker slots.

But I will ask the speakers if you already have a 10-minute speech, try to give it in 12 minutes, all right? Let us not be running far afield, but you can speak slower so that you can allow the interpreters to do their job very well.

And I would like to say parenthetically that I have been listening to the speakers from time to time and the interpreters are doing an excellent job of accurately and properly doing both English to Spanish.

(Applause.)

Very well. The program this afternoon calls for the first speaker to be the Honorable Mayor of the City of San Francisco, Mr. Willie Brown, but we have not heard whether he is on his way or not, so we are not going to prolong the meeting any longer.

We do know, however, that Congressman Tom Lantos, who is from this district is unable to be here, but we are very fortunate that Mr. Lantos has asked one of his key collaborators in the Congress, Mr. John Zucker, who is a member of his staff, he is a legislative assistant, and he is here with us to deliver a presentation on behalf of Congressman Lantos.

So I would like to ask Mr. Zucker to come forward to the podium.

Please proceed.

MR. ZUCKER: Thank you, Mr. Otero.

Thank you to the Bureau of International Labor Affairs. And I have timed this speech, it's only about 8 minutes.

My name is John Zucker. I am a legislative aide to Congressman Tom Lantos in his Washington office.

Congressman Lantos wishes to express his profound gratitude for being invited to participate in this important public forum and his sincerest regrets at not being able to attend. As you may know, the Congress is now back in session and several important votes were scheduled for today. He was therefore compelled to return to Washington. Nevertheless, he feels very strongly about the purpose and importance of this forum, and so he asked me to deliver his address to you exactly as he wrote it, so I will begin.

STATEMENT OF CONGRESSMAN TOM LANTOS: I would first like to commend you for holding this hearing which is the first of its kind under the terms of the NAFTA agreement on a case involving violations of workers' rights in the United States.

As you know, I was strongly opposed to NAFTA, but it is now the law of the land and we must live by its provisions. I will be the first one to make sure that the spirit and intent of the principles contained in NAFTA's side agreement on labor cooperation are given maximum attention in the enforcement of NAFTA's provisions.

The North American Agreement on Labor Cooperation states plainly that every effort will be made to guarantee to all workers the right of freedom of association and the right to union representation. The Sprint workers who are the subject of today's hearing were clearly denied these rights.

Sprint's shutdown of La Conexion Familiar demonstrated that reality falls well short of the goals of the NAFTA agreement on labor cooperation. This is the case of a company which willfully violated our labor law and which was cited with more than 50 violations. It is also a case of human pain and suffering.

As you know, on July 14, 1994, 235 individuals were thrown out of work by Sprint. Many of these workers live in my congressional district. Today we heard and will hear from several of these workers who have told us in their own words the turmoil they have had to endure. I have heard their pain from the beginning of this tragic situation and I have observed firsthand the wrenching consequences of Sprint's behavior on these workers' lives.

In a split second, these workers were unemployed. Their families were in disarray and the promise of the American dream was destroyed.

"How could this happen?" they asked, "After all, this is America where laws as supposed to mean what they say and are supposed to be enforced to the letter."

When Sprint abruptly shut its La Conexion Familiar facility 1 week before an organizing election, we had a classic case of U.S. labor law not adequately protecting American workers. Two hundred thirty-five workers lost their jobs, victims of an illegal campaign against workers' rights.

More than a year and a half after losing their jobs, the workers at La Conexion Familiar are still struggling and awaiting justice. Out of the 177 workers who were scheduled to vote in the union election, fewer than half are working. The rest are still out of work.

The National Labor Relations Board moved as quickly as current law permitted, but in spite of their efforts it took over 4 months until the case was heard and well over a year until a decision was issued and the process is far from over. As of today, this case is 593 days old and it will take many more months before the Board issues a final decision, even as they expedite the case.

It will take years before all parties exhaust available appeals. In the meantime, the workers are the ones paying the price for the inability of our system to provide prompt and effective remedies for this obvious and egregious violation of the law.

The Sprint case is not atypical. The latest data available from the NLRB show that by the end of 1994 the median number of days it took for an unfair labor practice case to reach a decision by an Administrative Law Judge was 360 days and the median number of days to reach a Board decision was 601 days. What this means is that half of all these cases took even longer.

The average age of cases pending before the Board as of September 30, 1994 was 758 days. After that, years of appeals through the courts and we have to recognize that our current system of labor law is in fact an easy and inexpensive tool for companies to use to break the law rather than abide by it.

It is simply unjust for workers who have lost their jobs as a result of unfair labor practices by their employers to have to wait so long for a remedy. Our labor laws and their enforcement mechanisms must be strengthened.

Under these circumstances, I admire the courage of the workers at La Conexion Familiar. They stepped up to the plate and took a swing at their rights. They did not know that the game was rigged against them and that Sprint was throwing a spitball.

What would you do if you were a worker in a plant or a facility such as La Conexion Familiar and you were told by your supervisor or your manager, look, don't even try to organize because we'll shut the plant down and it will take you 4 to 5 years to prove that the company did anything wrong? In the meantime, you'll be out of work.

Under these circumstances, would anyone try to organize? There's no question that the average worker would say no.

This is what's so admirable about the Sprint workers at La Conexion Familiar. In spite of all the threats, the coercion, and the spying, they still tried. They demonstrated that the importance of organizing a union is not from a bygone era but that organizing a union is more relevant than ever.

It is our system of labor law and its enforcement which must be brought into the 21st century. This is why I am testifying today in support of Sprint workers and all workers who want to organize. I will continue to do everything I can to seek a remedy in this case and will continue to push for labor law reform which provides prompt and effective penalties against labor law violators.

Workers must feel secure in their belief that they can exercise their right to organize without fear of retaliation by their employer and without running the risk of losing their job.

One reason I opposed the NAFTA agreement was that it perpetuated the ineffectiveness of U.S. law in protecting workers' rights. In the case of the right to organize, the NAFTA agreement provides only a mechanism for exposing violations of these rights and this forum is part of that mechanism.

It is important for workers to demonstrate the widespread abuse of workers' rights, but it's clearly not enough. The objectives of the NAFTA side agreement on labor cooperation are admirable, but the law itself should contain penalties against the companies who benefit from expanded trade opportunities but at the same time violate their workers' rights, whether in Mexico, Canada, or the United States.

I will fight hard to ensure that the NAFTA agreement is amended to include real penalties and appropriate enforcement provisions.

I support calls for an international code of conduct for all companies operating on a global scale. This code will ensure that workers' rights which we in the United States are at least committed to on paper and which are contained in the NAFTA side agreement on labor cooperation will become part and parcel of acceptable behavior in international commerce.

The promise of international investment and trade must go hand in hand with the promise of improved working conditions and living standards for workers both in the United States and abroad. By recognizing and protecting the rights of workers to form unions and engage in collective bargaining, we are not giving workers entitlements or handouts. We are giving them the tools to stand up for themselves and claim their fair share of economic progress that they had a hand in producing.

Thank you.

MR. OTERO: Thank you, Mr. Zucker, speaking on behalf of Congressman Tom Lantos.

Next on the list is Fernanda Recio, a former employee of La Conexion Familiar. We ask Ms. Recio to come forward.

MS. RECIO: Hello, everybody.

This is a very special day for those of us who used to work in Sprint La Conexion Familiar. We thank our union brothers and sisters in Mexico for caring enough about us to file a NAFTA complaint and today provide us with a unique opportunity to tell our story and give us hope that other workers won't lose their job in the future simply because they want a union.

This experience has provided me with both joy and sorrow. One positive result was an invitation I received from the telephone workers union in British Columbia to visit them and tell the La Conexion story. They were so outraged by Sprint's behavior they demonstrated outside a performance by Sprint spokeswoman Candace Bergen. It was a wonderful experience to meet with my Canadian union members who cared about our plight.

I continue to be amazed at the support this case has generated round the world. Although we were devastated by the closing, it is heartwarming to know others care.

When I began working in Sprint La Conexion Familiar in August of 1993, I had high hopes. I thought if I worked hard there would be opportunities for me to move ahead. But soon after my arrival at Sprint, I realized Sprint's public image is very different from its behavior as an employer.

From the start, I had problems getting paid my commissions. I was in sales and my motivation to sell was based on extra money I got for each sale. Every time I asked my supervisor to explain the payment procedure, I got the run around.

When I asked why I wasn't getting paid for sales I knew I had made, I was told I had to wait for the computer report. Then the report would be delayed. When it came, I was told it was wrong. I spent a lot of time meeting with my supervisor and the manager and got nowhere.

I felt I had to hire a lawyer. When I told my supervisor I was being represented by an attorney, suddenly he was able to give me a commission check. But it wasn't for the full amount due me. The check simply stated "commissions due." There was no breakdown of how many sales, when the sales were made, or anything. It was impossible to get an accounting from Sprint.

I kept a daily list of what I sold, so I had the records, even if Sprint didn't, and the check never matched my records. I still haven't cleared up the commission problem and I am working with a lawyer to get paid what Sprint owes me.

The difficulty in getting our commission was the main reason many of us were interested in forming a union. Everyone was having the same problem. We felt they weren't being fair to us and we weren't getting paid want we were owed. This was very frustrating.

There was a total lack of respect for us by management. The supervisors often yelled at us. They thought that we were children.

We had to sign a piece of paper to go to the bathroom. The paper lists the time that we left and the time we returned. We had to give this report to our supervisor each time we went to the bathroom.

We also were frustrated with the small cafeteria. There weren't enough chairs for us to sit and eat our lunches. We weren't allowed to eat at our desks. And there was only one microwave. We had 30 minutes for lunch and 30 people had to use the microwave in half an hour. We'd spend much of our lunchtime in line waiting to heat our food.

In October, I was promoted to an In Charge Supervisor. I was doing very well as a supervisor and still one of the top sales people. But, at the end of January 1994, I went with a few of my co-workers to a meeting with an organizer from the Communications Workers of America. When I returned to the office, my co-workers asked me where I had been and I told them about the meeting with CWA.

My supervisor heard me talking and started asking me all kinds of questions. He told me I shouldn't be talking with others about the union. I didn't know I needed to be secretive about wanting to form a union. In Chile, where I am from, being for the union is a good thing.

Many of us felt the union was our only hope.

On June 1st, we wore this T-shirt to show our support for the union. This is the only we thought we could make the things better.

We wanted to be treated fairly and with respect. We felt we didn't have anything to lose to join CWA, but we were wrong.

My supervisor asked me all the time about my connection with the union. My co-workers were told not to talk to me. If they did talk with me during a break, they were immediately asked what we were talking about, were we discussing the union?

For me, once they knew I supported the union, the rules changed. I was told to take a vacation day if I got sick. When I was too late to work, instead of getting a verbal warning like everybody else, I received a written warning in my file.

They couldn't bother me about my sales because they were so high, but they did other things to harass and intimidate me. One day there weren't any seats left in the cafeteria so I brought my soup to my desk. There wasn't anyone working in the area at the time. The supervisor came and told me I couldn't eat at the desk. He told me to go and eat in the bathroom. I couldn't do that. I threw away my soup.

After a few months of this pressure every day, I started getting palpitations. I went to the doctor, who gave me a monitor to wear to test my heart. A co-worker asked me about the monitor and how I was feeling. I said not too good. My supervisor came over and gave me a warning for talking.

I got so nervous. I couldn't talk to anyone and my co-workers were afraid to talk to me.

When I went to the bathroom, my supervisor would log out my computer so that when I returned I had to log back on. This took time to do which affected my productivity which affected my wages and commissions. No one else had to do this.

We heard over and over that if we voted for the union the office would shut down. We knew that this was against the law, that they couldn't shut us down, but they still told us all the time. Some employees did believe our supervisors and were afraid to support the union.

By April 1995, I couldn't take the pressure any more and my doctor advised me not to return to work and get in treatment for my stress. By the time I felt ready to try to return to work, Sprint had closed the facility.

I talked with my supervisor a year after the closing and I asked him, "Why did you treat me like that? I thought that you liked me."

And he said, "Fernanda, I had to follow instructions. I didn't have a choice."

My experience at Sprint has taught me many things. I am still a strong union supporter. I believe we would have been able to make things better at La Conexion Familiar if we formed a union. But I also learned that Sprint is a company that is willing to do anything to keep the union out and that frightens all of us.

Thank you very much.

MR. OTERO: Thank you, Ms. Recio.

The next presenter is Veronika Altmeyer, Managing Executive, from the German Post and Telephone Workers Union of Germany.

Ms. Altmeyer, welcome.

MS. ALTMEYER: Thank you.

(THROUGH INTERPRETER) Ladies and gentlemen, as a representative of the largest union in the postal and telecommunications industry in Germany with more than 530,000 members in Germany, I would like to thank you very much. I would like to thank the United States Department of labor and the representatives of Canada and Mexico for giving me the opportunity to express my union's point of view in front of this very important panel.

Through our international cooperation with the CWA, the union of communications workers in the U.S., we learned from Mr. Bahr in June 1994 about the case La Conexion Familiar and it was the first time we heard about Sprint Corporation violating labor laws and the right to organize.

In meetings of our international union organization, PTTI, on multi-national telecommunication companies, all member unions of this organization agreed to coordinate their activities with these multi-national companies. Since at that time it was already known that the German telephone company Deutsche Telecom AG and its French counterpart, France Télécom, intended to form a joint venture with Sprint Corporation, we, the CWA and DPG, decided to have the unions cooperate very closely.

After hearing about the complaints against Sprint Corporation, we acted in two ways. First, we wrote letters in July of '94, in August of '94, and in September of '94 and in February '95, we wrote letters to the chairman and chief executive officer of Sprint Corporation, Mr. Esrey, asking him to respect the right to organize in his company.

In addition, we also pointed out that Sprint's management guide contained a declared company object to keep Sprint union-free. We criticized this company policy and asked Mr. Esrey to guarantee the right of free choice of union representation and also to stop the threat to workers on the grounds of their union activities. To date, we have not received a satisfactory answer to these charges and indications.

Secondly, we informed that Mr. Esrey that the Supervisory Board of the Deutsche Telekom AG had decided in December of 1994 upon a code of conduct for the participation of the Deutsche Telekom AG in global telecommunications ventures. The then chairman of the board of the Telekom AG, Mr. Helmut Ricke, stated in an article of the employees' newsletter of the Deutsche Telekom that, and this is a quote, "Union rights will be respected. A common philosophy appears to be indispensable within the joint venture."

In view of the planned cooperation between the Telekom and Sprint, we asked Mr. Esrey to participate in joint talks with CWA and us. Unfortunately to date, these have not taken place.

We informed the board of Sprint Corporation that as a union of the telecommunications workers in Germany we had developed and established a high level of participation in German companies and that our working relationship was based on mutual recognition and respect.

As already mentioned, the board of directors and the supervisory board of the Deutsche Telekom, including the owners' representatives and the representatives of the Deutsche Postgewerkschaft, who are equally entitled members of the supervisory board, have set the code of conduct of the Deutsche Telekom AG in global telecommunications ventures.

These state as follows: "In all global ventures in the telecommunications industry, the Deutsche Telekom AG declares its support of its company principles. These company principles are announced to the partners in global ventures.

"These principles specifically the Deutsche Telekom AG's responsibility in society and responsibility towards its employees.

"The Deutsche Telekom AG recognizes the elected body representing interests of the employees, including unions, in any global venture.

"The Deutsche Telekom AG acts so that the company principles are taken up by the partners in the global ventures and are applied accordingly. This also means that the relations that are customary in Germany between employers and employees in all business areas and organizational departments in which the Deutsche Telekom AG works with global partners and their subsidiaries in Germany, are recognized and respected."

The company principles of the Deutsche Telekom AG further states as follows in one paragraph: "All employees contribute to the success of the company. We are willing to perform and take on our responsibility. A special feature of good cooperation is mutual give and take. The work has to be fairly compensated according to performance. In its decision-making process our company takes into consideration the effects on its employees. We cooperate with the elected representatives on a basis of trust."

Ladies and gentlemen, you probably all know that in the meantime the venture between Sprint Corporation, France Télécom, and Deutsche Telekom AG has been stipulated in a legally binding agreement and has been approved by the supervisory authorities of the United States and the European Union. In principle, we welcome this international cooperation. But on the other hand, we demand the acceptance of employee rights.

This venture between these companies means that more than previously in the telecommunications field the principle of freedom of association laid down in the Constitution of the International Labor Organization (ILO), and the Agreements 87 and 98 of the International Labor Organization have to be respected, even if these agreements have not yet been ratified by all member states of the International Labor Organization. The member states worldwide do support the control mechanisms of this special UN organization, especially regarding the principle of freedom of association.

Thanks in no small part to the United States of America, social criteria, and also the rights to freedom of union association, are still on the agenda of the World Trade

Organization (WTO). The European Parliament as well as the competent bodies of the European Union support taking the International Labor Organization's standards more into consideration in developing foreign trade policy.

I am pleased to say that there is a worldwide international trend which sees the freedom of association of employees as an integral part of social standards. Not least the World Bank has pointed out in reports that in many countries union activities have contributed to the establishment of free and democratic structures.

My union together with PTTI intends to make the "threefold declaration of principles on multinational companies and social policy" of the International Labor Organization an issue in the agreements between multinational telecommunications companies and their respective unions.

Subparagraph 41 of this threefold declaration states under the heading "Freedom of Association and Right to Form Associations" among other things: "The employees of multinational and national companies should have the right indiscriminately without prior authorization to form an organization of their choice and to join such organizations, the only condition being the respect of its bylaws. Furthermore, the employees should be protected from all discriminatory treatments and against freedom of association in connection with their employment."

Subparagraph 42 states: "In the areas of setup, actions, and administration, the organizations representing multinational companies or the employees of these companies have to receive adequate protection against interference from the other side, both for the organizations and for their representatives and members."

These aforementioned regulations of the so-called threefold declaration of principles on multinational companies and social policy are based on Agreements numbers 8 and 98 of the International Labor Organization.

Subparagraph 44 of this threefold agreement states: "The governments are called upon to apply the principles laid down in Article 5 of Agreement No. 97 if they do not already do so, since it is important in connection with multinational companies that associations representing these companies or their employees can join international associations of employers and of employees of their choice."

Today is a very important day for the development of workers' rights in the future also in the international sphere. The signal sent by this forum goes far beyond the United States. Thus, we welcome this kind of public forum because it contributes to show where the rights are infringed, where the workers' rights are violated, and it discusses this and it makes them public.

The results and the outcome of this public forum will also be followed closely outside of the United States. And in my union but also in the media of the Federal Republic of Germany the actions of Sprint Corporation against its employees have attracted a lot of attention. Hence, we would greatly appreciate it if the authorities of the United States of America continued to support their previous policy of social responsibility in the rules of the game as well as actions aimed at balancing relations between employers and unions.

Thank you very much for your attention.

MR. OTERO: Fraulein Altmeyer, Danke Schön. Thank you very much, Ms. Altmeyer, for your presentation. We appreciate you coming all the way from Germany to help us in this process.

The next presenter is Mr. José Luis Mendoza, Legal Counsel for the Telephone Workers Union of the Republic of Mexico.

Mr. Mendoza?

And I would like to say at the same time that Mr. Mendoza is part of the Mexican delegation to this event.

MR. MENDOZA: (THROUGH TRANSLATOR) First of all, I feel deeply committed for participating in this platform because as legal counsel for this union I was part of the procedures to bring all this into the open.

The Telephone Workers Union of Mexico, faced with a severe violation of workers' rights by Sprint and its subsidiary, La Conexion Familiar, based itself on the agreement labor cooperation in order to submit its protests against this company that had dismissed over 200 employees because they had decided to exercise their freedom of association because these workers wanted to claim their right of collective bargaining with their employer.

The doubts and concerns increased when we heard that throughout the United States there were 16,000 long distance operations or long distance workers who were not unionized either. NAFTA, the North American Free Trade Agreement, leads us to the fact that we have to confront new situations. It affects productivity systems. It affects organizational structures, it affects financial systems. Equally it affects company policies.

These new ways of existence bring us vis-à-vis of certain structures of the organizations. We are being affected at all levels. The agreement on labor cooperation consistently with this evolution foresees in the way it is drafted and in its principles and obligations the way the situation could be regulated. You could think that under their protection North America could make progress and achieve these new ways of existing based on respect for basic workers' rights.

The problem with Sprint can be analyzed from different points of view. From a legal point of view, we could arrive at the conclusion or at the analysis or ask ourselves if within the American legal system there is enough protection for the freedom of association and for the freedom of collective bargaining. We could also bring up the question of the procedural standards of the American legal system establishes proper penalization when certain infringement has happened and how compensation of damages can be brought about.

However, this would lead us away from the main issue. It would lead us away from those issues that are really transcendental.

I respectfully disagree with my colleague Sergio Tapia. The problem that we're living is not a problem of the good guys and the bad guys. It is a problem of ignorant and weak ones. Weak ones, the workers. Ignorant, the management who has forgotten that there are new ways of existing, of structuring. Sprint with its behavior creates damages in at least three ways. It creates a social damage, it damages the workers, and it harms itself.

Maybe the kind of management leadership, the destructive policy towards everything that has to do with unionization prevents the company from understanding that it's harming itself, that they do not realize that firing employees also bring about strong social economic and family hardship.

We have heard the presentations of our colleagues that have been really moving and dramatic and this is a result of ignorance.

The world of quality that is established or talked about in NAFTA and in the North American Agreement on Labor Cooperation demands that certain principles and institutions are fulfilled and upheld. It demands for certain resources and instruments to be implemented in a positive environment.

With what aim? For the purpose that within this positive framework team work can take place, participation in leadership, good communication and motivation.

We need to understand that within working procedures the human factor is of utmost importance and transcendental. The leaders who year after year meet in Switzerland have stated that at the top of the pyramid in the companies should be the client. This point of view changed recently, particularly at this international forum. Today, it is said that at the very top, at the very point, at the very tip of the pyramid the worker should be placed and it's very easy to understand and to explain how this change came about.

Productivity and quality are a result of workers' efforts and there can be no productivity or quality in a negatively determined working environment. Changes that are brought about are harmful for society, for the company, for the worker, when these principles are not fulfilled.

In the history of mankind, we have learned that unionism is a noble institution to defend the weak one. It is politically, legally, ethically, and philosophically defended and there is no doubt about it.

When we analyze the different effects that have been brought about by Sprint's behavior, we find that there are caused just by one factor, by one reason, to avoid unionization of workers, prevent them from defending their rights in a collective way. If we analyze the situation we are forced to reflect upon very basic elements such as management-labor relationships.

The world over it is understood that these relationships are integrated by three elements: trade union, workers, and management. In Sprint, it is understood that labor relations represented by just the management and the pressure they exert on the workers. Whereas in the modern world we are finding out that workers should be at the top of the pyramid, at Sprint they say they should be at the very bottom, that their rights should be stomped and that not even the most basic conditions need to be fulfilled.

We Mexican workers believe that the NAALC is a very good instrument to achieve its goals through its principles and it talks about situations through which we can bring about a change, a change where we can share wealth, a change where under the stewardship of workers and management we can create new living conditions for the world for the way work is performed.

There are countries, for example, certain Asian countries, that have demonstrated that if you give workers participation in decision making you can get excellent results. The lack of participation leads also to the lack of participating in solution of problems. We understand that by participating we satisfy a human need and we can solve problems that can exist within a company and we can arrive at more rational and more reasonable solutions.

It is said the standards of international law lack efficiency because there are no coercive measures. In the case of the NAALC, we can see a really exceptional phenomenon, an idea defined as the tool that will allow to wake labor conscious in North America where the outcries cannot be silenced by fear or oppression.

Mexican workers, in particular telephone workers of Mexico, support decidedly the plight of the workers at Sprint. they show their empathy towards them and with their effort they have brought about the fact that they are being noticed in North America and that we all reflect upon these measures, considering that they harm companies very severely, not only the workers involved. They affect negatively the society as a whole.

The consequences of the NAALC also suggest us to be more daring, to be more bold. We can find means to assure that progress of humanity is through a well balanced respect of workers' rights.

Thank you very much.

MR. OTERO: (THROUGH TRANSLATOR) Thank you very much, Mr. Mendoza.

The next presenter is a member of the Canadian tripartite delegation, speaking for the employer's side.

I ask Mr. Lawrence Bertuzzi to come to the podium.

Mr. Bertuzzi is a partner in the law firm of Miller & Thompson.

Mr. Bertuzzi.

MR. BERTUZZI: Thank you, Mr. Chairman.

May I begin by thanking our hosts, the U.S. Department of Labor, for this kind invitation and I thank the head of our Canadian delegation, Mr. Edmondson, for including me in the delegation.

I see that I will perform a rather unique function here today. There are very few of us from the management side and I think they all got used up before lunch. I may be the only banner carrier for the afternoon, but nonetheless, let me address you from a Canadian perspective.

Let me start by saying I am not here in any way, shape, or form to comment on the Sprint situation. It would be most inappropriate for me to do so and I will not pick up that particular baton.

I understood the purpose of the forum to be to study the effects of the sudden closing of a plant on the principle of freedom of association and worker's right to organize. I would like to take the word sudden out for a moment and say to you that the closing of a plant on the principle of freedom of association and the worker's right to organize is in Canada a relatively straightforward matter. The word sudden complicates it because it depends why.

I hope to speak of three things during my brief 10 minutes. One is to tell you a bit about the Canadian law covering this top. Two is to make a pitch for what I call balance. I think balance is critical as we approach the task with each other. And the third is to comment on the procedure, if I might, Mr. Chairman.

Firstly, under Canadian law, freedom of association and the right to organize unions of the employees' choosing is protected by every statute we have. As Mr. Edmondson said, we have 11 different labor statutes in Canada because we have 10 provinces, similar to your states, and each of them have primary jurisdiction over most matters except those which have been deemed to be federal like intraprovincial transport, telecommunications, et cetera. And for that, the federal government has thrown in their hat into the ring to create the 11th jurisdiction.

Every jurisdiction clearly recognizes, as does our constitution, the right to organize a union of the employee's choice. In fact, in most jurisdictions in Canada, the right to select a union can be done even without a vote. The presentation of membership cards of a certain amount, either 50 percent or 55 percent, in some jurisdictions more, will get a union organized, the union of the employees' choice, without a vote.

Now, all jurisdictions, all 11 jurisdictions, prohibit taking actions or threats against employees because of union activity. I believe that the Canadian law may well go further than the American law in this regard, Mr. Chairman, because as I understood it, you have the *Wright Line* test which essentially says ask two questions: one, was there anti-union reason for the decision and, secondly, was there any good business reason for the decision. And then if the answer to each is yes, then balance them.

The Canadian law in fact is less onerous on the unions and the employees than that. The test in Canada is was the decision motivated in any part by an anti-union motive. And, if so, if so, then the business interests may well have to take a back seat.

The second major distinction is the employer, while in the U.S. as I understand it bearing the onus of proving the business rationale, the employer in Canada bears a reverse onus of proving that it did not have an anti-union animus.

These are important distinctions but what the Canada law does and must continue to do even better is to attempt to put in a balance. We have a balance which in some respects comes from a sense of timing. It's not as good as it could be, but employers can decide to close or to relocate if that is not motivated by an anti-union animus.

Sound economic reasons, capital decisions, location considerations, especially in this era of in Canada increasingly older workplaces which don't meet environmental or safety concerns, these are all legitimate reasons for moving a location or closing a location and are not banned by our labor laws, nor should they be banned by our labor laws, if they are not accompanied by an antiunion animus.

Now, in many provinces, the scope of the union's jurisdiction is really only city or regionwide, so this right even can extend within only a few miles. And that is a right that they have in an attempt to have the balance in Canada and it's a right that seems to be working.

The certification system in our countries is rare in the commercial contract world and it is my suggestion and submission that the right to locate on business considerations, even if the impact is to deny union representation, is legitimate if it is not motivated by anti-union motivation.

It is the flip side of the certification procedure. In the commercial contract world, there are very few situations where an employer is told this is the party with whom you must make your commercial contract and under Canadian law told even further and here are key elements that must be contained within that commercial contract. When I go to buy my product, I have a number of suppliers to choose from. When I go to pick my energy, I have alternate sources. But in labor, under the certification system, you have one bargaining party. And so the quid pro quo is certain rights to manage your business effectively to stay viable.

Now, the collective agreement is in Canada pretty well the costliest commercial contract an employer signs. Of all the commercial contracts it enters into, it's the one that costs the most. And yet it is one of the few in which it has no choice with whom to bargain.

In Canada, we also have in most jurisdictions many mandatory provisions which I suggest give balance on the union side to the employer's right to move. For example, we have in most jurisdictions mandatory payment of union dues by every member of the bargaining unit, the very antithesis of your right-to-work states.

We have mandatory first contract arbitration in jurisdictions covering far and away the majority of our workers. We have in two provinces the banning of temporary strike replacements and in pretty well every province the prohibiting of permanent strike replacements.

So these are things that give leverage to the union side and things that tell me that I should continue to expose for a balance so that business can react accordingly in this environment.

Now, in recognition of the balanced approach, labor boards look at things like timing of decisions. For example, a decision made suddenly in the face of an organizing campaign may well attract a different response from the labor board than a decision made during the course of a mature relationship or even a decision made during a strike when the union demands are such that they make the business uncompetitive.

In one case, the realities have sent the labor board to say we must intervene. In the other cases they say we're all big players in a big market. When you exert your economic power as a union, you must do so within the context of realities and sometimes it doesn't work out that well. And employers have exactly the same difficult decisions to make. This is the balance that we must strive for.

An employer chooses his location for a number of reasons. Location, transportation, energy, cost of money, government incentives, government restrictions, health costs, very important in Canada, skilled and available labor and the cost of that labor. So long as no anti-union motivation exists, it must be permitted to take those matters, all of those matters, into consideration in deciding where to locate or where to relocate. The availability, quality and cost of labor are factors which must be weighed with all the other factors, whether as between provinces in Canada or as between states in Mexico and the United States or as between our respective countries. If moves in the right direction in any factor drive investment away, the parties and the government must take heed.

NAFTA is all about breaking down walls and recognizing our respective places in a bigger society, not about building walls to keep us in and others out. So, too, with our labor laws.

Now, Mr. Chairman, the third point I wanted to comment on, and gently, I might add, is a bigger concern I have with the potential interference with the internal administrative and court mechanisms in a country.

In Canada, we have a system of labor relations boards, 11 to be exact, in each jurisdiction and they have primary jurisdiction to consider matters of certification and matters of unfair labor practice when employees lose their job.

The matters have been removed from the court in first instance because of the recognition of the need for specialized, expert, independent tribunals to consider such issues. This has always been considered a positive development by both management and labor and it has been copied in a number of other areas in Canadian society. For example, environmental tribunals, real estate tribunals, et cetera. And those tribunals deal with their specialized matters, rather than the general court system.

Now, the courts are still there. They ensure review, to ensure fairness, natural justice, due process and to make sure the tribunals stay within their own jurisdiction, so they have a role.

I understand from my experience that the U.S. system, although distinct, is based on exactly the same principles.

Now, in view of this, the NAOs and the ministries of labor must be careful not to interfere with this system as it progresses. Such action, I submit would be most unwelcome as the parties rely on these specialized tribunals for consistency, direction, certainty and finality.

Public international fora on the merits of an incident or the merits of the review process while it is in process must take care that it not detract from a tribunal's independent and expert function.

So I urge caution. External interference in a working review system, even if it has imperfections will only add to its imperfections and likely extend the delays. This is especially so where the system has a specialized review process. It should not be usurped by this process.

In conclusion, let me say this. Bad facts invariably make bad law. It is a mistake to change the law because of an extreme case. That's the slippery slope to creating a set of laws and protections which makes a country uncompetitive, discourages new investment which, of course, is well beyond the arm of the law because it's not here yet. And ultimately does the greatest harm to those the law purportedly is created to protect, the workers and their jobs.

There must be a balance. Violations when proven by due process require appropriate remedies but they do not require legal amendment which further restrict others who willingly comply with the law.

In our workplace we sometimes joke about 95 percent of the rules are made to control 5 percent of the people. That should not be the principle in creating statutes. The statute should not be created to control the activities of 2 or 3 percent of the people.

Simply, as Mr. Anaya alluded to earlier, union organization is not a guarantee against normal economic decisions, whether they are good or bad from an employee's perspective.

Union organization has a vital and essential role in the employer-employee relationship. In Canada, the role of unions are influential well beyond their 37 percent coverage. The healthy push-pull between business and labor in our country has produced much success but only when a balance is kept because when it gets out of balance we do not have success.

Any analysis of the freedom of association and the right to organize must be seen in a realistic context which recognizes all the dynamics which go into running a business in the international marketplace. In Canada, we, and by that I mean business, labor, and the government, must always be cognizant of that as we sit in such close proximity to our two much larger and attractive neighbors.

Thank you for this opportunity to address you.

MR. OTERO: Thank you very much, Mr. Bertuzzi.

I have some comments to make but before you leave, I wanted to ask you a question. I am cognizant of the fact that labor law in Canada by your own determination is a matter of the provinces, unlike the United States where we have a single application of the labor law.

When you were alluding to the fact that the burden of proof on an employer in a contest for an election is to demonstrate that the employer had no anti-union bias, is this something that is applicable uniformly in Canada or were you speaking about one specific province?

MR. BERTUZZI: No. I can't answer the question that it's applicable uniformly, although I suspect it is. I can tell you that it is the law which covers at least 65 to 70 percent of the workers, because it is the law of Quebec, Ontario, British Columbia, and the federal law and that would represent 65 percent or better of our workers.

If there's an unfair labor practice charge laid against an employer, the onus is on the employer to prove that it did not commit an unfair labor practice. That's the check on one side and the rights go on the other side.

MR. OTERO: Thank you very much.

As you take your seat, I want to make some comments. First of all, I would like to thank you very much, Mr. Bertuzzi for bringing back the discussion to a broader picture of the impact that sudden closure of plants have on the freedom of association separating that from the instant case of Sprint which is what generated this forum in the first place. But that was the intent of the three countries in conducting this hearing, was to look at the Sprint case, since it was the case that we had before us, but also to broaden the inquiry to try to ascertain with a model of clarity what happens in similar instances, not only in the United States but in the other two countries as well. And, in fact, we have, as I said before, tasked our labor secretariat in Dallas to undertake an empirical study of this matter, looking not only at the Sprint case but going as far afield as the information will permit us.

And so I thank you very much for refocusing the discussion of this afternoon. You made a lot of very interesting points.

I only want to assure you and the public here assembled that the United States and Mexico and Canada indeed in the process of conducting the ministerial consultations that were requested by the government of Mexico were extremely careful and cognizant of protecting the process.

I would like to say for the record that shortly after Secretary of Labor Bonilla from Mexico requested ministerial consultation from Secretary Reich who promptly accepted, at the time the judge of the NLRB had not rendered his decision and the parties, Mexico and the United States, agreed to suspend the ministerial consultations until the judge had concluded his analysis and rendered a decision so as not to give any appearance, however slight it may be, that this process that we were instituting under the treaty had in any way any design to influence the outcome of that decision because we, like you, recognized the importance of separating this process on the two tracks. And so it was not until the judge in this case had rendered a decision that we decided then to proceed with the ministerial consultations and enter into an agreement as to how we could deal with this problem without doing any harm.

In fact, I would like to say also for the record that we were also very careful in consulting throughout the process with the NLRB itself to make sure that any of our steps did not in any way interfere because it would have been in reality improper for this process to have anything to do with that. This is being handled, as I said earlier, on two tracks.

And so your caution is very well taken. We appreciate the fact that you thought about it and that you brought it to our attention, but at the same time, we have been extremely cognizant of our responsibility to protect the process because one case does not change the process, in our opinion.

And I would like to say finally as another commentary, is that whatever maybe the result of these endeavors which our objective here is to find more specificity as to what impact this either closure, like you said, without the word sudden or sudden closures have on the principle of the right to organize and the freedom of association to which Mexico, Canada and the United States attach the greatest of importance, that is our objective here.

And I think that you have made a significant contribution this afternoon by putting this discussion in the context that we thought from the very first moment, which was to look at the Sprint case, of course, but also look beyond at the entire picture and you have been most helpful in your presentation and I want to thank you for doing so.

Let me now recognize the next presenter.

Mr. Philip C. Bowyer is the General Secretary of the Postal, Telephone and Telegraph International known as PTTI which is one of the 14 international trade secretariats associated with the International Confederation of Free Trade Unions and Mr. Bowyer has come from Europe. We also thank him very much for crossing the Atlantic to be here with us today.

Mr. Bowyer.

MR. BOWYER: Thank you very much.

Mr. Chairman, as you said, I am the General Secretary of the Postal, Telegraph and Telephone International, the PTTI, to which various colleagues have referred to earlier. The PTTI represents 4.6 million workers in 22 affiliated trade unions in 117 countries of the world who work in the communication industries.

I would like to begin by first commending the Mexico Secretary of Labor and the U.S. Secretary of Labor for their decision to initiate this public forum on the closure of La Conexion Familiar. And I would like also to thank you for presiding over this forum and for allowing me to share the views of the PTTI and its affiliates around the world concerning this case and the question of freedom of association.

As you said, the PTTI cooperates with the International Confederation of Free Trade Unions. Within the European Union, which is probably the largest trading block in the world, we represent telecom workers. Also, and I think more relevant to this particular hearing, we participate in the activities of the Trade Union Advisory Committee of the Organization for Economic Cooperation and Development, the OECD. And we are also active within the ILO, the International Labor Office.

Now, in particular, the latter two organizations have a great deal of work, have done a great deal of work in connection with the question of freedom of association and, of course, the United States of America is a member of both of these organizations and we believe has certain obligations to try and implement the standards which those organizations make.

We think, therefore, Mr. Chairman, that given our activities we are in the PTTI well positioned to try and place the sudden closure of Sprint/La Conexion Familiar within a global context.

We do believe that the U.S. Government must now face the responsibility that comes from liberalized trade and a more open scrutiny of practices in enforcing trade union rights in the U.S.A. and we are very clearly interested in the practical outcome of these proceedings.

Throughout most of the world, the telecommunications industry has had one of the highest unionization rates of any industry. It's a highly profitable industry; it's characterized by continuous innovation, high productivity, and a highly skilled work force.

It's also a key industry in the development of trade and for the strengthening of democracy. And here in the United States, the telecommunications and information industries hold the promise of creating more and better jobs.

The fact that telecommunication workers enjoy relatively high standards of living we do not think is an accident or an achievement of benevolent employers. It is the legacy of this high unionization rate. But we also recognize that over the past 10 to 15 years we have undergone extremely rapid change.

Competition and liberalization in the sector as the result of liberalized trade have propelled an economic war with giant multinational companies buying each other out as they try to win part of the market. And, of course, U.S. telecommunications companies with some $170 billion of revenue at their disposal are amongst the most aggressive players in this economic battle.

And for us there is clearly a social dimension to this war because when companies penetrate a foreign market, generally they also take with them their labor relations practices and, of course, Sprint is one of those companies and that is why we are so concerned about this particular case, because it can affect our members wherever they might be working in the world and wherever Sprint decides that it wants to be active in the future.

Telecommunications around the world, I must say, are determined to ensure that Sprint respects its workers' right to freedom of association and to bargain collectively and they are determined that the company will not be successful in undermining their right to a decent standard of living. These rights are embodied in the conventions of the International Labor Organization, of which the U.S.A. is a member, and they are referred to in Annex 1 of the North American Agreement on Labor Cooperation. And the PTTI has been cooperating with our colleagues in the Communications Workers of America and with the Union of Telephone Workers in Mexico to try to ensure that Sprint is in compliance with these internationally recognized principles of labor law.

And, Mr. Chairman, I will submit in writing an analysis of the relevant international standards, particularly of the ILO and of the OECD, the ways in which the actions of Sprint have violated these standards and also the ways in which the U.S.A. has failed to implement its obligation under those standards.

We in the international trade union movement were shocked to hear that Sprint had closed La Conexion Familiar only days before a scheduled union election. Since then, Sprint was found guilty of committing over 50 violations of the U.S. Labor Code, Sprint has been permission by the U.S. Government and by the European Union, to enter into a multi-billion dollar alliance with France Télécom and German

Telekom, the project known as ATLAS, but in the meantime 235 Latino workers faced a loss of income, the uncertainty of finding other jobs and, in many cases, having to uproot their families from the communities in which they lived. And in these circumstances, it would be hardly surprising if they have lost faith in the ability of the U.S. government as the guarantor of their rights as workers and as citizens to form a trade union.

As an international observer, the Sprint case in my view is one of, if not the most, outrageous examples of the violation of workers' rights to form a union to occur in our industry worldwide. Even more shocking for us is the fact that the entire law enforcement apparatus of the U.S. government, and even of the U.S. federal court systems, have proven inadequate or unwilling to either prevent or to remedy the flagrant violation of basic trade union rights by Sprint.

The company's actions against these 235 Latino workers would be considered morally reprehensible, socially intolerable, and most certainly illegal in many other industrialized countries. As we have heard from spokesmen today, in Canada, the labor code would have facilitated recognition of a trade union based on a simple review of employees' legal signatures.

In Europe, under the treaty and the directives established by the European Union, all member states are obliged to enact legislation strictly regulating collective dismissals. For example, the European Court of Justice, one of those special institutions of the European Union which don't exist under the NAFTA agreement, but the European Court of Justice in a case against the United Kingdom confirmed the following principles:

They confirmed that governments must require an employer contemplating collective dismissals to consult the workers' representatives with a view to reaching an agreement.

Even more important, they confirmed that governments must provide for the designation of employee representatives even where an employer does not agree to this.

And, finally, they say that governments must provide for effective sanctions in the event of a failure to consult workers' representatives.

In other countries in the region, in Europe, in countries such as the Scandinavian countries or the country in which I live, Switzerland, Sprint would have been obliged to recognize industrywide agreements on working conditions.

Now, our view of the inadequacy of the U.S. labor code to deal with such cases is shared by the International Confederation of Free Trade Unions.

In its *1995 Survey of Violations of Trade Union Rights*, the ICFTU concludes that in the United States, "Workers often have no effective redress in the face of abuses by employers. Inadequate remedies available to workers who have been fired illegally for trade union activity and ineffective penalties against employers who illegally fire them place severe obstacles in the path of workers seeking to join trade unions."

According to the ICFTU survey, at least 1 in 10 union supporters campaigning to form a union is illegally fired and 1 union supporter is fired for every 30 people who vote for a union in union elections.

The ICFTU also quotes a poll conducted in 1994 which found that 79 percent of all Americans believe that workers are likely to get fired if they try to organize a union at their place of work.

And, finally, the ICFTU concluded that the example of La Conexion Familiar was one of the most blatant illegal actions in 1994.

The cumulative effects of this anti-union behavior on the part of employers in the U.S.A. is nothing but shocking. While thousands of workers are fired every year during union organizing drives, the U.S. government can take years to make decisions on illegal firings and anywhere from 3 months to 3 years to effectively conduct union representation elections.

And, finally, as the Sprint case demonstrated, employers in the United States appear to have the ultimate weapon at their disposal, which is to close the facility all together in order to avoid unionization without any fear of effective sanctions being taken against them.

Now, in the written analysis which I said I would submit, after looking at the conventions of the International Labor Organization, it must be said that even if one could accept Sprint's extremely improbable economic necessity argument, then the company's conduct would still be incompatible with the international recognized standards of the ILO of which the U.S.A. is a member.

To Sprint, the cost of breaking the law has been negligible, but 19 months after the closure those workers remain fired and the company is still bidding for government contracts. In our view, this indicates that the U.S. labor code and its enforcement mechanisms need to be overhauled in the most pressing manner and in full consultation with the trade union movement.

I agree with the president of CWA, President Bahr, that Annex 1 of the North American Agreement on Labor Cooperation contains all the necessary objectives. However, the aggressive anti-union behavior of companies like Sprint show that we need to add strong economic sanctions to prevent companies from closing down facilities and shattering workers' lives under the guise of global competition.

The PTTI believes that the violations of their rights that workers suffer in the United States must be prevented by the introduction of the Code of Conduct that President Bahr and STRM General Secretary Francisco Hernandez Juarez outlined during their testimony, which is based on the principles of the ILO and the other international institutions of which the United States is a member.

It's our expectation that this recommendation should be given full consideration as the NAO considers steps to be taken as a result of this examination.

In my view, and also that of many other observers, the NAO investigation must ensure that the practical outcome goes far beyond an intellectual exercise on the inner working of U.S. labor laws.

Mr. Chairman, what began for us in the PTTI as a simple exercise in international solidarity with our colleagues in the CWA has grown into a campaign with a life of its own. Telecommunications workers around the world are taking the initiative and opposing entry of Sprint and its brand of anti-union practices into their countries. Just since 1993, workers in the United Kingdom, France, German, Mexico, Canada, Portugal, Brazil, and Nicaragua, to name a few, have acted to oppose Sprint's anti-union activities.

In fact, I've heard just recently that Sprint is about to bid for a part of the privatized telecommunications in Nicaragua and our affiliate in Nicaragua will be opposing that and they will be supported by the PTTI and our affiliates around the world.

Mr. Chairman, the lives of more than 200 workers, most of them women, were shattered in an instant simply because they were determined to exercise their right to freedom of association, to speak collectively through their union, and to negotiate their way out of injustice. Until this is resolved, the PTTI and its affiliates will continue to undertake whatever actions are necessary to deny Sprint Corporation entry into other telecommunications markets and we will do whatever is necessary to ensure that Sprint is brought into full compliance with internationally accepted standards.

Thank you.

MR. OTERO: Mr. Bowyer, thank you very much indeed for your presentation and for coming all the way from Europe to be with us. We share your interest in the practical outcome of these proceedings and, of course, we welcome your offer to provide us with analysis of the ILO and the OECD standards that may have been involved in this case.

I think I feel compelled to say that shortly after President Clinton was installed in office in consultation with Secretary Reich we proceeded to install the so-called Dunlap Commission, fully aware that American labor law is in need of some re-examination and revamping. And the Dunlap commission has labored long and hard with the participation of several former Secretaries of Labor from both political parties, I might say, as well as representatives of the AFL-CIO and representatives of the business community. And the Dunlap report has been recently completed and forwarded to the White House for presentation to Congress.

Of course, at the present time, the climate for labor law reform in the United States is not entirely conducive to success and so I believe that their report itself is worth reading for those of you who may not be familiar with that effort because it offers significant changes to expedite the process and to make it easier for both employers and workers to have a more expeditious process of settling these disputes and, of course, making the organizing of workers more in tune with the ILO standards. But I appreciate very much your offer to give us an analysis of the ILO and the OECD standard from your perspective and I will ask you that you kindly forward that to our office in the Department of Labor in Washington, D.C.

Thank you very much, Mr. Bowyer.

At this point now, I would like to call on another presenter, Ms. Marie Malliett. If I am not pronouncing your name correctly, please, I apologize. The president of Local 9410 of the Communications Workers of America, CWA, AFL-CIO.

Ms. Malliett. Good afternoon.

MS. MALLIETT: Good afternoon.

My name is Marie Malliett and I am the president of Local 9410 of the Communications Workers of America located here in San Francisco. My local provided the support and assistance to the workers of La Conexion Familiar in their organizing drive.

My local was privileged to observe the tremendous worker solidarity and resolve to unionize their workplace. In a little more than 4 months, the La Conexion workers came within 1 week of achieving what no other workers in Sprint's long distance division had been able to accomplish. We observed this worker solidarity on a daily basis. By pure chance, the La Conexion Familiar moved into a building right next to our local union in 1993. It didn't take long for the La Conexion workers to hear about CWA and, in fact, the workers made contact with us in February of 1994.

From that point on, the Sprint workers held regular, daily meetings in our union hall. They came before reporting to work, during their breaks, during lunch hours, and after work. They asked us a million questions about how to change their working conditions at Sprint and how to organize themselves into a union. They really became part of our local family.

We shared with them the day-to-day painstaking tasks of building an organization and the exhilaration of imminent success.

We soon recognized that an overwhelming majority of the Sprint workers wanted a union. I have been through many organizing drives and we do not evaluate lightly the potential of a drive nor the timing of an election. I have always been aware of the risks that workers face in organizing and I am especially aware in today's current environment of a tax on workers' rights and particularly Sprint, which has an anti-union corporate culture.

During the organizing campaign, we assessed very carefully the business conditions at La Conexion and Sprint, the company's anti-union campaign, the strength and resolve of the workers to overcome these incredible odds.

At every turn we concluded that these workers were committed to unionize the workplace. Based on these assessments we filed for an election with the National Labor Relations Board on June 3, 1994. The NLRB subsequently set the date for an election on July 22, 1994.

Management itself confirmed our estimate of La Conexion/Sprint's prospects. In one of Sprint's own employee newsletters, it reported in the June 1994 issue, and I have provided it in an exhibit for you, just 1 month before the closure that, and I quote, "La Conexion Familiar is different than other carriers and very successful.... Using the grass roots strategy in conjunction with the power of Sprint's Marketing and Operator Groups, La Conexion has grown at an astounding rate in the last three years because it has targeted cities with large Spanish speaking populations."

Other statements by Sprint management also confirm that La Conexion was financially prospering.

During the last weeks of the campaign I devoted myself full-time to the drive. I participated in daily meetings and made home visits to the workers. Based on this intimate knowledge of the campaign and 70 percent of the workers who had signed their name to the petition for an election, I can tell you with absolute confidence and certainty that the union would have prevailed in the July 22nd NLRB election.

On July 12th, I was informed by our national union staff that Sprint Vice President of Labor Relations, Carl Doerr, had requested to meet with CWA in San Francisco on July 14th. I attended the meeting, which was held at our district office in Burlingame. As I and other CWA representatives were waiting for Mr. Doerr to arrive, we received a telephone call from my local. We were told that a Sprint worker had just reported that Sprint had shut down La Conexion and it was shut down effectively immediately.

When he arrived for the scheduled meeting, Mr. Doerr confirmed the announcement. As Mr. Doerr spoke, never as a union representative have I heard a corporate executive trash the integrity of his employees at the very same time that he was throwing them into the street. He said, and I quote, that La Conexion workers only spoke "Hispanic," that they were all "illegal immigrants" who had "bought" their $7.00 an hour jobs. To find out later that this same executive was deeply involved in a conspiracy to submit evidence to an agency of the federal government only added more insult.

The workers took the announcement very hard and so did I. Nothing could have prepared us for the suddenness nor the brutality of the mass execution. Upon hearing the brutal announcement over loudspeakers, workers burst into tears. One woman fainted and paramedics had to be summoned. The workers were told to immediately gather their things and leave the building. As they left, Sprint security searched all their belongings and in some cases, workers were bodily searched.

As you can imagine, my local became a second home for many of these workers. We worked very hard to document their legal case against Sprint to ensure that workers received the social services that they were entitled to and to supplement the wholly inadequate training and outplacement services provided by Sprint.

We continued to hold regular meetings with the workers to keep them informed. We organized a food bank. We worked with them to take their case to the public. We held an all night vigil in San Francisco to make the public aware of Sprint's anti-union/anti-worker philosophy. And we took our case home to the Latino community and to the Latino businesses that Sprint had been courting.

We took their case to our local elected representatives of the San Francisco Board of Supervisors, to members of Congress, and to you, our elected federal officials.

Through it all, the workers have shown amazing stamina. In spite of their unemployment and the burden that places on their family, they have kept up the fight. What they can't understand is why it's taking so long to get a remedy from Sprint.

Why do these workers have to pay the price of months and years of waiting? Why is it taking so long to get justice?

I try to give them hope. I tell them that we will get justice, Sprint will be forced to pay for what they have done. But in my mind I wonder how long will it take, what will it take? You see, to me there is a very fundamental issue at stake. The Constitution of the United States guarantees freedom of speech and freedom of association; therefore, it logically follows the freedom to organize and become members of a union. However, Sprint in this country has been allowed to place themselves above the law. They fired the 177 La Conexion workers because they had dared to exercise their lawful rights to unionize their workplace.

You would have had to have lived through this organizing campaign with me to understand the human fallout of illegal corporate behavior and the inability of our political system and our legal system to stop Sprint. From this entire experience, I am a changed person.

Sprint didn't suffer at all. The same day they shut down La Conexion they mailed out a notice in Spanish to all La Conexion customers with the heading "Good News." They promised better service, $100 of free calls, lower rates, and a calling card. And to this day, Sprint continues to market its services to the Spanish-speaking community. La Conexion became the first runaway shop on the new information highway and Sprint's customers were never told about the more than 50 violations of the federal laws which it had committed against its employees.

The workers of La Conexion did what they had to do. They believed in the American dream, they believed in the rule of law, and they acted upon it.

Now, it's time for you, our elected representatives, to act upon what you have learned from this tragic experience. This forum is the first national opportunity these workers have had to state their case to the public.

On behalf of all the La Conexion Sprint workers, I want to personally thank your brothers from the Mexico Telephone Workers Union for making this all possible. We hope the results of this forum will match its promise, so that other workers will not have to relive the trauma which befell the workers of La Conexion Familiar.

Thank you.

MR. OTERO: Thank you very much, Ms. Malliett.

By agreement between the next scheduled speaker and the last speaker on the list, we are going to switch the order because Mr. del Campo has a problem of child care and he has to go home by 4:00.

Let me introduce formally Frank Martin del Campo, President of the San Francisco Chapter of the Labor Council for Latin American Advancement.

Mr. del Campo.

MR. DEL CAMPO: Muchas gracias, Jack, y Jaime.

The issue of responsibility I will touch on today and I am very pleased to be able to have the support of my associates in LCLAA in being able to secure my own personal responsibility with respect to child care.

I will offer my words in both English and Spanish, which will reflect the binational perspective of those of us who have the great fortune of having lived in two wonderful countries.

(THROUGH INTERPRETER) First of all, I will speak in English and then in Spanish. Addressing the topics that we have discussed today on labor organization, I will offer some remarks trying to focus on workers' organizations in our countries of origin and also in this country. As a Mexican and as a Latin American, I would say that in this country, we have many millions, many million colleagues working here, seeking dignity.

I come from a family that has a lot of pride. We are in Jalisco, in Guadalajara, there is a town called Ameca. On the way to Ameca, halfway through, there is a farm called Encalison. On this farm, my parents and my relatives have lived for 100 years. Recently, I went back to Ameca because there is no country like Mexico and all of us Mexicans go back to Mexico and in talking with my relatives, it was said that all my childhood friends, all of the people that I grew up with, summer after summer, year after year, none of us, none of us stayed in Ameca. Nobody, I repeat, stayed in Ameca.

(IN ENGLISH) In many ways, we did not decide to leave Ameca. In many ways, although we as people in our family made the decisions personally, the decisions that were made that had an entire town leave Ameca, Jalisco had more to do in the boardrooms of New York City and San Francisco, and in some regards, perhaps, in some regards, perhaps, in other countries of the world.

But really these decisions that were made for us affected us much deeper than anyone else. Effectively, it is the central point of my offering today that the transnationals who make decisions in New York and San Francisco have dominated the political decision making of all three countries.

The irony of this particular case is, of course, that this particular company makes its living off of the separation of our families. The very process of immigration and our need to stay in touch with our families was the endeavor which united the companera La Conexion Familiar.

In many ways, however, we remain the recipients of these decisions. The movement toward the global economy and the corresponding decisions around privatization and layoffs are the results of the political and economic dominance of a few that affect all of our countries.

Let's talk about the waves of immigration.

My father came to this country looking for opportunity. Those who come to this country now are looking for survival and escape from repression in their countries of origin. The circumstances of that have a lot to do with the domination that I have described.

What have the recent immigrants found? Speaking as a Latino workers, they find an environment of 1800 that denies them the very right to exist, incarcerates them in a prison of subemployment for the rest of their lives. They find a climate of retreat on affirmative action that deprives not only them but their children of the very fact of education which in my case it was employment and education which was the path to the middle class and it's now currently being deprived.

These decisions around moving from La Conexion Familiar can be hidden behind a very nice trapping of legal argument. Fundamentally for the workers of La Conexion Familiar to whom I am privileged to be with here today, what we have is a case that has been described as to what the outcome is, alcoholism, difficulty with your children, et cetera. They pay the price.

In many ways, many of us here in the labor movement have examined the lack of enforcement of labor laws and the illegal process ad infinitum which means we are effectively disenfranchised of our rights and it's a sad reflection on the U.S. labor laws today that we search for ways around them rather than submitting to them, that in SEIU and many other unions of this country we reject the NLRB. We think it's a trap and what we look for is to find justice in the workplace, evading that trap which is an employer-dominated trap for us.

To conclude, I believe that there should be concrete recommendations offered here today and I would respectfully offer the following:

Strengthen NAFTA and put some teeth into it so that rather than informational gathering here that we have a court where we can have sanctions to protect the employees from La Conexion Familiar.

With respect to the question of Latino workers in this country, stop the racist immigrant bashing which encourages the denial of their rights and the racism that they exhibited on their final day of employment which denied them their language, their culture, and their heritage.

For the United States government from whom I have learned much and can thank for my education on the GI bill, I would submit respect the political decisions of other countries. Treat other countries as a cooperative arrangement and not one of domination and respect their political decisions with respect to the directions to which those countries wish to go.

There must be cooperation, not domination, internationally and in the absence of that, in the absence of incorporation of the various sectors of society, we will always have disputes.

Two last comments.

With respect to Mexico and the country to which I have my most affinity given my cultural upbringing and the way in which I was raised, I would respectfully offer that perhaps you might resolve the question of Ruta Cien in Mexico to find a resolution through a negotiation.

I'll conclude my remarks in the following way.

For those of us in U.S. trade union movement who have knowledge of Latin American unions, we know we will never go back to the days of Lazero Cartinas and Franklin Delano Roosevelt. Nor are we attempting to. However, the principles that were involved in both of those governments in a historic period, that workers should be included, respected, and find dignity in the process of their own labor and that their rights must be respected should be incorporated and that the lack of balance that we find today is because workers do not have the same rights as those who employ them and there is this disequilibrium, we will continue to have the problems that we face until such time as we address the problem of disequilibrium between those forces that employ us and those forces who are employed at the workplace.

Thank you very much.

MR. OTERO: Thank you very much, Mr. del Campo.

The next presenter is a member of the Canadian tripartite delegation speaking for the Canadian labor movement.

I would like to invite Mr. Dick Martin, Secretary-Treasurer of the Canadian Labour Congress, CLC, to come forward.

Mr. Martin.

MR. MARTIN: Thank you very much, Mr. Chairman.

Perhaps before I just proceed, I should for the information of the delegates here explain that the Canadian Labour Congress is the major central labor body in Canada and represents some 82 affiliated unions and 2.3 million members.

My role in the congress as secretary-treasurer amongst other administrative matters is responsibility for Latin America in terms of all issues, including human rights, trade union rights, economic matters, and, of course, issues circulating around NAFTA.

I want to pay, first of all, my personal regards to the workers of Sprint who have testified here today and certainly educated me as to what had happened in your situation. You have courage, I know, to even come here and speak out.

I also want to complement Francisco Hernandez Juarez, the president of the Mexican telephone workers, on his determination and courage to insist on laying these complaints and then coming here to testify in particular in view of his comments this morning that it was certainly suggested that he not come here and put his views forward.

I also want to pay my regards to the leadership in terms of the Secretary of Labor, Robert Reich, and to Jack Otero for holding these hearings because at least in spite of the criticism that will follow from me at least it allows the workers here in this city and in this state and perhaps across the country to air their grievances and it also allows the representatives of the working people of the United States and Canada and Mexico to put their opinions forward. And so I think from that extent it's beneficial and I do know that the department has taken some risk in order to have these hearings.

When we look at what has happened here, I think you should know that the Canadian Labour Congress strongly opposed NAFTA along with the AFL-CIO in the United States, for a great number of the reasons that we are here today.

We were very, very concerned that this was going to have a major push, a downward effect on the standards that we enjoy in terms of Canada both in terms of labor legislation but ancillary legislation that is very important to us, such as occupational health and safety, workers compensation and, indeed, our social programs.

Of course, we were considerably worried that there was going to be a dramatic loss of jobs, simply because the discrepancies and differences between the three countries.

In a report that has been put together by us, it goes on to talk about, and this was a joint report of which the AFL-CIO and a number of community action groups in the United States and Canada put together, we talked about the U.S. firms that break promises in both Canada and the United States.

Large corporations made sweeping predictions that free trade would enable them to hire more workers. Studies conducted in both countries indicate that just the opposite has occurred.

A U.S. consumer organization, Public Citizens, followed up on the jobs promise of about 80 pro-NAFTA companies. In nearly 90 percent of the cases surveyed, the companies had made no significant steps toward fulfilling their promises of U.S. job creation or export expansion.

In fact, according to the U.S. Department of Labor, a number of leading NAFTA promoters have laid off U.S. workers as the result of NAFTA, such as Allied Signal, General Electric, Proctor & Gamble, Mattel, Scott Paper, Xerox, Baxter International, Alcoa, and Zenith.

Likewise in Canada, most of the corporations which promised to create more jobs if the Canadian U.S. Free Trade Agreement known as FTA was signed have instead destroyed hundreds of thousands of jobs. The Canadian Center for Policy Alternatives has monitored 48 of the country's largest corporations and found that 37 of them have slashed more than 215,000 jobs since the FTA passed in 1988. The other 11 companies created only 11,993 jobs. All of the firms are members of a powerful business council on national issues in Canada which lobbied strongly for the FTA and NAFTA.

Throughout Canada and the United States there is now, and indeed I will corroborate that which Mr. Edmondson talked about this morning that we do have in relative terms a good record of certification, applications and certifications, in Canada relative to the United States and certainly it seems up here Mexico. But that does not mean that there are very, very strong interests, and in fact some provincial governments in Canada have stepped substantially backwards in terms of a number of laws that are very important to workers in our country and certainly this happens in the United States.

They have stripped away or are attempting to strip away the enforcement power in the U.S., OSHA, and, indeed, in provincial legislation in Canada, occupational health and safety legislation. There are attempts to legalize company unions, abolish overtime pay, outlaw corporate campaigns targeting company's lenders, suppliers, or customers for picketing or other actions, reduce workers compensation, outlaw union shops, and repeal laws that guarantee prevailing wages for construction workers on federally funded projects. That is just the beginning.

What we as labor have to understand and those that are in the general community have to understand is that the corporate world is not created nor exists nor continues to exist to make anything better for anyone except to generate profits. That's what they're created for, profits for the shareholders, and indeed give CEOs some very big paychecks.

Private corporations are not created nor do they exist to enhance or sustain social programs. They are not created to enhance the environment or make sure workers have clean and healthy working conditions. They are not created by individuals to enhance the betterment of the state or create a new era of health, prosperity or peace.

They are created, as I simply said, to create dividends and increase their share prices for shareholders.

The concept of being a good corporate citizen is alien to their creation and on-going operations. If being a good employer and good corporate citizen is beneficial to their bottom line, then smart management will do it. But also we do not necessarily have a lot of smart management.

Consequently, they use confrontational, legal, bullying, and threatening ways to meet their bottom line of increasing profits. The corporate group, U.S.A. and NAFTA, for example, proclaimed that NAFTA itself will improve working conditions by generating economic growth which will enable all three countries to provide more jobs with higher pay and a better working environment. There is not one shred of evidence that NAFTA has done that.

For example, in the United States and Canada, whipsaw bargaining is taking place, where a corporation threatens to shift production to Mexico unless unions agree to concessions. There abounds all kinds of examples of this. There is whipsaw legislation. For example, when President Clinton proposed an increase in the U.S. minimum wage, Newt Gingrich and his gang of Contract of America fought back by arguing that this would force more U.S. firms to move to Mexico.

Although Mr. Edmondson talked of success rates of Canadian unions obtaining certification, and he is right, we are haunted by the specter that if a law is so weighted in the U.S. and in Mexico against workers organizing, we shall eventually be at those dismal statistics.

It is ironic, I find, in a country like the U.S. that has probably more elections for anything than any of the other countries, certainly in terms of obtaining and sustaining a public position, that the will of the majority right down to the very bottom in terms of election for dog catcher or sheriff must be sustained at the same time that when workers try to organize by a majority vote they are thwarted at every turn. They seem to be harassed, intimidated, fired, sometimes beaten, sometimes jailed. And that's from their colleagues in the United States. Democracy for all things, but not for workers who want a union.

With all due respect to my American friends here, the United States, as has been repeated before, needs a complete overhaul of its labor laws and enforcement of its labor laws.

A previous speaker from Mexico spoke of employers becoming nervous if a new trade union comes into their company that they don't know or can't control, a union that won't impose discipline and order. With all due respect to my colleague, Mexico has signed more ILO conventions than either the United States or Canada and indeed has obeyed the least in our opinion.

The United States and Canada should be castigated for not having signed more and not enforcing many of their provisions, but nevertheless the record stands for itself.

Quite bluntly, it is not the business of the company to approve or disapprove of a union the workers choose. As long as the workers democratically choose their union, their officers and approve or disapprove collective agreements, it is their business and no one else's.

We are fed up. We are very fed up with corporations saying to government, "Don't intervene in our business but intervene in the rights of the workers."

We demand as the Canadian Labour Congress that NAFTA and new trade agreements implement social charters that address and enforce basic human rights or our opinion will be of little value and the workers and citizens of all our countries will be the worse off for it and a very small top elite will be very much more wealthy.

Thank you very much.

MR. OTERO: Thank you, Mr. Martin. Your remarks are well taken and I appreciate it.

The Chair now calls Ms. Janice Wood, Vice President of District 9, Communications Workers of America, CWA, AFL-CIO.

Ms. Wood?

MS. WOOD: Thank you, Mr. Otero. As you said, my name is Janice Wood. I am vice president of CWA District 9, which covers in part the states of California and Nevada. CWA represents 56,000 union members in these two states who work in telecommunications, broadcasting, publishing, the public sector, and other fields.

I have some brief prepared remarks which I'll turn to in a moment, but I did want to comment briefly, if I may, on some things that I heard here today.

There were three speakers who to my ears seemed to defend the actions of the Sprint Corporation and each of them said something that I found very interesting. There was Professor Corrada who said that the *Wright Line* standard gave Sprint the right to do what they did at La Conexion Familiar because they had dual motives, one of union animus and a second of financial interest. But we believe that that's just not the case, that there was a single motive for the closing of La Conexion Familiar and that motive was anti-union behavior.

Never was there any discussion, indication, or intimation of non-profitability of LCF until that issue was raised as a shield against the charges brought by the CWA and the workers at LCF against the Sprint company.

And, Mr. Anaya, I believe that I understood you to say that collection bargaining should be a demonstration of goodwill and cooperation, and I would agree with that.

But, frankly, sir, the obstacles to organizing non-union workers in the United States are so enormous that it is nearly impossible to unionize workers at any company where an employer is willing to show even the smallest demonstration of goodwill or cooperation with its own workers.

And Mr. Tapia said that it seemed that we were attempting to create an impression of good guys versus bad guys and he reminded us of the right of employers to close non-profitable businesses. We don't have to prove who the bad guys are. That proof has already been made in federal court. The bad guys are Sprint. They were found guilty of 50 different violations of federal labor laws.

They may have the right, they may have the right to close a non-profitable business, but that isn't what they did. They closed LCF and moved the work, the customers and the profits to other facilities in the Sprint Corporation, after they assured the workers at LCF that they were profitable, that Sprint benefited from their labor, after they spent tens of thousands of dollars to remodel the office of the manager who directed the threats against employees at LCF just a couple of months before the facility closed.

If finances were the issue in the closing of LCF, why in God's name would Sprint have paid every worker there the equivalent of 60 days' pay for no work at all? Why would LCF not have stayed open so that people could continue to work profitably for Sprint Corporation until the 60-day notice period had passed?

Because LCF did just what they said they'd do. They threatened to close the facility if people wanted a union and they did it.

The problem, however, is not that the La Conexion Familiar closed. The problem is that there are thousands of American employers who can and who will do the same thing, that it is the very industry in which we work that has created the technology to make this possible.

Work can be moved from one facility to another instantaneously using the telecommunications network and that worked for Sprint.

I am not here to prove who the bad guys are. I am here because I am an officer of the union that promised people that they had the right to organize and to be members of a union, that they had the right not to fear if they did what the law allowed, to say that they wanted to be unionized.

I am here because we asked the workers at LCF to put their jobs on the line and they did. And because the government that promises that they can't be fired for doing so has nothing to offer them but the chance to come here to tell their story and to hope that having heard their story that you will act to change the system that makes these promises we all know won't be kept.

The practice of union busting is so common in the United States that we have a term of union busting, that there are people who make their living as union busters, advocating openly to employers that it is cheaper to violate the law because the penalties for having done so are less expensive than the cost of wages and benefits under a union contract. I am ashamed to be from the country that allows this.

But my report is about the freedom to associate and the right to organize and I want to focus for a minute on the impact that the actions of employers like Sprint have on broader social and economic trends, on the decline in living standards among working people in our society.

Just 3 weeks ago, the federal government passed a sweeping new telecommunications law that ushers in a new competitive age in telecommunications.

California got a jump start on this legislation when it opened the in-state long distance market to competition earlier this year.

These changes have been heralded as creating millions of new jobs in the growing information sector of our economy and only time will tell if this is true or just more hype from an industry eager to get into new markets. But one thing is certain: unless workers in the fast-changing information industry have the right to organize free from threat of plant closure and job loss, there will be a constant downward pressure on workers' wages and benefits in this industry.

Historically, telecommunications has been the model of a high-wage, high-scale industry. Advanced technology, a skilled workforce, and a union wage standard have translated into productivity improvements and rising wages and benefits for telecommunications workers.

Telecommunications is the only U.S. private sector service industry with a middle-income wage standard and comprehensive benefits. Average annual earnings of non-supervisory telecommunications workers are $37,500 annually, which is twice the average annual earnings of other service sector workers.

What makes these statistics all the more impressive is that women comprise half the telecommunications workforce. In general, the higher proportion of women in the work force of an industry or occupation, the less its pay. And yet the telecommunications industry has been the exception to the rule of low pay for female-dominated work.

It has also provided access to middle-class jobs for minority workers. According to a study by the Washington, D.C., research group The Institute for Women's Policy

Research, in 1994 nonsupervisory women in telecommunications earned on average $27,040 annually, twice the average earnings of $13,000 of all non-supervisory women workers in the service sector.

Minority workers in telecommunications are also an exception to the rule of low pay. Nationally, minority workers in other service industries earn low wages, averaging $14,300 annually. This is just under the poverty level for a family of four. But minority workers in telecommunications average almost twice that much at $26,000 annually, closer to a middle-class living standard.

And what explains this pattern? Simply put, it's the high rate of unionization in the telecommunications industry. Through 50 years of collective bargaining, workers in this industry have achieved middle-class wage and benefit levels. Collective bargaining has enabled women and minorities in telecommunications to overcome labor market based pay discrimination that sets the standard in other female and minority dominated service industries.

But this model of a high-tech, high-wage union future in the industry is now threatened. Non-union telecommunications companies such as Sprint are pursuing a low wage, minimal benefits path. They are choosing to compete by undercutting middle-income wage standards.

Women are particularly threatened by these trends. The pay systems that companies like Sprint Long Distance use widened the gap between predominantly female and male jobs, undermining the progress achieved through collective bargaining by women in our industry.

New developments in the industry threaten the progress made by women and minorities also. New technologies and regulatory changes provide opportunities for telecommunications employers to follow the low wage, non-union business strategies of the rest of the service sector.

In the face of changes in the industry, it now seems likely that unless union representation is extended to the growing non-union segments of the information industry, average wages of all telecommunications workers will shift downward. The promise of the information age is to create millions of high-skill, high-wage jobs but that promise will not be realized if this trend continues.

I thank you very much for the opportunity to address this panel.

MR. OTERO: Ms. Wood, thank you very much. Is it appropriate for us to assume that this paragraph that you put in your testimony where you allude to the pay of minority workers in the telecommunications industry which average about $14,300, are you equating this pay with what actually transpired at La Conexion Familiar? Is this the kind of wage that was prevalent in the company?

MS. WOOD: The $14,300 figure is for the service sector generally. And, yes, if you figure it out, LCF was paying about $7.00 an hour. That would be significantly less than the average $26,000 paid to most minority workers in telecommunications. Or significantly less than the average $27,040 a year paid to female workers in telecommunications. Certainly I believe one of the reasons that the workers wanted to organize and form a union, to improve their wages. To be paid like union workers at the Sprint Corporation are paid.

MR. OTERO: Very well. Thank you very much.

MS. WOOD: You are very welcome.

MR. OTERO: We appreciate the clarification.

Now I would like to invite to the podium Ms. Kate Bronfenbrenner, Director of Labor Education Research, New York School of Industrial Labor Relations at Cornell University.

Welcome, Ms. Bronfenbrenner.

MS. BRONFENBRENNER: Thank you.

Deputy Under Secretary Otero and forum members, thank you for this opportunity to present the findings of my research on the impact of plant closing and the threat of plant closing on the right of workers to organize.

I am the Director of Labor Education Research at Cornell University. Starting in 1988 and continuing to the present, I along with my colleague, Tom Juravich, from the University of Massachusetts, Amherst have conducted a series of studies to analyze which factors contribute most to union success and failure at organizing and first contract campaigns.

Today, this research provides the most comprehensive analysis of the determinant role played by employer behavior, both illegal and legal behavior, in election and first contract outcomes and it's the only research that controls for other factors such as election background, bargaining unit demographics, union and employer characteristics and union pay.

As you have heard in testimony today, Sprint Corporation engaged in an extremely aggressive campaign to prevent its workers at La Conexion Familiar from organizing.

Throughout the campaign, Sprint threatened and harassed union supporters, used electronic surveillance and coercive interrogations to ascertain and undermine union support, vowed to never bargain with the union, and threatened repeatedly to shut down operations if the workers voted the union in.

After the union staged a solidarity day where 100 of 170 workers wore the T-shirt we saw here today, the company knew for certain the union was going to win the election and they shut La Conexion Familiar down. They even went so far as to fabricate documents to fraudulently claim that the decision to close La Conexion Familiar had been made long before the union campaign got off the ground.

As you have learned here today, even the company did not dispute those facts. Neither does the NLRB administrative law judge who found Sprint guilty of more than 50 different egregious labor law violations.

Yet, despite the mountain of evidence that this was an extremely successful marketing division in the process of expanding operations and that Sprint's sole reason for shutting down the operation was to maintain their union-free status, the judge did not find that the shutdown itself was in violation of labor law.

What I can tell you based on my years of study in this area is that Sprint's actions during this period represent an all too familiar pattern of aggressive union avoidance on the part of American private sector employers. The judge's decision also reflects a labor law that in both its standards and enforcement provides weak and ineffectual protection of the right to organize free of coercion and intimidation, which is the stated mission of the National Labor Relations Act.

Given the extent and intensity of employer opposition to union organizing, we should not be surprised that less than 50 percent of elections in the private sector are won by unions and that less than a third of all workers who attempt to organize end up under a union collective bargaining agreement.

This contrasts sharply with the data that we've found about the public sector, where win rates average 85 percent and unions win with 85 percent victory margins in public sector elections, in a climate where very few if any employers oppose union activity. In fact, we found 25 percent of employers in the public sector don't campaign against the union whatsoever and only 8 percent run aggressive campaigns.

What my research shows is that more than three-quarters of private sector employers run aggressive anti-union campaigns, including some combination of discharges for union activity, threats, surveillance, captive audience meetings, bribes, promises of improvements, illegal wage increases, anti-union committees, leaflets, letters, meetings.

As shown in Table 1 that's attached to my testimony, most of these tactics were associated with win rates 10 to 20 percent lower than in units where these tactics were not used. And the individual employer tactics, when included in a regression equation, were found to decrease the probability that the union would win the election by between 3 and 22 percent. That's individually. In combination, it's much, much higher.

Under the free speech provisions of the National Labor Relations Act, employers have virtually unlimited opportunities to aggressively communicate with their employees, in letters, in leaflets, in captive audience meetings, and in supervisor one-on-one conversations.

Under our law, these employer communications can and often do include distortion, misinformation, threats, and intimidation with very little chance of censure or penalty by the board or courts.

Not surprisingly, win rates decline dramatically as the number of employer meetings and letters increase. In fact, the probability of winning the election decreases 1 percentage point for each additional letter, for each additional meeting.

In these letters, leaflets, meetings and supervisor one-on-ones, employers tend to focus on three primary issues: strikes, dues, fines and assessments, and the threat of plant closing. In fact, my research shows that close to 30 percent of all employers make the threat of plant closing a primary focus of their campaign. In some cases, like La Conexion Familiar, the threat is very clear and direct. In others, it's more subtle, with management pointing to other places that shut down when there was a union drive. But the impact is consistently negative.

Where there are no such threats, the win rate is 59 percent. Where those threats are, the win rate goes down to 41 percent.

This aggressive anti-union behavior does not stop when the union wins the certification election. In fact, the majority of private sector employers continue to aggressively fight the union during the first contract process. They continue to fire workers for union activity. They continue captive audience meetings. And they continue to threaten to close the plant down. In fact, a quarter of employers even though the election is won, threaten the plant will close if there is a union contract. Four percent of employers actually shut their plants down rather than operate union.

In some cases, a third of the cases, the threat of a plant closure successfully erodes support for the union and the union is never able to get a first contract. In others, such as the laundry workers' campaign in the late '80s in NASDCO in Chelsea, Massachusetts, the union wins the election, bargains a first contract, ratifies the agreement, only to be told that corporate headquarters decides to shut the plant down as they count the ratification ballots.

In still others, the threats serve to undermine union bargaining power, weakening the agreement but still reaching a settlement.

These data, however, do not include cases such as La Conexion Familiar, where an election is never held because the employer initiates a full or partial plant closing before the election takes place.

We will not have quantitative data on the percentage of union campaigns that never get off the ground or never get to an election due to plant closings or serious threat of plant closings until we get the results of the 6-month study commissioned by the secretariat and unless the secretariat addresses that specific issue.

However, we do know from case study data collected by the Industrial Union Department of the AFL-CIO that plant closings and the serious threat of plant closings are significant both in number and impact in campaigns that never make it to an election.

For example, we have a 1991 UAW campaign at Flex Cable and Furnace Products in Morley, Michigan. First, the employer threatened to shut the plant down if the workers unionized. When that threat didn't work, the employer then on the Friday before Memorial Day had the workers watch as they padlocked the gate. On the Monday after the holiday, they called back those workers who had not supported the union campaign, but the union supporters were never called back to work.

Six months later, in an NLRB settlement, some of the workers got reinstatement, some got back pay, but the union campaign had been effectively broken.

Some employers even go so far as to threaten the NLRB with plant closings. During the 1980s, what was then ACTWU and what is now UNITE campaigned at Farris Fashions in Arkansas. The employer repeatedly made statements such as "If you don't quit messing with this union, I will close the plant down, turn it into a chicken coop and manure."

Although the union lost the election, they were able to establish at the NLRB hearing that a clear majority of the workers there wanted a union and the Board issued a bargaining order supporting the union's argument that it was employer threats and coercion that had undermined union support.

In their post-trial brief, the company went so far as to state, "The Respondent will close if it ultimately has to bargain with the union. This is a fact that the union and that CGC," the counsel for the General Counsel of the NLRB, "should not doubt."

What these cases show is that although Sprint's anti-union behavior at La Conexion Familiar was extreme, it is not uncommon. I am afraid, Mr. Bertuzzi, that Sprint's actions represent not the exception but the norm of employer behavior in the American private sector.

Under our labor laws, employers have virtually free rein to threaten, to intimidate, to bribe, distort, with only minimal penalties for the most gross infractions of the law. If they fire half the workforce, as they did at ACTWU's campaign in Lichtenburg in Georgia, the worst penalty they face is reinstatement and back pay. There are no possibilities for punitive damages.

If they absolutely refuse to bargain, after bargaining order after bargaining order, the worst penalty they face is another piece of paper telling them to cease and desist from failing to bargain in good faith and to go forth and bargain in good faith.

And in the case of La Conexion Familiar, the only penalty was that Sprint be required to send a letter to employees informing them that they had a right to organize and pledging not to harass them in the future.

As Arizona Congressman Ed Paster said, this ruling "would be laughable if it were not so heartless."

Professor Corrada is correct that there are legal precedents for shutting down a plant for business reasons in the midst of a contentious organizing campaign, but the facts in this case speak otherwise.

Sprint has shut down other facilities for business reasons and in all those cases they gave at least 60 days' notice. And in all those cases, they gave the employees an opportunity to bid for other Sprint jobs. But in this case, there was no notice and there were no jobs offered.

It is clear that in this case, it was not a business decision, it was a decision based on anti-union animus alone.

In the end, when we hear the testimony of the courageous women at La Conexion Familiar, I think we are struck by how workers still manage to fight for unions despite the odds.

The only way that we can ever create the environment envisioned by the drafters of the National Labor Relations Act is through significant expansion of both worker and union rights and employer penalties in the organizing process. This will require not only more vigorous and rapid enforcement of current law, but also serious financial penalties and injunctive relief to restrain the most egregious employer violations, particularly plant shutdowns, and the threat of plant shutdowns.

It will also require expansion of union access to the workplace in order to counteract the captive and coercive nature of employer communication with workers during the organizing campaign.

As CWA President Morton Bahr testified earlier today, these changes need to be accomplished not only by significant reform to U.S. labor laws but also by amendments to the North American Agreement on Labor Cooperation to provide an enforceable code of conduct for countries covered under NAFTA. This code must include both restrictions on the ability of companies to shift their operations to other countries to avoid unionization and guarantee for the right to organize free of management interference and intimidation.

Most important of all, these new codes must include meaningful penalties for the violation of those rights. Then and only then will workers be able to exercise their democratic rights to have an independent voice of their own choosing to represent their interest in the workplace, and then and only then will employers such as Sprint Corporation no longer be able to flagrantly violate labor laws at the expense of their workers' dignity and well-being.

I sincerely hope that this forum, along with the 6-month study to be conducted by the secretariat, will be an important first step in that direction.

Thank you.

MR. OTERO: Ms. Bronfenbrenner, thank you very much. I have a couple of questions. On page 3, you went off your prepared text and you cited some statistics which I failed to write down.

MS. BRONFENBRENNER: I condensed it.

MR. OTERO: Would you please repeat them for me? What you were talking about is no surprise that less than half the NLRB elections held this year in this country result in union victory and then you went on and cited some —

MS. BRONFENBRENNER: The public sector?

MR. OTERO: Right. But I was not able to copy that.

MS. BRONFENBRENNER: Okay.

MR. OTERO: Would you repeat that?

MS. BRONFENBRENNER: Okay. That's in the written testimony, by the way, but I'll go over it again. It's in the written testimony on page 8.

MR. OTERO: Page 8?

MS. BRONFENBRENNER: Yes. The second paragraph on page 8.

In the public sector, win rates are 85 percent across all unions and there are very few employers who engage in any kind of employer opposition.

MR. OTERO: I see. Okay. My second inquiry deals with your intriguing statement on page 5 to 6, when you state that "We will not have quantitative data on the percentage of union campaigns that never get off the ground or never get to election due to plant closings until we get results from the 6-month study."

And I'm wondering if you're telling us that in your research you have been able to quantify that and, if that's the case, could you outline why?

MS. BRONFENBRENNER: I have not done that study to this date.

MR. OTERO: I see.

MS. BRONFENBRENNER: It can be done. It's very extensive and expensive research. Now, Lance Compa from the secretariat met with me last week to ask my advice in designing a study and I explained to him that — and what data we had and I explained to him the only way we can find out whether the threat of plant closings and plant closings truly affect workers' ability to organize is if we look at campaigns that never made it to an election and that can only be done by taking all campaigns where a petition was filed but then withdrawn and surveying those campaigns to find out whether there was a threat of plant closings or plant closings, which would be difficult but not impossible research to do.

MR. OTERO: That's very good.

My final question deals with the research that you have done. Is this limited to the United States only?

MS. BRONFENBRENNER: Yes.

MR. OTERO: Okay. Thank you very much. We appreciate your help.

I now call to the podium Ms. Giselle Quezada, union steward of Local 9410, Communications Workers of America.

Ms. Quezada, please?

MS. QUEZADA: Thank you very much. My name is Giselle Quezada and I am originally from South America, from Peru. I am a mother of four and I am a union steward and also very active in my community.

Approximately 3 years ago I became a U.S. citizen because I realized that no matter how active I am I have no voice in this country, so I became a U.S. citizen.

I want to also tell you how I met the workers.

I was asked to help organize the workers from La Conexion Familiar, since I was a union steward and active in my union and they had lots of questions in regards to how does the union work, what are the contracts, and so I went in and helped.

I was very impressed with the workers. At first, they were there, they had a lot of questions and were uncertain about where all this was taking them. But the injustices they endured were so great, you heard some of them, that it just empowered them and at the same time gave me so much energy that I wish I could share that with you with my words. They were empowering. They believed in what they stood for. They realized that the struggle was hard but they knew that in this country they had the opportunity and the chance to speak out and become part of a union, that that was a right they had, that they had the freedom of speech, and that they would be heard.

And this is amazing when we hear of the stereotyping that takes place, that they'll only come here to this country to have children, just to reap the benefits that we have to offer, so that they could receive welfare and be taken care of. But yet these workers before you all wanted to have a decent job. They wanted to be very much a part of the American dream. They wanted to be able to become citizens, make a better living, and for their children, offer them the chance and opportunity of a good education.

And I feel that the workers would have accomplished that if they would have been given the opportunity to have a chance to vote. But yet the place was closed, the doors were slammed shut in their faces without any regard of who they were or what they were.

They also were told, well, where else could you get a job? All you do is speak Spanish. It's amazing when we stop and think that when they want our business, all of a sudden we are valuable, but when we become the workers then we are treated so differently with a lot of injustice and put down.

When we stop and we think what is it that in shutting down La Conexion Familiar by Sprint it devastated the community which, by the way, it had promised that it would hire people and it would be a part of the community, and they were out there campaigning, selling, they had booths everywhere, saying this is a service, that we care.

Let's look at the name they gave this company, La Conexion Familiar, which involves the family, but yet when it came to the workers and giving them their rights, they did not.

The other part of who I feel feels the greatest part is the children as they watch their parents struggle up to this day without jobs. And when we talk about their chances and their opportunities, that we are in a land that they can speak out and voice their opinions and vote in a union and yet all they look at is having to move from one place to another because of the fact that their parents don't have a job, their mom.

And some of these people, by the way, also contrary to what was said by Sprint to the president of my local, Marie Malliett, that they were illegal people, they had people in there of high education but the only unfortunate part was they did not speak the language, the English language. But yet if it weren't for the fact that they spoke Spanish, they wouldn't be employed, they wouldn't have been employed by Sprint to begin with.

I think that I would like to see that we never forget these workers, these workers who gave up a great deal, who stood up and believed for their rights, who believed in the kind of power and what it took to be able to be recognized and stand up and to be treated equally with respect and dignity.

I hope that we send that message loud and clear from one end of the earth to the other that what would happen to them as workers was wrong, unfair, and unjust.

Now, if I may say a few words in Spanish.

(THROUGH TRANSLATOR) The fight as workers for us is very difficult and it's very rough and tough, but all of us together, we will never be divided.

Thank you.

MR. OTERO: Thank you very much y muchas gracias, Ms. Quezada, for your presentation.

And we now come to the final presenter of the day, who by personal decision shifted with Mr. del Campo.

Let me ask Jaime Gonzalez, the field representative of the California Federation of Labor, AFL-CIO, to come forward.

MR. GONZALEZ: (THROUGH TRANSLATOR) First of all, Mr. Otero, I would like to thank you, to share with you and all your colleagues this present opinions.

I bring you greetings from the treasurer, Jack Kenney, who was unable to be here.

I congratulate you by the way you used this dialogue, utilizing the manipulation of La Conexion Familiar.

(IN ENGLISH) This forum is to examine the impact of sudden plant closures on the freedom of association and organizing by workers. The inference and common-sense assumption based on the track record of corporate America is that the closing is done in order to prevent the successful organizing by workers.

My intent is not to repeat the facts as stated by the workers of La Conexion or CWA and accepted by any common sense individual who has firsthand experience with labor-management relations and is not rendered naive by personal interests or potential business contents, but rather to share with you an opinion of possible consequences of further plant closures in an effort to prevent successful worker organizing.

This opinion is based on an understanding gathered from different comments that have been made here today.

It has been stated that there is an interest in reconciling the interests of both workers, unions, and capital corporations.

The reconciliation of the interests of what under NAFTA are considered units of production, not people, not workers, but units of production, and the interests of corporations begs the question what interests are more common, what interests are more important to our society if a decision had to be made between the interests of workers' well-being and corporate profits?

The answer would depend on what type of society we would want. Some would want a society where only a minority would have the opportunity to fulfill aspirations and human potential and the majority live in subsistence standards and economic insecurity.

These individuals would choose the interest of corporations in which they have a vested interest to live better than the majority. These individuals would welcome company unions that are not too radical or threatening. They would want free applause simply because of their title and not because of the substance or merit of their words.

On the other hand, others would take a more risky attitude. They would choose the interests of workers, the people, the families, the majority. These would seek a society where people play by the rules according to the law, even if the law is not intended to lay a level playing field.

They would choose to seek a society where the majority of the population, not the vested elite minority, get an opportunity to enjoy even the most simple of pleasures, a job, respect, dignity, and even some free time and money to nurture a family.

These individuals would choose the interests of the people, the workers or, as stated, the units of production.

I thank those of you on this board who have a proven record of concern and commitment to the interests of people and not of capital profits for a noble attempt to bring justice and credibility to a deal that was not meant to produce justice but rather profits.

I thank you for refusing to be accomplices to the exploitation of people by un-checked capital. I share with you this opinion. If justice is not rendered through some just resolution to this matter and other corporations continue to close their plants suddenly in order to prevent the organizing of workers, there will be other martyrs and other workers and their families will suffer as those of La Conexion Familiar.

But these economic martyrs will become a powerful reminder that workers cannot depend on an enlightened government or a benevolent corporate agenda to secure a humane society. They will continue to remind us that a humane world for the major-ity will only come about through worker organization and international solidarity.

These proceedings will at the very least strengthen and stretch the bond of coop-eration and solidarity between and among the workers of the Americas.

(THROUGH TRANSLATOR) And those who speak Spanish, I would like to remind you that everybody looks after their own selves and maybe that's why so many of them didn't show up here today.

Thank you very much.

MR. OTERO: Thank you very much, Mr. Gonzalez. Please convey my best wishes to the Secretary-Treasurer of the AFL-CIO, Jack Kenney, a long-time friend.

We have come now to the conclusion of this event, ladies and gentlemen, and be-fore we all go on our own merry way, I would like to take the prerogative of the chair to make a few final comments.

First of all, I must express my personal appreciation on behalf of the Department of Labor to each and every one of the presenters for their brief, useful, insightful, and enlightening presentations. Most particularly, I am thankful to each and every one of you for the discipline and the cooperation you lent the chair in ensuring the orderly process of these proceedings in a manner in which everyone had the opportunity to say his or her piece.

Let me also say that as we prepare to leave this room, everything that has been said here by every person must be respected as their own opinions, even if as they spoke some felt the opposite viewpoint. That is the beauty of the democracy in which we live, that we are able to be tolerant of others in expressing opinions, even on matters as controversial and as painful as some of these presentations here have demonstrated today.

We came here with the hope that we would be able to learn more about the impact that cases where companies' shutdown have on this very precious right of freedom of association. I am going away today enriched by the contributions of each and every one of you. I hope that my colleagues from Canada and Mexico feel likewise.

And, of course, we will pursue this matter to an even greater degree by working with our labor secretariat in Dallas in developing more empirical data, not only as these cases have occurred in the United States, but also in Canada and Mexico, and we hope that by the end of this summer we will have a report that we could elevate to the three ministers of labor who compose the Ministerial Labor Commission under the North American Labor Agreement, for it is they, the ministers of our countries responsible for labor matters, who are ultimately the judge of what can and should be done either collectively or individually by each country with regards to the problems at hand.

Let me say also that on behalf of the Department of Labor we in the United States recognize that American labor law is far from perfect. We recognize that there are a number of areas that need to be changed. As I said before, Secretary Reich and President Clinton sought immediately upon ascension to power to undertake a study of these problems and commission a very respectable, highly respectable, commission, I should say, led by Professor Dunlap to undertake this study.

We appreciate the constructive criticism and we hope that there will be more for only in true transparency can we hope ever to be able to change something that is not working very well and make it work even better for the benefit of those who toil every day for their livelihood.

The report of these proceedings will be made public in a few days, hopefully, as soon as we get all of the technical aspects and they will be available as a public available information document through the Department of Labor, specifically through our National Administrative Office. If you have looked at all of our materials, the telephone number, the fax number and the address of our National Administrative Office at the Department of Labor is available in the documentation.

I would also like to request that those of you who may have developed or who may have other information to offer upon return to your homes please feel free to do so. The record will not be closed because we have allowed a number of people who did not want to present testimony in public to have sent it to us in writing and we will keep the record open for the next two weeks so that we can have the opportunity to collect even more materials that would be useful to us.

Finally, let me express my sincere appreciation to my colleagues, Mr. Warren Edmondson from Canada and the tripartite delegation that accompanied him here to participate in these proceedings; also to Dr. Luis Miguel Diaz of the Mexican Labor Secretariat along with the Mexican delegation, for their presence and the contributions that they have made to this process today.

I would also like to say thanks to my very effective, very efficient, but silent colleagues, Irasema Garza. She does have a tongue, believe me. And my legal advisor, Mr. Widom, who is very knowledgeable on matters regarding American labor law. He is in the Solicitor's Office now but he was for many years one of the principal people at the NLRB. They have been able to provide the technical support and the necessary legal advice that is required for us to do the job.

I also would like to express my appreciation to our logistics and public relations director, Mr. Bob Z. I can't pronounce his last name. He was responsible in dealing with all of the arrangements for this event and also with the press.

And I think also that we owe a debt of gratitude to the technical people, the interpreters, the people who actually wired the room and made sure that technically we were up to par. There was not a hitch in the communications today. And all of this only happens because of the dedication of these people who are behind the scenes and make people like me look very good.

So I would like to thank everyone. And, of course, I say to them also the check is in the mail, you will be getting paid, I hope.

And to all of you, ladies and gentlemen, unless you have anything else that anyone cares to say at this point, I bid you all goodbye. May you have a very safe and happy return to your respective homes and thank you very much for being here with us today.

This concludes the forum officially at 5:04 p.m.

Thank you very much.

[Whereupon, at 5:04 p.m. the forum was concluded.]

UNITED STATES DEPARTMENT OF LABOR
REPORTER'S CERTIFICATE

TITLE: Public Forum/ILAB
DATE: February 27, 1996
LOCATION: San Francisco, California

This is to certify that the attached proceedings before the United States Department of Labor were held according to the record and that this is the original, complete, true and accurate transcript which has been compared to the reporting or recording accomplished at this hearing.

BAYLEY REPORTING, INC.   February 27, 1996

BIBLIOGRAPHY

American Airlines, Inc., v. Brotherhood of Railway, Airline, and Steamship Clerks, 3 C.L.R.B.R. 90 (1981).

America's Best Quality Coatings Corp. and Staff Right, Inc., Joint Employers, and United Electrical Workers, 313 NLRB No. 52 (1993).

Arthurs, II. W., et al. *Labor Law and Industrial Relations in Canada*, Toronto: Butterworths, 1988.

British Columbia, s.8(6); Manitoba, s.7; Ontario, s.89(5); Quebec, s.17; Prince Edward Island, s.11(5); Canada, s.98(4).

British Columbia Government and Service Employees' Union v. Humanacare Counselling, unreported, November 30, 1995, B.C.L.R.B. 292–39, (1995).

Bruce, Peter G. "State Structures and Processing of Unfair Labor Practice Cases in the United States and Canada." In *The Challenge of Restructuring: North American Labor Movements Respond.* edited by Jane Jenson and Rianne Mahon. Industrial Relations Centre, Queen's University, 1993.

Brudney, James J. "A Famous Victory: Collective Bargaining Protections and the Statutory Aging Process." *North Carolina Law Review* 74 (1996): 939.

Cable-Masters, Inc., and Communications Workers of America, 307 NLRB No. 139 (1992).

Carillo, Jorge, and Alfredo Hualde. "Maquiladoras: La restructuración industrial y el impacto sindical." In *Negociación y conflicto laboral en Méxic*, edited by Bensusán and León. 1990.

Chaison, Gary N., and Joseph B. Rose. "Continental Divide: The Direction and Fate of North American Unions." In *Advances in Industrial and Labor Relations*, edited by Donna Sockell, David Lewin, and David B. Lipsky. Greenwich, Conn.: Jai Press, 1991.

City Buick Pontiac (Montreal) Inc., 81 C.L.L.C. 14,108 (1981).

Climent, Juan B. *Elementos de Derecho Procesal del Trabajo* (Edit. Esfinge). 1989.

Consolidated Bathurst Packaging Ltd. v. Int'l Woodworkers of America, Local 2–69, 68 D.L.R. (4th) 524 (S.C.C.), (1990).

Contec Division, SPX Corp. and UAW, 320 NLRB No. 52 (1995).

De la O., Mar'a Eugenia, and Cirila Quintero. "Sindicalismo y contratación colectiva en las maquiladoras fronterizas," *Frontera Norte* 8 (July-December 1992).

"Dislocated Workers: Worker Adjustment and Retraining Notification Act not Meeting Its Goals." Washington D.C.: U.S. General Accounting Office, February 1993.

"Displaced Workers: Trends in the 1980's and Implications for the Future." Congressional Budget Office, Congress of the United States, February 1993.

Ekos Research Associates, Inc. "Industrial Adjustment Services Program Evaluation." Ottawa, Ontario: Employment and Immigration Canada, November 1993.

Estadisticas Laborales, Segundo Semestre, STPS, Subsecretaria "B" at 123.

"Estudio del Grupo de Expertos Independientes." In *Consultas Ministeriales: Registro de asociaciones sindicales*. March 1996.

First National Maintenance Corp. v. NLRB, 452 U.S. 666 (1981).

Freeman, Richard. "On the Divergence in Unionism among Developed Countries." Working Paper no. 2817. National Bureau of Economic Research, 1989.

Gambrill, Mónica Claire. "Sindicalismo en las maquiladoras de Tijuana: regresión en las prestaciones sociales." In *Reestructuración industrial: Maquiladoras en la frontera México-Estados Unidos*, edited by Jorge Carrillo. 1986.

General Electric Company and United Electrical, Radio, and Machine Workers of America (UE), 321 NLRB No. 86 (1996).

Hualde, Alfredo. "Industrial Relations in the Maquiladora Industry: Management's Search for Participation and Quality." In *Regional Integration and Industrial Relations in North America*, edited by Maria Cook and Harry Katz. Ithaca, N.Y.: Cornell University Press, 1994.

Humpty Dumpty Foods Ltd., 78 C.L.L.C. 16,136 (O.L.R.B.) (1978).

Hunter-Douglas, Inc., v. NLRB, 804 F.2d 808 (1986).

Informes de Labores de la Secretaria del Trabajo y Prevision Social (STPS), 1989–1994.

Insurance Courier Services and UFCW, Loc. 175, 18 Can. L.R.B.R. (2d) 286 (Can) (1993).

Int'l Woodworkers of America, Local 2–69 v. Consolidated Bathurst Packaging Ltd., 83 C.L.L.C. 16,066 (O.L.R.B.) (1983).

ITT Automotive and United Auto Workers, decision of Judge Marion C. Ladwig, NLRB Division of Judges, JD–79–96 (1996).

Kennedy Lodge Inc., O.L.R.B. Rep. 931 (1984).

Kennedy Lodge Nursing Home, 81 C.L.L.C. para. 16,078 (O.L.R.B.), at 473 (1980).

Kochan, Thomas A.; Harry C. Katz; and Robert B. McKersie. *The Transformation of American Industrial Relations.* Ithaca, N.Y.: Cornell University Press, 1986.

Kopinak, Kathryn. *Desert Capitalism: Maquiladoras in North America's Western Industrial Corridor.* Tucson, Ariz.: University of Arizona Press, 1996.

Langille, Brian. "Equal Partnership in Canadian Labour Law." *Osgood Hall Law Journal* 21 (1983): 496.

LCF, Inc., d/b/a La Conexion Familiar and Sprint Corporation, 322 NLRB 137 (1996).

Ley del Seguro Social, Instituto Mexicano del Seguro Social, 1997.

Marrero, Guillermo. "Labor Issues for Maquiladoras." *Latin America Law and Business Report* 4 (May 31, 1996).

Meredith, Robyn. "Despite Election, a Wal-Mart Goes Union in Canada." *New York Times*, 18 February 1997, C3.

Middlebrook, Kevin J., and Cirila Quintero Ramirez. "Conflict Resolution in the Mexican Labor Courts: An Examination of Local CABs in Chihuahua and Tamaulipas." U.S. National Administrative Office, 1995.

Mills, Mike. "With Click of a Mouse, White-Collar Jobs Go Overseas." *Washington Post*, 17 September 1996, A1.

Ministry of Labour Task Force. *Seeking a Balance: Canada Labour Code Part 1 Review.* 1996.

National Bank of Canada v. Retail Clerks' International Union, 9 D.L.R. (4th) 10 (S.C.C.) (1984).

Newfoundland *Labour Relations Act*, R.S.N. 1990, c. L–1, s. 26.

NLRB v. Champion Laboratories Inc., CA 7, No. 95-2433 (October 24, 1996).

NLRB v. Gissel Packing Co., 395 U.S. 575 (1969).

NLRB v. Village IX, Inc., 723 F.2d 1360 (7th Cir. 1983).

Ontario *Labour Relations Act*, 1995, S.O. 1995, c.1., s. 70.

Picot, Garnett; Zhengxi Lin; and Wendy Piper. "Permanent Layoffs in Canada: Overview and Longitudinal Analysis." In *Business and Labour Market Analysis*. Ottawa, Ontario: Statistics Canada, May 1996.

Portz, John. "WARN and the States: Implementation of the Federal Plant Closing Law." Paper presented at the annual meeting of the Midwest Political Science Association, 1992.

Pries, Ludger. "Volkswagen: Un Nudo Gordiano Resuelto?" *Trabajo* 9 (1993): 7

Programa Nacional de Desarollo 1995–2000, Programa de Empleo, Capacitación y Defensa de los Derechos Laborales 1995–2000, Informe de Avance de Ejecución del Plan Nacional de Desarollo 1995, Informe de Labores de la Secretaría del Trabajo y Prevision Social 1995–1996.

Revenga, Ana; Michelle Riboud; and Hong Tan. "The Impact of Mexico's Retraining Program on Employment and Wages." WPS 1013. World Bank, 1992.

Roblaw Industries, Inc., and International Brotherhood of Teamsters, Case No. 12–CA–17901 (1995).

Rosen, Howard. "Training: Who Gets It; Does It Work?" Working paper. Competitiveness Policy Council, March 1996.

Saskatchewan *Trade Union Act*, R.S.S. 1978, c. T–17, s. 11(1)(I).

Sawyer, Kathy. "Unions Striking Out in High-Tech Firms." *Washington Post*, 18 March 1984, C1.

Saxenian, AnnaLee. *Regional Advantage: Culture and Competition in Silicon Valley and Route 128*. Cambridge, Mass.: Harvard University Press, 1994.

Schmenner, Roger W. *Making Business Location Decisions*. Englewood Cliffs, N.J.: Prentice Hall, 1982.

Secretaria del Trabajo y Prevision Social, "El Mercado de Trabajo en Mexico, 1970–1992."

Semanario Judicial de la Federación, época 7A, Tomo XXXIII, p.15, Precedentes: Amparo Directo 6486/68, Unión de Abridores de Ostión, Trabajadores en las Industrias de Empacadores de Pescado, Mariscos y Productos Similares del Golfo de México, 8 de septiembre de 1971, 5 votos. Ponente: María Cristina Salmorán de Tamaño. Cierre Total de una Empresa, Demanda a la Reanudación de Labores en Caso De.

Semanario Judicial de la Federación, época 6A, Tomo LVIII, p. 9, Precedentes: Amparo Directo 3273/56 Moisés Cosío Gomez, 12 de abril de 1962, 5 votos. Ponente: Agapito Pozo. Contrato Colectivo de Trabajo, Terminación, Causas De.

Semanario Judicial de la Federación, época 5A, Cuarta Sala, Tomo CXIX, p. 2528, Precedentes: Tomo CXIX, p.2528 Alvarez del Castillo Efrén , 3 de julio de 1953, 4 votos. Contrato de Trabajo, Terminación del Por Cierre Total de la Empresa;

Semanario Judicial de la Federación, Cuarta Sala, época 5A, Tomo CVII, p.1965, Precedentes: Tomo CVII, p. 1965, 14 de marzo de 1951, 5 votos, Tomo CXXV, p. 1982, Tomo XCIV, p. 54, Tomo LXXXVIII, p. 2046. Cierre de Empresas, Con Autorización de la Junta. Despido Injustificado.

Semanario Judicial de la Federación, época 5A, Tomo LXXVI, p. 6207, Precedentes: Tomo LXXVI, p. 6207 Ojeda Manuel, 28 de junio de l943. Cierre de Negociaciones por Incosteabilidad.

Semanario Judicial de la Federación, época 5A, Tomo LX, p. 4276, Precedentes: Tomo LXIX, p. 4267, Munos Munoz, Nieves, 17 de septiembre de 1941; Semanario Judicial de la Federación, época 5A, Tomo LVII, p.1267.

Semanario Judicial de la Federación, época 5A, Tomo XLVII, p. 1991, Conflictos de Orden Económico.

Semanario Judicial de la Federación, época 5A, Tomo LVII, p. 1768, Juntas, Conflictos Económicos Ante Las.

Statement of Kary L. Moss, Executive Director, Sugar Law Center for Economic and Social Justice, to Senate Committee on Labor and Human Resources Subcommittee on Labor, July 26, 1994.

STPS/INEGI, 1995 National Employment Survey.

Stroehmann Bakeries, Inc. [Division of George Weston Ltd.] v. NLRB, CA 2, Nos. 95–4159(L), 95–4207(XAP), September 9, 1996.

Texas Electric Steel Casting Co. and United Steelworkers, decision of Judge James S. Jensen, NLRB Division of ALJs, JD (SF)–19–94.

Textile Workers Union v. Darlington Mfg. Co., 380 U.S. 263 (1965).

Tiano, Susan. *Patriarchy on the Line: Labor, Gender, and Ideology in the Mexican Maquila Industry*. 1994.

UEW, Local 504 v. Westinghouse Canada, Inc., 80 C.L.L.C. 16,053 (O.L.R.B.) (1980).

UFCW Local 751 v. Brown Group, Inc., ___ U.S. ___ (May 14, 1996).

United Food and Commercial Workers, Local 175 v. Insurance Courier Services, 18 C.L.R.B.R. (2d) 286 (1993).

United Steelworkers of America and Wal-Mart Canada, Inc., Ontario Labour Relations Board, nos. 0387–96–R, 0453–96–U, February 10, 1997.

U.S. Department of Labor and U.S. Department of Commerce, Commission on the Future of WorkerManagement Relations. *Fact Finding Report*. May 1994.

Waldie, Paul, and Marina Strauss. "Windsor Wal-Mart Wins Right to Union: Firm Intimidated Staff, Board Rules." *Globe and Mail*, 11 February 1997.

"Wal-Mart Canadian Unit to Appeal Labor Ruling." *Wall Street Journal*, 28 March 1997, A13.

Weiler, Paul. "Promises to Keep: Securing Workers' Rights to Self-Organization under the NLRA." *Harvard Law Review* 96 (1983): 1769.

Westfair Foods and RWDSU, Local 454, S.L.R.B.D. No. 2 (1993).

Westinghouse Canada, Inc. v. UEW, Local 504, 80 C.L.L.C. 14,062 (Ont. Div. Ct.) (1980).

Williams, Edward J. "Attitudes and Strategies Inhibiting the Unionization of the Maquiladora Industry: Government, Industry, Unions and Workers." *Journal of Borderlands Studies* VI (1991): 51.

Wright Line, A Div. of Wright Line, Inc., 251 N.L.R.B. 1083(1980), *enf'd*, 662 F.2d 899 (1st Cir. 1981), *cert. denied*, 455 U.S. 989 (1982).

REPORTS FROM CONTRACTORS
AND CONSULTANTS

Contributions from contractors and consultants used in the preparation of this report are available from the Secretariat upon request, with a binding, copying, and shipping charge. All materials are available for public review at the office of the Secretariat and at the National Administrative Offices (NAOs) of the three NAALC countries.

Analysis of Court of Appeals Decisions (1986–1993) for Secretariat
Plant Closing Study
—Professor James J. Brudney (39 pages, in English: $5.00)

Summary of NLRB Cases on Plant Closings and Threats of Plant
Closing
—Professor David Weinstein (69 pages, in English: $8.00)

The Effects of Plant Closing or Threat of Plant Closing on the Right
of Workers to Organize
—Dr. Kate L. Bronfenbrenner (with copies of questionnaires, 78 pages, in English: $9.00)

Report to Labor Secretariat of the North American Commission for
Labor Cooperation on Canadian Administrative and Judicial Decisions on the Issue of Plant Closings in the Context of Unionization
—Professor Brian Etherington; John C. Murray; Jeffrey Sack, Q.C.; and Andrea Bowker (119 pages, in English: $15.00)

*Efectos del Cierre Repentino de Empresas o Establecimientos Sobre el
Principio de Libertad de Asociación y el Derecho de los Trabajadores a
Organizarse en México*
—Néstor de Buen Lozano and Carlos E. de Buen Unna (24 pages, in Spanish: $5.00)

Efectos Sindicales en el Cierre de Empresas
—Arturo Alcalde Justiniani (30 pages, in Spanish: $5.00)

Copies of Mexican press clippings on plant closings
—appended to Alcalde report (49 pages, in Spanish: $7.00)

Problemática Terminación Colectiva de la Relación de Trabajo
—Humberto Flores Salas (10 pages, in Spanish: $3.00)

Estudio Relacionado con Cierre Repentino de Empresas sobre el Principio de Libertad de Asociación
(Summary description of plant closing cases before the Federal Conciliation and Arbitration Board and Summaries of Supreme Court Cases on Plant Closing Issues)
—Juan Jose Ríos Estavillo (32 pages, in Spanish: $5.00)

Chart of Case Files on "Conflictos Colectivos de Naturaleza Económica"
(Case file summaries)
—Juan Jose Ríos Estavillo (38 pages, in Spanish: $5.00)

LIST OF ABBREVIATIONS AND ACRONYMS

AFL: American Federation of Labor

ALJ: Administrative Law Judge

BLS: U.S. Bureau of Labor Statistics

CA: collective agreement

CAB: Conciliation and Arbitration Board (Mexico)

CBO: U.S. Congressional Budget Office

CIMO: *Programa de Calidad Integral y Modernización* (Integral Quality and Modernization Program)

CIO: Congress of Industrial Organizations

CLRB: Canadian Labor Relations Board

COBRA: Consolidated Omnibus Budget Reconciliation Act (United States)

CSTEC: Canadian Steel Trade and Employment Congress

CWA: Communication Workers of America

d/b/a: doing business as

DWS: Displaced Worker Survey (United States)

EB: Extended Benefits

EDWAA: Economic Dislocation and Worker Adjustment Act (United States)

EI: employment insurance

FLL: Federal Labor Law (Mexico)

GAO: U.S. General Accounting Office

HRDC: Human Resources Development Canada

IAS: Industrial Adjustment Services (Canada)

IDB: Inter-American Development Board (Mexico)

ILO: International Labor Organisation

IMF: International Monetary Fund

IMSS: *Instituto Mexicano del Seguro Social* (Mexican Institute for Social Security)

INEGI: *Instituto Nacional de Estadística Geografía e Informática*

INFONAVIT: *Instituto del Fondo Nacional de la Vivienda Para los Trabajadores*

ISSSTE: *Instituto de Seguridad y Servicios Sociales de los Trabajadores del Estado* (Institute for Security and Social Services for Public Servants)

JTPA: Job Training Partnership Act (United States)

LABA: Labour Adjustment Benefits Act (Canada)

LCF: *La Conexion Familiar*

LMAS: Canadian Labour Market Activity Survey

LMRA: Labor Management Relations Act (United States)

MSS: Mexican Social Security Institute

NAALC: North American Agreement on Labor Cooperation

NAFTA: North American Free Trade Agreement

NAFTA–TAA: North American Free Trade Agreement Transitional Adjustment Allowance

NAO: National Administrative Office

NLRA: National Labor Relations Act (United States)

NLRB: National Labor Relations Board (United States)

OECD: Organization for Economic Co-operation and Development

OLRA: Ontario Labour Relations Act

OLRB: Ontario Labour Relations Board

PARAUSSE: *Programa de Acción para Reforzar el Acuerdo de Unidad para Superar la Emergencia Económica* (Program to Reinforce the Unity Agreement to Overcome the Economic Emergency)

PCMO: *Programa de Calidad de la Mano de Obra* (Human Resource Training Program)

PEET: *Programa Emergente de Empleo Temporal* (Short-Term Employment Program)

PMMT: *Programa de Modernización del Mercado Laboral* (Labor Market Modernization Program)

POWA: Program for Older Worker Adjustment (Canada)

PROBECAT: *Programa de Becas de Capacitación para Trabajadores Desempleados*

PROSSE: *Programa de Servicios Sociales Esenciales* (Essential Social Services Program)

RC: representation case

SAR: *Sistema de Ahorro para del Retiro*

SEDESOL: *Secretaría de Desarrollo Social* (Ministry of Social Development)

SLID: Canadian Survey of Labour and Income Dynamics

SNE: *Servicio Nacional de Empleo* (Mexican National Employment Service)

STPS: *Secretaría del Trabajo y Prevision Social* (Ministry of Labor and Social Welfare)

STRM: *Sindicato de Telefonistas de la República Mexicana*

TAA: Trade Adjustment Assistance

TRA: trade readjustment allowances

UAW: United Auto Workers

UE: United Electrical, Radio, and Machine Workers of America

UI: Unemployment Insurance

ULP: unfair labor practice

WARN: Worker Adjustment and Retraining Notification Act (United States)